CHRISTIAN UNIVERSALISM
Maybe God Isn't Such A Bad Guy After All

Surprising answers to perplexing questions people ask about the God of the Bible

Fifth Edition

by Richard H Goyette

Published by

Richard Goyette Enterprises

Phone: 530-588-5075

Email: richardinparadise@gmail.com

Cover Photo: Isabella Perez

My lovely granddaughter

This book is dedicated to three beautiful ladies:

my wife, Arlene,

and my two daughters, Amanda and Wendy.

Foreword

By Amanda Northouse

Our minds, like candles, try to make things clearer and brighter in an often dark and confusing world. We would like to understand more about why things are the way they are, to try and make sense of our existence and purpose, and most of all, to try and understand more of the mystery and immensity of God. This book is one man's, my dad's, delving into the fundamental questions of human existence, and the mind and purposes of God. It is his candle to the world, offering a new, but truly biblical, glimpse of God. Allow this faith journey, both surprising and genuine, to enlarge your vision, allowing you to see more of the splendor of our Creator and the beauty of His interactions with and purposes for humanity. You may even catch a glimpse of His heart you had never seen before.

This journey of thought comes from a man irresistibly drawn to the biblical portrayal of the love of God in Christ, but who is not content to accept paradoxical concepts, and who values truth enough to seek it with all his heart and mind, following wherever that path may lead. It has led, through many winding ways and turns in the road, to a place of peace and faith for him. For him, and I would say, for most people, the Bible contains many difficult to understand, and often seemingly contradictory, truths. This methodical work attempts to make sense of how a God of love is also a God of judgment, and how a God who is wholly good allows evil to exist and invade our lives. It poses the question that if God is all loving and all powerful; can hell itself be defeated, with all of God's creatures eventually finding their way back to Him? Are we meant to ask such questions? Do we dare hope to find answers to such questions? God gave us our minds (and hearts), and I believe we should dare to travel these paths of thought, whether or not the answers will ever be found this side of eternity.

While growing up, I always had plenty of theological questions for my dad, and he never responded with a "pat" answer. He would take the time to describe various schools of thought on the issue and bring up relevant Bible passages. He would then tell me I would have to come to my own conclusions. I grew up in a home where thinking was valued, and searching for answers was never easy, but vitally worthwhile. This book is for the intellectually curious, questioning, or confused, but also for anyone, who would value one more "school of thought" regarding many theological difficulties. It is written in an easy to read, conversational style, where complex ideas are made understandable. You will find yourself on a new and exciting journey for your mind and soul, where you will be expertly led into a deeper understanding of God as our "Abba," our Father.

Table of Contents

Prologue

The Events of My Life, Which Have Led to the Writing of This Book

My earliest recollection of church is walking along a curb in front of the Armory Building in Lowell, Massachusetts, on a bright sunny day, at the age of four or five. The church which my parents attended, Calvary Baptist, had burned down and was in the process of being rebuilt. To this day I associate church attendance with warm sunny days and new Easter outfits that my sisters and I received each year, despite the fact that my parents during those early years had very limited financial means. We did not regard ourselves as being poor, but money was very hard to come by and finances were always a deep concern. Most of my childhood activities centered in and around the newly re-built church. It was such a happy place. On Children's Day each year we all received potted geraniums in the Social Hall in the church basement. The annual Children's Christmas Party was also held down there. Of course, the highlight of that event was the appearance of Santa, with presents for all the children in attendance.

I remember the chart on the wall of my Sunday School class, with rows of Smiley Faces and Gloomy Gusses beside each name. Oh how I loved those Smiley Faces! Each year, for many years, I would receive an additional bar to attach to my Perfect Attendance Pin. After Sunday School the Children's Choir would sit in the balcony at the rear of the church sanctuary, totally bored with the service, and entertaining ourselves by observing the people below. I especially remember the interesting variety of hats the women wore to church in those days. The Children's Choir director, Frank Horn, was the man I admired most on this planet. He was also the Boy Scout Master of the troop that met in the Church Social Hall on Tuesday nights. Finally, after turning 11 years of age, I was permitted to join the troop. My parents couldn't afford the complete Boy Scout uniform, but there was at least enough money for the shirt, cap, and neckerchief. Most of the guys I ran with were members of the church and the scout troop. They also lived roughly in the same neighborhood as I, within a one mile radius. During my primary and secondary school days, the church activity which I absolutely loved the most was Vacation Bible School. Oh how I loved the singing, and the arts and crafts. My favorite songs were *Itsy Bitsy Spider, The Wise Man Built His House Upon The Rock, and Hallelu, Hallelu, Hallelu, Hallelujah.*

During those formative years, I was not in the least bothered by any doctrinal issues. At the age of 11, I attended a series of classes, led by the pastor, and was baptized. I remember memorizing Psalms 23 and 100 in Sunday School. My relationship with God was superficial at best. Occasionally I would pray *The Children's Prayer* before going to bed at night, which went like this: *Now I lay me down to sleep; I pray Thee Lord my soul to keep; If I should die before I wake, I pray Thee Lord my soul to take.* I remember wondering, after praying that prayer one night, if God was really there. I remember being very frustrated and upset that God didn't make Himself known to me in a more direct way. I was so frustrated that I literally banged my head against the wall. Although that was an isolated incident, the frustration of not knowing for sure if God was really there remained with me throughout my childhood and young adulthood.

In 1957, when I was 12 years old, my parents moved our family to Southern California to find better jobs and get a new start financially. We joined a large Baptist church in Riverside, with a large youth group. This church was more conservative and evangelical that the one we left in Massachusetts. It was here that I was exposed to a more intense evangelical religious environment, with many, though not all, of the trappings of Christian fundamentalism. The Sunday services were energetic, especially the evening service, and the gospel was part of every sermon. At the conclusion of each service, several verses were sung of an "invitation hymn," and those in attendance were urged to go forward to the front and publicly declare their intention to receive Christ for the first time as Savior and Lord, or to rededicate themselves to Christ, or to commit themselves to full-time Christian service as a pastor or missionary.

As was the case previously in Massachusetts, my life revolved around the church. I was there every time the doors were open. On Sunday evenings there was a youth group meeting, followed by an evening service during which the youth choir sang, followed by a youth fellowship singspiration at the home of one of the young people in the youth group. On Wednesday evenings we attended youth choir practice, followed by youth Bible study, followed by informal recreation in the fellowship hall or on the church parking lot. I especially loved the singing during the evening services, and the after-church singspirations. Young people were given various positions of responsibility in the youth group, and I served in various leadership capacities, and led the singing most of the time during the singspirations. I was even given the opportunity of preaching the sermon during the evening service on two occasions. Every summer, the youth group attended summer camp for a week, along with youth groups from other churches. In the winter, we attended winter camp. The camp experiences had a strong evangelical flavor to them, and I experienced many spiritual and emotional highs, sometimes referred to as "mountain top experiences," at those camps.

As much as I loved church and the fellowship of both the youth and adults who attended, I always felt inferior to them because I could never rid myself of the nagging doubts that I had experienced since childhood about the existence of God and the truth of the Gospel. I desperately wanted to be a "real" Christian, but always felt that I was prevented from achieving this because of my lack of faith. I listened to hundreds of sermons during this period, and the main teaching was that faith or belief in Christ and the gospel message was the primary condition that had to be met in order to become a Christian. The point was emphasized over and over again that salvation could not be obtained by doing good works, only through faith. For some, that would make it easy to become a Christian. Believing in Christ is much easier for some of us than doing good works, but not for me. Although I experienced many emotional and spiritual highs during my years of association with that church and its youth group, I never really experienced full assurance that I was truly saved. It did not seem to help that I walked down the aisle many, many times to rededicate myself to the Lord's service.

One evening, on New Year's Eve, after a youth event, during my junior year in college, I felt particularly frustrated by my vain attempts to find assurance of salvation. I drove around town for hours, praying to God as hard as I could for the faith I needed to become a Christian. I was in absolute misery. Finally, somewhere in the wee hours of the morning I knocked on my pastor's door and begged him to let me in so that I could pray with him to receive Christ. This was a big step for me because it was the very first time that I admitted to anyone that I had been a "hypocrite" all these years and had not really been a true believer. We prayed together. The next morning I went to the home of my youth group sponsors to tell them the news. A girlfriend of mine was also there. When they greeted me at the door they told me that they knew that I had been saved the previous evening. They could see it on my face. They told me that the girl friend of mine had stayed up all night praying for me, despite the fact that I had never revealed to anyone that I had a problem of unbelief. I took this as confirmation from God that He truly was real and that my conversion was genuine. Later, I was re-baptized in my church and made my decision public.

Eventually, however, the emotions related to that experience faded, and I again found myself plagued by doubts about the existence of God and the truth of the gospel message. I suppose you could say that on a scale of 1-10 my level of belief was about a 7 or 8. Not a bad score. But "close" only works with hand grenades and horseshoes. How was one to know what level of belief God requires for salvation? It appeared from my study of the Scriptures, and all the sermons I listened to, that you can't be just 80% saved. Either you are saved or you are not! Period! So how is a person like me to know whether his measure of faith is sufficient? Exactly where does God draw the line? To this very day I have never heard a satisfactory answer given to this question in any sermon I have heard or book I have read. Many other questions have arisen in my mind that are directly related to this. For example, I was taught that babies go to Heaven without having to believe in the Gospel because they aren't able to understand the Gospel message and they are not yet aware that they are sinners. When they reach the so-called "age of accountability" the awareness of sin is awakened in them and they then become accountable to God for it. At that point, they must receive Christ as Savior or they will be lost. Logic would indicate that this process of awakening and awareness of sin would be a gradual process, with no sharp line of demarcation between the two categories of children, those who have reached the age of accountability and those who have not. Where does God draw the line?

In addition to being perplexed by the above questions there were a host of other unresolved doctrinal issues for which I could find no satisfactory answer. I had serious questions regarding the relationship between science and religion. I had serious doubts about the literal inerrancy of the Scriptures. If the Scriptures were not literally inerrant in every respect, how could they be trusted to provide reliable information about God? I had a big problem understanding how a loving God could condemn most of the human race to everlasting torments in Hell. I had trouble enough finding assurance of my own salvation, but to make matters worse, what chance was there for the heathen who have never heard the Gospel, or those who might have rejected the Christian message due to strong religious and cultural biases for which they were really not to blame?

Despite all the unanswered questions, I nevertheless held onto my core Christian beliefs, although tenuously at times. I reasoned that somehow God must have understood my predicament and would someday provide the answers I needed. In my heart I was irresistibly drawn to Christ, and I wanted to serve Him as best I could under the circumstances.

As a college student at Redlands University, I attended the Baptist church most closely associated with the University, where most of the professors attended. It was a good church, with a membership comprised of liberal and conservative Christians, and everything in between. Redlands University was a Christian school, supported in part by the American Baptist Convention, but with a somewhat liberal theological orientation. Despite the unresolved doctrinal issues I had with fundamentalist conservative orthodoxy, I had bigger issues with liberalism. It seemed to me that Christian liberals were throwing out the baby with the bathwater. They didn't agonize over the same issues as I. It seemed to me that the central truth of Christianity was that Jesus was God incarnate and that He died and rose again to atone for the sins of mankind. The liberal has no problem with Hell. He simply doesn't believe that Hell exists, or else redefines the term to mean something far less serious. He doesn't have to reconcile apparent contradictions in the Bible because he doesn't believe the Bible to be inerrant. The Christian liberal can call himself a Christian because he respects many of the core spiritual and ethical teachings of Christ, but does not believe in the resurrection and has no personal relationship with Christ. Not all who regard themselves as liberals are that extreme in their beliefs. They might regard themselves as orthodox in their doctrinal beliefs but would espouse a more liberal and open view of the Scriptures. The popular term for this movement was Neo-Orthodoxy. It seemed to me that when you took this view of the Scriptures, you were in a sense opening a Pandora's box, filled with serious problems, the biggest of which is not knowing which parts of the Bible to believe and accept as God's truth.

Matters came to a head one day when I delivered a sermon in my church in Riverside. In this sermon, I lashed out at Christian liberalism and the liberal orientation of many of the professors at the university. I singled out the University Pastor in particular, who once told me that he did not believe in the atonement, at least not in the way I understood it. The sermon was full of self-righteous indignation. After the sermon, I was approached by a member of the college group at the Riverside church, an intellectual whom I respected. He told me that he was disappointed with my sermon and that he had expected better of me. He did not elaborate beyond his short, terse statement, but it had a huge impact on me. That night, in my bedroom at home, I wept bitterly. I realized that by lashing out at Christian liberals I was only compensating for my own feelings of inadequacy.

During my junior and senior years at Redlands University, in reaction to the somewhat liberal orientation of the church I was attending, I joined an extremely conservative, fundamentalist Baptist church across town. In that church I found warm fellowship and secure, familiar surroundings. There was a price to pay for this luxury, however. I was forced to endure weekly Sunday school lessons, steeped in fundamentalist dispensational theology. The worst part of it for me was the huge chart on the classroom wall with lurid depictions of beasts, dragons, angels, and other symbolic imagery from Ezekiel, Daniel, Revelation and other apocalyptic passages of the Bible. I absolutely did not buy into all that stuff, even though it was all right there in the Scriptures. Despite my aversion to certain aspects of fundamentalist theology, I felt very much at home in this church.

After graduating from Redlands University, I attended Seminary at California Baptist Seminary, now called the American Baptist Seminary of the West. The overall theological orientation of this school was somewhere between liberal and conservative. There was a mixture of both, and I found the environment there to be supportive and healthy. I only stayed one year for two reasons, one being financial and the other relating to my suitability for the ministry. Although I enjoyed the academic aspects of school, I really was not a "people person." I have always been somewhat of a loner, with few primary relationships. I enjoy the company of people in a church or work atmosphere, but do not care about people in the personal way that a pastor should. Despite the fact that I worked a graveyard shift at a local hotel to support myself at Seminary, and often suffered from sleep deprivation, I earned good grades. I would have made an excellent Seminary professor, I believe, had I stayed in school and obtained an advanced degree. However, the timing would not have been right because, at the time I was experiencing way too much ambivalence regarding the many perplexing and unresolved theological issues in my life.

There are two major take-a-ways from my experience at seminary, that have contributed the most to my current theological positions. The first is that belief (or faith) in Christ does not refer to intellectual assent to the existence of God or any prescribed doctrine about Christ. Instead, it refers to the process of entering into relationship with Christ. In the New Testament, the word "believe" is often followed by the preposition "in" or "on" which in the original Greek implies motion toward the object. In later years, I was able deduce from this that in order to become a Christian it is not necessary to have perfect faith. What is most important is that you exercise the faith that you have, whether it be strong or weak, and enter into relationship with Christ. You cannot imagine how liberating this has been to my soul.

The other take-a-way from my seminary experience is that salvation may be more correctly regarded as an ongoing process rather than an all-or-nothing event that takes place at only a single moment in time. In the New Testament, salvation is described in past, present and future terms. It is something that we experience partially in the present and more completely in the future. This concept has been the catalyst that I have used in subsequent years to successfully resolve, at least to my own satisfaction, many difficult and complex theological issues.

During the summer following my year at Seminary I served as youth director for a small church in Bremerton, Washington. Overall, it was a very enjoyable experience. I liked working with the young people, planning events, and playing my guitar and leading them in singspirations and devotional times. What stands out most in my mind about my time in Bremerton, however, is the single occasion of a brief visit I made to the home across the street from the church of two charming and elderly brothers who lived together. On that occasion they introduced to me to the concept of "universal reconciliation." They explained to me that Jesus paid the price for everyone on the Cross of Calvary and that everyone would eventually be saved, even those who went to Hell. They further explained that the words translated "eternal" and "everlasting" did not mean "unending." In the original Greek, these words meant an "age" or "age upon age" or "into the ages," with each age, or succession of ages, having a beginning and an end. Eventually, they explained, all will be reconciled with Christ. They showed me some Scripture passages which seemed to support this view. They explained that the purpose of Hell was remedial and that eventually everyone in Hell would be brought to repentance and be saved. As much as I wanted to believe them, I absolutely could not. This teaching seemed to contradict so much of what is taught elsewhere in the New Testament, and I could not get around the argument that if eternal damnation must come to an end, so shouldn't eternal life, because the same word was used to describe both. And, at least for the time being, that was the end of that.

After my experience as Youth Director in Bremerton, I joined the Air Force, during the Viet Nam War. I was an administrative officer at a small pilot training base in Big Spring, Texas, for two years, and was the chief of an armed forces courier station in Bangkok, Thailand, for the remaining two years of my tour of duty. During this period nothing significant happened regarding the development of my theological views.

In Texas and in Thailand I served in Southern Baptist Churches. I taught Sunday School in the Southern Baptist Church and also taught English in the language school established in Bangkok as part of the Southern Baptist missions program. The most rewarding of my experiences in Thailand, however, was the time I spent teaching English in the homes of Thai Christians. We met in small groups in their homes on a regular basis to teach English from the Bible. I was especially moved and touched by the presence of God when I listened to them sing hymns and pray in their native tongue. I benefited far more from those experiences than the people I was serving.

After my discharge from the Air Force, I left my parents' home in Riverside and went to Redding, California, to seek my fortune. I had little money and no job, so for me this was a somewhat risky undertaking. I chose Redding because of the beautiful lakes and trees there, which were reminiscent of the area where I grew up in Massachusetts. I quickly found a place to live and decided I would try to make a living teaching classical guitar. I rented a very small studio, gathered up a few students, and earned a little money, but mostly I spent my time fishing in Lake Shasta and Whiskeytown Lake. I attended the local Baptist Church in Redding, and one week in August I found myself counseling at a high school church camp sponsored by a group of Northern California American Baptist churches. The pastor of the First Baptist Church in Paradise, California, observed my interactions with the young people at the camp, and at the conclusion of the week-long camp asked me if I would consider moving to Paradise and joining their church staff as youth director. At the time, I had no job, and nothing better to do, so I agreed to give it a try and see what happens.

The church in Paradise had about 250 members and was comprised mostly of retired people. There was no youth group in this church. As a matter of fact, there were only two high school-aged girls and one junior high school-aged boy in the entire congregation. It was my job to build a youth group, pretty much from scratch. So out I went into the parks and streets, looking for young people to talk to and invite to church. One afternoon, as I was walking by the swimming pool at the apartment complex where I lived, I saw a young woman lounging by the pool who aroused my interest. In order to break the ice, I asked her if she knew of any young people who might like to join my church youth group. She said she thought she might. One thing led to another and we not only became friends, but ended up working together in the youth ministry. About a year and a half later, Arlene and I were married.

I modeled the youth ministry in Paradise after the one I was most familiar with from my experiences at First Baptist Church in Riverside. Every Sunday evening, the young people, eventually numbering about 40, filled up one side of the sanctuary, with the adults on the other. The evening service was informal, with lots of gospel singing and testimonies. After each service, all the young people were transported to a private residence for a singspiration and fellowship time. On Wednesday evenings we had song practice, followed by a Bible study. Times were changing, and youth choirs were no longer in vogue, so we formed a singing group, called Faith Incorporated, and performed programs and musicals at various locations.

About a year into this ministry, I was introduced to a Bible teacher named Roger Bagley, who earned a living of sorts by teaching in homes. He was not affiliated with any church, and one of his Bible study locations was the home of one of my youth group sponsors. Roger was an interesting fellow, deeply committed to Christ, and very intellectual in his approach to Bible study. We invited him to speak to our young people on a few occasions, and eventually he became the teacher of the Sunday Morning High School/College class. Many of the young people in the high school and college groups were highly intelligent and were drawn to Roger's teaching style. The first time anyone would attend one of his classes, they would come away from it bewildered and thoroughly confused. The concepts he shared were complex and difficult, if not impossible, to grasp in a single sitting. His teaching had a positive affect on the young people and they thrived under his teaching. We installed Roger as the teacher of the Sunday Morning Sunday School class because that was the only way we could entice many of the young people to attend the Sunday Morning worship service, which they regarded as very boring. Most of the young people came from unchurched families and would not otherwise be required to attend Church on Sunday Mornings.

The main themes of Roger's teaching centered around the Lordship of Christ. According to Roger, becoming a Christian results from receiving Christ as both Savior and Lord (see Romans 10:9-10). Yielding to the Lordship of Christ equated to repenting of the sin in one's life and deciding to follow Christ, instead. This did not negate the teaching in Ephesians 2:8-9 that salvation is given to us as a gift by grace, apart from works. The way I liked to explain it was that a person becomes saved when he repents and turns to Christ, before he is able to take even a single step of obedience to the other commands of Christ. This concept fit very well with my view of faith in Christ as describing a process of entering into a relationship with Christ, rather than being just a static form of intellectual assent to a set of theological propositions. Years later, I gradually came to the realization that this teaching embodies a very subtle form of legalism that can create serious doubts in the mind of the believer regarding the assurance of salvation. The question that plagued me in later years was this. To what degree must one repent of one's sins and yield to the Lordship of Christ in order to "qualify" for salvation? The answer, although simple, eluded me until very recently.

After about three years as Youth Pastor at First Baptist in Paradise, I felt it was time to move on, partly due to financial considerations and partly due to the fact that I felt myself getting a little "burnt out" and needing a change. I sold insurance for a year, and then relocated to Sacramento to take a sales job that did not materialize as expected. During this period, I had opportunity to meet my replacement at First Baptist, who happened to be an ardent hyper-Calvinist. Up until this point in my life I had given little or no thought to the doctrine of predestination, which I believed to have for the most part died out after the time of Jonathan Edwards. The notion that God arbitrarily predestines some to eternal life and others to eternal damnation, without giving anyone a say in the matter, was in my view absolutely detestable and completely contrary to God's nature, as reflected throughout the Scriptures. After reading up on the subject, I quickly realized that this doctrine is not only alive and well today, but it is the predominant view of many Christian denominations and is prevalent even in the Baptist church. A very strong case can be made in the Scriptures for this doctrine, and, as I soon discovered, it is very difficult, if not impossible, to refute many aspects of this teaching. The knowledge of this was a tremendous shock to my system.

A greater shock came when as a result of my research into the subject I discovered that Arminianism, the popular alternative to Calvinism, presented equally difficult problems. According to the Armenian view, we are all free to choose, and when God's "elects" or "chooses" us for salvation His decision is based on His foreknowledge of what our choice will be. Upon closer examination of the processes involved, however, I soon realized that no decision to follow Christ can be "self-caused." Although we are free to choose, the reason we choose differently from one another is that we are all created unique and different. What is it about you that makes you want to be saved? What "caused" you to be different? It doesn't make any difference whether God directly "caused" you to want to be saved, or whether God indirectly "caused" it by creating a random series of events which led to your birth and the particular life circumstances which predisposed you to want to make that decision. Seemingly, your decision to receive Christ was ultimately "caused" by forces outside of yourself. This being the case, how can it be fair that God saves some and not others? I was not able to resolve this issue to my complete satisfaction until very recently.

The next phase of my spiritual journey I shall call my "know-it-all" phase. After a disappointing experience with a sales job in the Sacramento area, I felt led to give youth ministry another try, and I accepted a position as Youth Director at First Baptist Church in Placerville. In this church there were more young people to start with and the youth group grew more quickly. During this period of my life, despite many unanswered theological questions that continued to vex me, I felt I knew enough of the truth to write and publish a Bible study guide. I called it "The Learning Factory," and the central theme was the Lordship of Christ. In this work I carefully explained many Bible doctrines as they related to the issues surrounding faith and works and the Lordship of Christ. One unique aspect of this study guide was its structure. It was a type of programmed study, similar to the ones which I was exposed to at Officer Training School in the Air Force. I would present a paragraph or two of information, with the important points in bold faced type. The paragraph was then followed by one or two questions, the answers to which were bolded in the preceding text. After the next informational paragraph, the question from the previous paragraph was repeated and another was added, and so on. As one progressed through the guide, new questions were added and older ones dropped off. Each question was repeated about three times, and then once again at the end of the work. I thought it was quite ingenious, and I thought the information contained in the work was so helpful and informative that I could perhaps make a living by publishing these guides. After "burning out" once again in the Youth Ministry, I tendered a partial resignation and worked part-time for the church, while a transition was made to a new Youth Director. This gave me time to self-publish my book and make a brief stab into the publishing industry.

Well, I was unable to find a printer who was willing to print my study guides cheaply enough to suit me, so I bought a table top press and printed copies in my home. Unfortunately, I was able to sell only a few copies, and that was the end of that. While trying to sell my study guides I took in printing jobs from local businesses to pay for the press and help make ends meet. One thing led to another, and I soon found myself in the printing business, which for the most part was the basis of my livelihood for the next 20 years or so.

Sometimes new theological insights come from unexpected sources. Not long after entering the printing business in Placerville, I received fresh insights from two unrelated incidents, one involving a crabby, complaining neighbor, and the other from a television show featuring a panel of atheists.

A few months after leaving the youth ministry, Arlene and I moved into a small home which had just been built on the edge of a very strange piece of property. It was about a two or three acre parcel which was somewhat of an eyesore due to the unchecked growth of weeds and blackberry vines along a small creek that ran through it. In the center of the property there was a small, run-down house, with lots of junk and debris lying in piles around it. The owner of the property was an older gentleman, of Russian descent, who was somewhat eccentric and who mostly kept to himself. The parcel on which our house stood had been split off from this man's larger parcel, and there was a deeded easement along the edge of his property that we used to access our house. One day, as I was clearing brush and weeds from the edge of the easement that gave me access to my property, the police showed up and told me the old man who owned the property next door was upset that I was trespassing on his property and wanted me to stop what I was doing. Well, to make a long story short, eventually the relationship between this neighbor and myself grew more cordial and we established a friendly relationship. One day the topic of our conversation turned to religion, and the subject of salvation and the eternal security of the believer came up. It turned out that he was raised in the Russian Orthodox tradition. I explained to him that one of the reasons I believed in "eternal security" had to do with the definition of the word "eternal." Since the word, "eternal" means "forever," and since the Bible describes eternal life as something that the Christian currently possesses, then it would logically follow that a person, once saved, could never lose his salvation. Otherwise, the "eternal" life, which the Christian was once in possession of, could not have been "eternal" to begin with. It would have been "temporary" life, at best.

He countered with an interesting argument. He told me that in the Russian Orthodox tradition, eternal life is not something that the believer actually possesses. Instead, eternal life belongs only to Christ, and the believer only experiences eternal life when he is in relationship with Christ and spiritually united with Him. If the believer withdraws from that relationship, then he would no longer experience the benefits of salvation, which is only to be found in Christ. Now, the old man did not word it exactly the way I just did, but that is the gist of his argument. At that time, I realized that there was much Scriptural support for this line of thinking, and it immediately brought to my mind Jesus' illustration of the vine and the branches and the necessity of abiding in Christ. It also fit well with the parable of the sower, which is troublesome to those who espouse the doctrine of eternal security. Many of the seeds sprouted, but for various reasons eventually died off. This teaching also explains the many admonitions in the New Testament epistles regarding the necessity of continuance or perseverance in the faith as a precondition of receiving the promise of eternal life as a future inheritance from Christ. Of course, I could not accept the old man's argument at the time, because there was just too much Biblical support for the doctrine of eternal security that did not rely just on the definition of the word "eternal." It was not until more than twenty years later that I was able to resolve these two seemingly irreconcilable doctrines to my complete satisfaction.

It was also during this period of my life that I became greatly disturbed by a statement made by one of the panelists on a television show I happened to be viewing as a result of a bit of channel surfing. At that time, the group led by Madelyn Murray O'Hair produced a television show espousing an extreme form of atheism that was highly critical of Christianity. While watching the show, I was completely taken back by a comment made by one of the panelists. He pointed out that the Christian God hides Himself from the world and then commands people to believe in Him. He makes it nearly impossible for any intelligent person to believe in Him, and then condemns to everlasting torments in Hell all those who don't. As much as I detested Madelyn Murray O'Hair's brand of atheism, I had to admit to myself that the panelist did have a point. The case that that panelist presented continued to vex me for many years. I was particularly sensitive to his argument because of the difficulties I, myself, had experienced as a youth when trying to "muster up" the necessary belief or faith which I thought was required for salvation. I often wonder how many non-Christians today, who would otherwise be sympathetic to the message of Christ, are prevented from embracing Him because of this distorted view of what God is really like.

Getting back to the story of my life, I wasn't the best business person in the world, and as a result I subjected my family to many serious financial stresses during my 20 years as a business owner. I involved myself in many side businesses that my family referred to as "get-rich-quick schemes" in order to dig myself out of the many financial binds in which I regularly found myself. During this period, we lived in nice homes and never wanted for the necessities of life, but through it all there was nearly constant financial pressure. At the end of this period came total financial collapse. For the past several years, however, we have enjoyed a measure of financial stability and freedom from financial worry. I am semi-retired now and own and operate an internet-based guitar sales business in Folsom, California. For the time being, my wife,

Arlene, and I are quite content. We have two wonderful daughters and sons-in-law who are all serving the Lord. The photo on the cover of this book is of our beautiful granddaughter, Isabella.

I am telling you all this because it relates to some of the doctrinal issues covered in this book. Some of the chapters in this book were written during times of extreme financial difficulty and discouragement. When times get bad, especially when most of the problems have resulted from our own misdeeds, it is easy to regard our distress as a kind of punishment from God. It is difficult to understand and believe during times like these that despite our own guilt God really wants to bless us. Our relationship with God is totally based on His grace. He loves us unconditionally and will permit nothing to occur in our lives that He cannot use as His instrument of blessing. I have learned to never underestimate the love of God and His willingness to bless me beyond expectation. When I look back on those difficult years I can now praise and bless God with every fiber of my being because in hindsight I can now clearly see God's loving and redemptive purposes through all of it.

A few years ago, in 2004, I decided it was time to finally make an all-out assault on the many unresolved doctrinal issues which have bothered me throughout my life. I decided to rigorously pursue the truth, no matter where it led. Each day, I asked God to lead me into truth and help me find the answers that I somehow knew must exist. Each day during my morning run, I would talk to myself, and to God, and ponder these issues. Most of my insights and creative thoughts occurred during these morning runs, which usually lasted about an hour and fifteen minutes, and which continue to this day. As a result, I wrote a series of essays, each addressing a different issue. Over time, I began to see connections among the various issues, and the pieces began falling together. Sometimes weeks and months would pass before new insights came, and I continually revised and updated previously written essays as new information presented itself to me. Eventually, it occurred to me to compile these essays into chapters of a book, which I could make available to others like me, who have been troubled by these issues.

Please understand that I do not presume to have all the correct answers, or that this book represents the final word in any of the matters discussed. I fully expect that virtually no one will agree with all of my conclusions. My thinking regarding these issues will always be a "work in progress." For the time being, I am satisfied with the answers that I have found. They work for me. My prayer is that regardless of whether you agree with my conclusions or not you will be helped by this publication and will find answers that will work for you.

Chapter 1

Summary of the Theological Views Expressed in this Book

This book is all about God's immense love for ALL of his created beings and His intention to eventually redeem us all from sin and death! God's judgments in this life and the next are completely fair and equitable and are expressions of His love for all mankind.

Let me say right up front that I consider myself to be an evangelical Christian, and I believe my views to be entirely consistent with the teachings of Scripture. I believe in the Trinity, the Deity and Resurrection of Jesus Christ, the Son of God. I believe in salvation by grace apart from works through faith in Christ. The major difference between my views and those of the majority of evangelical Christians today is my belief that if Jesus made atonement for the sins of all mankind on the cross of Calvary, eventually all mankind will be saved. I believe that all of God's judgments in this world and the next are remedial in nature and have a redemptive purpose. Eventually, after time as we know it comes to an end all of God's created beings will be fully reconciled to God through Christ (see 1 Cor. 15:22-28). Contrary to what many think, there is overwhelming Scriptural support for this view.

With that in mind, let me begin by summarizing the main theological positions which I have taken in this publication.

The main unifying theological position that I have taken is that God is both loving and just and that these are not contradictory aspects of His nature. Everything that God does in relation to His created beings is entirely consistent with every aspect of His nature. There are no "buts" in the equation. God doesn't have to say, "I love all mankind, 'but' because I am also just, or because I want mankind to have 'free will,' I must do things that I would really rather not do."

The God I believe in is the God of the Bible. The Bible, although not to be identified as the actual words of God Himself, may be relied upon for accurate information about the nature of God and how we may relate to Him. The writers of the Bible did write under the inspiration of the

Holy Spirit, and I believe they communicated to us exactly what God wanted us to hear. Being inspired by God, however, does not guarantee inerrancy. If it did, then all Holy Spirit inspired preachers in our own day and age would be preaching exactly the same message, and we wouldn't have hundreds of different Christian denominations. I believe that the most important truths about God are clear and unambiguous. My primary rule of Scripture interpretation is this: the least important doctrines are the ones that are the most highly disputed, while the most important ones are the ones on which most people agree.

Jesus said that unless we become like children we won't enter the Kingdom. All that the children of Jesus' day knew theologically was that Jesus loved them, and they loved Him back. Over the years the simple message that Jesus and His followers taught has evolved into a highly complex and detailed set of beliefs that have been used as a means of excluding most of the human race from the salvation that God has provided for all on Calvary. Theological correctness is not a prerequisite for Christian salvation. All of the gaps in our spiritual knowledge will be filled in after we die.

Although God is completely sovereign over His creation, He mostly uses indirect means to accomplish his purposes. Rather than imposing His will on mankind and intervening directly into our affairs and orchestrating our every move, He allows us to operate within the context of free choice (not the same as free will). He accomplishes His purposes in a mostly indirect manner by inspiring and empowering fallible and imperfect human vessels to do the job on His behalf by the power of the Holy Spirit.

The penalty for sin is spiritual death, or estrangement from God. This is not a permanent condition. That which is dead can be made alive again. Christians who were once dead in their sins have been made alive in Christ. According to Ephesians 2:4-5, *" because of his great love for us, God, who is rich in mercy, made us alive with Christ even when we were dead in transgressions—it is by grace you have been saved."* If the penalty for sin were everlasting torture in a place called Hell, then Jesus could not possibly have paid the price of our sins on Calvary. He rose from the dead less than three days later and is alive and well today.

God's ultimate purpose is to redeem all mankind from sin and death. On Calvary Jesus acted as a surrogate for all mankind when He endured estrangement from God, died physically, and was physically and spiritually raised from the dead. According to 1 John 2:2, *"He Himself is the propitiation for our sins; and not for ours only, but also for those of the whole world."* The difference between those of us who are saved and those who are not saved has to do with our awareness and experience of the connection that we all have with God through Christ. God is technically omni-present. He exists everywhere. He dwells within His creation, which includes all of us. By faith we are awakened to this connection and experience God's love, mercy and forgiveness in a personal way.

I like the way Paul puts it in Ephesians 2:6, *"and God raised us up with Christ and seated us with him in the heavenly realms in Christ Jesus."* What we fail to realize when interpreting this passage is that Paul was not just talking metaphorically here. Christians were actually raised up with Christ at the time of His resurrection. By using the past tense to describe this event Paul was telling us that we were saved in Christ before we became Christians. When Christ was raised so were we. Technically all who are destined to become saved were already saved in Christ 2000 years ago, before they were even born. The Bible clearly states in 1 Corinthians 15:22 that all will eventually be *"made alive in Christ."* All humanity will eventually become saved. If that is true, then according to Ephesians 2:6 all are saved already. Everyone who was ever destined to be saved was saved 2000 years ago in Christ. They just don't all know it yet. Most haven't yet experienced salvation in their conscious awareness. Sin is a form of blindness. The estrangement from God that sinners experience in this life is an illusion. When God saves us He merely removes the blinders.

I would take this one step further and state that in the mind of God the crucifixion and resurrection of Christ actually occurred before the universe was even created. God is timeless, and every event that has ever occurred, or will occur, is part of God's present. According to Revelation 13:8, Christ *"was slain since the foundation of the world."* There is good news and bad news in this passage. The good news is that some of us were *"predestined"* before the foundation of the world to receive or be awakened to life in Christ sooner than others (Rom 8:29). All will eventually experience salvation, but not until after undergoing a second death of sorts. Many will be required to do a "few more laps around Mount Sinai," to put it metaphorically, before fully experiencing the fullness of their salvation. According to 1 Timothy 4:10, *"God is the Savior of all men, and especially of those who believe."*

The goal of Christian "salvation" is to "grow" into the likeness of Christ. It is not an instantaneous event based solely on a single act of repentance or the belief in and recitation of a sinner's prayer. The Bible speaks of Christian salvation in past, present and future terms. It is process that will not be complete until the end of the ages. Christian salvation should not be equated with being saved from the consequences of our sinful behavior, or receiving a get-out-of-jail-free pass. God loves each of us unconditionally, and because of that we often find ourselves on the receiving end of His "tough love." The purpose of our sojourn here on earth is to learn through positive and negative interactions how to love like God loves. Christian salvation should not be regarded as a ticket into Heaven or escape from a place called Hell. Instead, when we enter into relationship with Jesus Christ and seek to apply in our lives the principles He taught us, we are saved from those destructive attitudes and behaviors that lead to unhappiness and misery. The rewards we receive in Heaven are not things but instead are the joy and satisfaction of knowing that we have made progress towards our goal of becoming like Christ. This, I believe, is an ages-long process.

Christian believers today have been elected or chosen in Christ not for salvation to the exclusion of all non-Christians, but as a royal priesthood and ambassadors for Christ (1 Peter 2:9). It is our mission to reach out to those who are still lost and act as Christ's body, His hands and feet, as it were, in eventually redeeming all mankind.

"Aionian" life, often mistranslated "eternal" life, does not refer to the duration, but instead, to the quality of our life in Christ. The Greek term *"Aionian"* literally means belonging to or pertaining to an age or ages. It means exactly the opposite of "eternal" and "everlasting." Nowhere in the Bible does it refer to an infinite, unending period of time. When Jesus gives us *aionian* life, the life He gives us is Himself. He is the *"way, the truth, and the life."* Everyone will live eternally, both Christians and non-Christians alike. All people continue to live after death in the sense that their conscious existence will never come to an end. *Aionian* life does not refer to never ending conscious existence. Even those who believe in everlasting punishments of the wicked in Hell, will acknowledge that the wicked possess everlasting "conscious existence." Instead, *aionian* life refers to our quality of existence IN CHRIST (See Rom: 3:24; 6:3-4; 8:1-2, 1-11; 1 Cor. 1:30; 2 Cor. 5:17; 15:22; Eph. 1:1-9; Col. 3:4; 2 Tim. 1:1; 2:19).

If *aionian* life referred to the length of our life, the meaning of the phrase would be completely lost. The emphasis should not be placed on the word *aionian*, but instead on the word "life." What distinguishes the Christian from the non-Christian is not the length of his life, but the nature of it. Bible passages which refer to *aionian* life are referring to spiritual life vs. spiritual death, not physical life and death. As Christians, we experience spiritual life in our present walk in this world and during the ages to come. To have *aionian* life is to be alive spiritually in Christ.

Those who do not have *aionian* life are dead spiritually and separated from Christ in this life, a condition which sometimes, but not always, continues after death. Technically Christ still resides within all of us, but not all are consciously aware of this. As a result, not all are experiencing *"aionian"* life.

Belief, or faith, is not a prerequisite for salvation. The term merely describes the means by which we enter into a relationship with Christ. Faith enables us to "open the door" of our hearts and receive Christ as Savior and Lord (see Rev. 3:20). It is not our faith, but the "opening of the door" that brings us into relationship with Christ. Faith is not an all-or-nothing proposition. It is something that we all have in varying degrees. Jesus died on the cross of Calvary once for all mankind and for all time (See Rom. 6:10). There now remain no obstacles preventing anyone from having a relationship with God through Christ. God accepts us just as we are, with no preconditions. It doesn't matter how sinful we have been or how weak our faith may be. All who come to Christ with an attitude of repentance and gratitude will be received by Him. *"Everyone who calls on the name of the Lord will be saved."* (Romans 10:13) There is nothing we can do to deserve or earn our salvation. We receive it by faith, no matter how weak or halting that faith might be, not by works. There is absolutely no room for boasting.

Although this sounds contradictory to what I just said when quoting Romans 10:13 above, I don't believe it is technically necessary to receive Jesus Christ by name in order to become saved. Calling on the name of the Lord should not necessarily be equated with calling the Lord by the name, Jesus. There is an important difference. There is no magic in the name Jesus. Names and titles meant a lot in the Jewish and early Christian culture, but have much less relevance in today's culture, and no relevance at all in Heaven (ie. the spirit world or the afterlife). In the Jewish and Christian cultures of the first century A.D., names were very important. We are told in Acts 4:12 that *"there is no other 'name' under heaven, given among men, by which we must be saved."* The Apostle Paul told us in Philippians 2:10 that Jesus was given a "name" which is above all names and at the name of Jesus every knee will bow. Of course, the Old Testament passage from which this was taken does not mention Jesus by name, but refers to God the Father instead (see Isaiah 45:23). The name Jesus was given to Jesus during his earthly existence. It actually means to "rescue" or "deliver," and was the same as "Joshua" in the Old Testament, who was also a deliverer. But Jesus would not necessarily be called by that name in the afterlife. The Jesus of history and the Christ of faith are indeed one and the same, but the name Jesus belongs for the most part to the earthly life of the Christ, who in a larger sense is the divine "Logos," the co-creator of the universe. When the Bible speaks about every knee bowing at the name of Jesus, those worshippers were not technically bowing to a name, but instead to the person who bore that name during His earthly sojourn. It is not the name Jesus that we worship. Instead, we worship Christ Himself. According to Matt. 25, when the sheep are separated from the goats many of those sheep will be admitted into the kingdom who never knew Him by the name Jesus.

This brings me to the topic of the deity of Christ and the doctrine of the Trinity. This is a highly controversial and divisive topic, even within the relatively safe confines of orthodox Christianity. If God is loving by nature, as the Bible attests, then for any kind of loving interactions to occur there would need to be at least two or more persons or entities participating in those interactions. It would seem logical to me that God's first act in time would be the creation one or more persons or entities with whom He could interact. According to the Bible, Christ was the first (Col. 1:15). So Christ did have a beginning in time. Based on my knowledge of quantum mechanics and the conservation of energy (God Himself being made up of pure energy) I do not believe that Christ was created out of nothing. He was created out of God's own essence (pure energy). He came from God in the sense that a human baby is made from the body parts of the mother and father. Jesus was "begotten" from God in the same sense that human parents "beget" their children. Jesus was divine in the sense that everything that comes out of God is part of God Himself. He was fashioned from God's DNA, so to speak. He also had a separate and distinct personality with whom God the Father could interact.

I believe there is another reason for Christ's existence. He is the personification of a God, who otherwise would be invisible, impersonal, and unknowable. *"No one has ever seen God, but the one and only Son, who is himself God and is in closest relationship with the Father, has made him known."* (John 1:18) In other words, Christ exists for the benefit of all humanity, that we might have a way to know and connect with God the Father.

Now I would turn your attention to the Holy Spirit. In the Bible, God is described as being a spirit. *"God is spirit, and his worshipers must worship in the Spirit and in truth."* The same is true of Christ. He exists in Heaven today in spiritual form, in a "spiritual" body, not made of flesh and blood. According to 1 Cor. 15:50, *"flesh and blood cannot inherit the kingdom of God, nor does the perishable inherit the imperishable."*

In addition to being in spirit form, both God the Father and the Son have a spirit. Christians are said to be indwelt by both the Spirit of God and the Spirit of Christ, and the two are used pretty much interchangeably. *"You, however, are not in the realm of the flesh but are in the realm of the Spirit, if indeed the Spirit of God lives in you. And if anyone does not have the Spirit of Christ, they do not belong to Christ."* (1 Cor. 3:16-18).

For me, the conclusion of the matter is this. Both God the Father and God the Son are different manifestations of a single divine Godhead. The term "Spirit" simply refers to what they are made of. As God's only begotten son, Christ is made up of "God parts," ie. spirit. Both the Father and Son share the same spirit, but also exist as separate entities. A very literal translation of John 1:1 expresses this connection: *"In the beginning was the Word* (ie. the Christ), *and what God was, the Word was."* Because both the Father and the Son exist in spirit form they can divide themselves into an infinite number of smaller pieces and focus their attention in many different places at once. Each piece is intimately connected with the whole and knows what all the other pieces are up to. The Spirit of God can listen to millions of different prayers at the same time. God is omnipresent. His Spirit and the Spirit of Christ are everywhere. All creation is infused with the Spirit of God and of Christ. Christ is the image of the invisible God and in Christ all things hold together. *"He is the image of the invisible God, the firstborn of all creation. For by Him all things were created, both in the heavens and on earth, visible and invisible, whether thrones or dominions or rulers or authorities – all things have been created through Him and for Him. He is before all things, and in Him all things hold together."* (Colossians 1:15-17)

As for the rest of us, I would conjecture that we are made up of "Christ parts," if we are to believe the Bible when we read in Colossians 1:6 that both the heavenly and earthly realms in existence, and all the people in them, were created by and through Christ. (See Colossians 1:16) We are spiritual beings because we are part of Christ, and Christ is a part of God. One day Christ will gather all of us up in Himself, completely perfected, and present us to the Father, and we will merge with God the Father, and God will finally be *"all in all."* (See 1 Cor. 15:22-28)

As for unsaved people being lost and tormented forever in a place called Hell, nothing could be more unbiblical. A better term for "Hell" would be "the righteous judgments of God" which for the most part are self-imposed and only temporary. The words "eternal" and "forever" in the Bible are mistranslations of the Hebrew word *"Olam"* and its Greek counterpart *"Aion"* and their derivatives, which literally mean the exact opposite of "forever" and "eternal." Their literal meaning is "age-during" or "pertaining to an age or ages," each of which has a beginning and an end. God allows us to suffer the negative consequences of our sins in order that they might be used by God to lead us to repentance and restoration.

The terms Heaven and Hell (Hell is not a biblical term) may best be described as states of being, rather than places. They represent opposite ends of a continuum of sorts. Heaven may be regarded as a state of sinless perfection in the presence of God. Hell may be regarded as living in a state of unrepentant sin, totally isolated from God. Just as there are degrees of reward and exaltation in Heaven there are degrees of suffering and torment in Hell. There is virtually no difference between the "lowest" place in Heaven and the "highest" place in Hell. Because Christ made atonement for the sins of all mankind there is no reason for God to punish anyone in the punitive sense. The suffering and torment that one experiences in Hell are self-imposed. Everything that happens to us is part of God's plan of redemption. Even while living in our own self-imposed versions of Hell Christ is still with us, just not in our conscious awareness. *"Where can I go from your Spirit? Where can I flee from your presence? If I go up to the heavens, you are there; if I make my bed in the *depths, you are there."* (Psalms 139:7-8) *Note: in the King James version, the word *"depths"* is translated *"Hell."*

So why does God allow this to happen? Why does He permit sin and evil? If He is the original cause of everything wouldn't that make God directly, or at the very least indirectly, the cause of evil? Why did a perfect God allow His creation to become so imperfect? To understand why, we need to realize that God's idea of perfection is not the same as ours. The material world that God created is filled with imperfections. It is precisely because of those imperfections that the world is so perfectly suited for God's purposes. Love and goodness cannot exist in isolation from their evil counterparts. Traits that we admire such as love, joy, peace, patience, kindness, goodness, faithfulness, gentleness and self-control have no meaning except in contrast with their opposites. When we view God's creation and his created beings in this way we should have no problem with God being the author of both good and evil. One cannot exist without the other. Even at the culmination of history, after evil is finally done away with, there must always be at least the remembrance of evil in order to understand and appreciate the good. Knowing this, we can better understand why God loves us and uses us to carry out His purposes despite our imperfections. It also helps us understand why sufferings, trials, difficulties and hardships can be used by God to bless us and help us grow stronger spiritually. *"I form the light, and create darkness: I make peace, and create evil: I the Lord do all these things. Drop down, ye heavens, from above, and let the skies pour down righteousness: let the earth open, and let them bring forth salvation, and let righteousness spring up together; I the Lord have created it."* Isaiah 45:7-8

Finally, I would like to address the subject of extra-biblical sources of information. The Apostle Paul has told us that God reveals Himself to us not only in the Scriptures, but also through the things He has made (see Romans 1:20) and through our own intuition. God's laws are *"written"* in our hearts and consciences. (See Romans 2:15). All truth is God's truth, no matter what the source. We learn from the study of the things God has made, especially from the findings of Quantum physics, that the material world exists only in our minds and that human consciousness exists independently of the human brain and the physical realm in which we temporarily reside. We learn from Near Death Experiences (NDE's) and "past-life" and "between-lives" hypnotic regressions that after death people are welcomed and received in Heaven and immersed in God's love, regardless of their religious beliefs during their earthly existence. This does not negate the truth of the Christian Gospel. It only affirms those truths as I have described them above. In my view, the evidence for the reality of NDE's, past-life recall, past-life and in-between lives hypnotic regressions is absolutely overwhelming.

I have been convinced beyond any reasonable doubt that these experiences and communications from the "other side" and our "inner-mind" are indeed real and genuine. Due to the highly subjective nature of these experiences care must be taken to harmonize these truths with one another and with the teachings of Scripture. The only way that these experiences could be untrue or false would be for them to be part of a huge demonic conspiracy to disseminate false information about God's universal love for mankind. If this were the case, many ardent Christians would be subject to this same deception because both Christians and non-Christians report exactly the same experiences.

I believe this summarizes fairly well the substance of the issues discussed in this publication. May God bless you as you read this book and seek a closer walk with Him*.

**Technically, God the Father, Son and Holy Spirit, are genderless.*

Chapter 2

The Problem with Proof Texts

The problem with so-called Bible "proof texts" is that they don't really "prove" anything. There are many reasons for this. Most individual Bible passages that deal with important doctrines are open to more than one interpretation. Quoting a scripture that has more than one reasonable interpretation proves nothing at all, and it would make no sense to suggest that an opposing point of view is not supported by Scripture.

Your acceptance of one interpretation over another would depend on the following:

1. Your views regarding the inspiration of Scripture.
2. Whether you would favor a literal or figurative interpretation of a given passage.
3. Your knowledge and awareness of other related Scriptures dealing with the same issue, including the immediate context and the broader context of the entire body of Scripture.
4. Your knowledge and understanding of the background and motivation of the writer.
5. The way in which a given interpretation fits into your over-all theological belief system.
6. Your level of understanding of the original language in which the text was written.
7. The various interpretations to which you have already been exposed.
8. The ways in which you process information. Some of you tend to emphasize reason and logic, while others depend more on personal experiences and intuition.
9. The degree to which you are willing to accept logical inconsistencies as part of your belief system.
10. Your willingness to change your views in the light of new information.

11. The degree to which you are satisfied with your current views.
12. The amount of time you are willing to devote to your theological study and inquiry.

Based on the above variables, it is no wonder there is so much disagreement regarding the many theological issues discussed in my book. My obvious intention in writing this book and creating the companion website is to inform and persuade. In order to do this effectively I believe it is important to begin by establishing some common ground with my audience (that would be you), and establish a sound basis for productive dialog.

I would like to begin by describing to you where I am coming from and the ways I have approached the study of the Scriptures relating to theological issues that are important to me. If you can identify with and relate to my experiences, and are in fundamental agreement with my approach to Bible study, then we would have a solid basis for productive dialog. My mission in life is to provide substantial help to people like myself who are troubled by logical inconsistencies with traditional theological views that are widely accepted by the evangelical Christian community.

I grew up in the evangelical Christian tradition and have always been bothered by logical incongruities relating to many traditional evangelical Christian doctrines. I was emotionally drawn to Christ and the gospel message, but was very uncomfortable with those doctrinal contradictions. We didn't call them contradictions, however, as that would be an admission that the Bible contradicts itself. So whenever we were confronted with firmly held contradictory doctrines we would call them paradoxes instead. A paradox is not a contradiction. Instead, a paradox may be defined as two truths which only seem to be contradictory. The way we dealt with these paradoxes was to throw our brains out the window and accept logical opposites as both being true, and pride ourselves on our ability to believe them by faith. In such instances faith would take precedence over logic. These contradictory truths have become so firmly engrained in our thinking that most of us refuse to believe that there is any way to logically reconcile them by means of sound Scriptural exegesis and interpretation. Most of the proof texts that are quoted in support of these opposing doctrines seem incontrovertible, and we don't look for solutions and resolutions to the conflicts because we don't believe that there are any.

Even if we became aware of alternate interpretations that might resolve some of these conflicts, we would be extremely reluctant to accept them because we would be bucking centuries of established evangelical Christian tradition. How can so many sincere and dedicated Bible scholars be wrong? Why would God allow such deception to continue for such a long time? Who am I to take issue with centuries of Christian scholarship? I discuss this issue in greater detail in a later chapter of this book.

Here are some examples of paradoxical truths that are commonly believed and accepted by evangelical Christians:

Most evangelicals believe that God is loving, fair and just, and commands us to follow His example and forgive our enemies. At the same time they also believe that God does not forgive most of His enemies and punishes their finite sins with infinite punishment in Hell.

Many evangelical Christians (Calvinists) believe that God is loving and is able to save all mankind and no one can resist His will, but for reasons known only to Him He decides only to save a few and send the rest to eternal damnation in Hell without giving any of them a real choice in the matter.

Many evangelical Christians (Arminians) believe that God is loving and all-powerful and desires that all men be saved, but is unable to save most of them in the interest of preserving their freedom to choose. He is either unwilling or unable to change their thinking and bring them to repentance.

Many evangelical Christians accept both the Calvinistic and Arminian positions as true despite the contradictions between them because the Bible apparently teaches both.

Most evangelical Christians believe that Christ paid the penalty of death for the sins of all mankind, and that the penalty only had to be paid once. At the same time, most believe that most of mankind will still be required to pay the penalty that supposedly had already been paid by Christ, and as a result will spend eternity in hell.

Most evangelical Christians believe that Jesus was telling the truth when He said that in the next life we all will reap what we have sown. Yet they also believe that in the next life Christians will be rewarded for their good deeds and not be punished for their sins and that non-Christians will reap a far greater punishment than what they would justly deserve and not be rewarded for their good deeds.

Most evangelical Christians believe that we are saved by faith alone, apart from works, and our salvation is of God, not ourselves, lest anyone should boast. Yet they also believe that man must qualify for salvation by believing the Gospel, repenting of his sin, and producing good works as evidence of his salvation. Many believe that if a person does not continue in faith and good works he may lose his salvation at some time in the future.

In addition to paradoxical truths, there are other evangelical doctrines which, though not paradoxical, still don't square with reason and logic. The main teaching of this sort, that has bothered me to no end, is the teaching that Salvation is an all-or-nothing condition that occurs at only one instantaneous point in time. It is commonly taught that one becomes instantly saved when he or she believes the Gospel message and receives Christ as Savior and Lord. A problem arises in my mind when I try to understand exactly what level of belief or repentance is required and how God draws the line between "saving" faith and faith which doesn't quite cut it. If Salvation does not always occur instantaneously, how does a person determine whether or not he or she is saved? At what point, for example, does a child reach the "age of accountability?" If repentance is required, at what level of repentance does one qualify for salvation? This question is discussed in more detail, and answered, in a later chapter of this book

So here's what I'm leading up to. If the issues discussed above are not troubling to you, then there is no need for you to read this book. If, on the other hand, you are troubled by these issues I believe you may be greatly helped by the information that I am sharing with you. Please understand, however, that in order to successfully resolve these doctrinal conflicts to your own satisfaction you must be willing to temporarily set aside many traditionally held views and open your mind to new ways of viewing them. You must not be afraid to think "outside the box" and be open to new interpretations of many familiar Scriptures. I will not be interpreting any Scriptures in unnatural ways. As a matter of fact, because of our entrenched traditional theological views we in the past have avoided accepting the most natural and obvious interpretation of many Scriptures.

As a result of setting aside all of my previous views and approaching the Scriptures directly and actually letting them speak for themselves, I have arrived at a point in my understanding where I can now accept and believe the Scriptures at face value without having to do work-a-rounds or resort to awkward interpretations of anything I read in the Bible. A few years ago I decided to begin a serious study of the Scriptures with a completely open mind to see if I could interpret them in such a way as to avoid contradictory or paradoxical conclusions. The result was a strengthening, not an abandonment, of most of my core Christian beliefs.

I discovered that it was possible to responsibly and naturally interpret the Scriptures and arrive at a systematic theology that successfully resolves nearly all of the conflicts which had troubled me so much in the past. Today, I love the Scriptures and my God as never before. My prayer life has been tremendously enhanced, and I can accept without reservation all that the Scriptures teach.

When reading the information in this book, please keep an open mind and try to free yourself from the above-mentioned obstacles to correct Scripture interpretation.

Chapter 3

Why I Believe in the God of the Bible

If you are like most people, you have struggled with the question of God's existence and more specifically the truth of the Bible. The purpose of this chapter is to help you understand why I believe in the God of the Bible, and in so doing help you to believe as well. One of the major obstacles I personally faced in this regard is the fact that if God does exist He does not overtly make His existence known to us. His presence in the world and in our personal lives remains undetectable by our physical senses. He seems to hide himself from us. I will only briefly address this issue in this chapter because I will be covering it in more detail in a later chapter. My reasoning is that in order for us to develop qualities of Godly character, our choices must be freely made without coercion by God. Ultimately God is sovereign in our lives, but his purposes are mostly accomplished through human agency rather than by direct intervention. As a result we are able to develop Godly character and engage in useful and purposeful ministry in partnership with God. If God forced all our choices and accomplished his purposes by direct intervention, then we could not be morally accountable for our actions. We would like Pavlov's dogs, who's responses were conditioned solely by external stimuli. It has taken me the better part of a lifetime to understand this and remove God's invisibility as an obstacle to my personal belief in Him.

I now draw your attention to the main purpose of this chapter, which is to present evidence of God's existence and the truth of the Bible. Please understand that I will be presenting mostly circumstantial evidence, not irrefutable proof. It is impossible to irrefutably prove anything. I cannot prove that you or I even exist. Everything in life, even the strictest of scientific disciplines, is based on probabilities, not certainties. The fact that I cannot prove God's existence in the absolute sense, however, does not prevent me from exercising faith in God and acting on what I believe is most probably true. My goal in writing this chapter is to help remove major obstacles to your faith and give you sufficient reason to embrace the truth of the Scriptures and develop a meaningful relationship with God through Jesus Christ.

Many believers do not require hard physical evidence to support their belief in God. They base their faith on their own intuitive thought processes and use a form of inductive reasoning to support their conclusions. They intuitively believe in God and seek validation for their belief by observing the life experiences of themselves and others. For example, when they pray for something and get what they asked for, they conclude that God may have answered their prayer. If that experience is repeated in their lives and the lives of people they know, they generalize, through a process of inductive reasoning that God must exist. Many such "evidences" are used to support a belief in God and the truth of the Scriptures. Support for their faith is drawn from God's apparent intervention in people's lives. Another example of a type of inductive reasoning would be inferring the existence of God from the fact that the majority of people in almost every culture believe in some form of higher power. If the vast majority of people on Earth believe in a god or gods, then there must be some factual basis for those beliefs. Although persuasive, such examples of inductive reasoning cannot conclusively prove the existence of God. They may be used to support one's belief system, but cannot be used as irrefutable evidence.

Conclusive evidence of the existence of God can only result from a process of "deductive" reasoning whereby conclusions are deduced from universally accepted scientific facts and historical truths. An example of this kind of reasoning would be calculating the probability of certain natural processes occurring without divine, supernatural intervention. According to Dr. Hugh Ross, a highly respected astrophysicist and pastor, the mathematical probability of even one planet existing in the universe which is capable of supporting life is much less than one chance in a hundred thousand trillion, trillion, trillion, trillion, trillion. A probability that small is for all practical purposes zero. Dr. Ross lists 75 criteria that must be satisfied for a planet to be capable of supporting life. He then calculates the probability of each of those criteria of existing in any one planet. If just one of those 75 criteria were not satisfied, then life would be impossible. When you multiply the 75 individual probabilities, you arrive at the probability of a planet existing that could support life. You will find these 75 criteria listed, along with their respective probability factors, on Dr. Ross' website www.reasons.org.

Using simple mathematical formulas, probabilities can also be calculated for other natural processes occurring without divine intervention, such as the creation of life on this planet or its evolution into higher forms. These probabilities are so infinitesimally small that they are basically zero. It would logically follow then, that the probability of the intelligent design of our universe, the planet Earth, and life on Earth, is infinitely great and for all practical purposes certain.

Additional scientific evidence for the existence of God may be found in the study of quantum mechanics and general relativity. Many scientists, especially theoretical physicists, are coming to realize that we don't actually live in a physical, material world, but a supernatural world instead. Their belief in a natural world, subject only to the natural laws of Newtonian physics, has given way the idea that the world we observe and experience consists solely of immaterial wave functions that may be described only as probabilities and possibilities, and do not "collapse" into reality unless observed by conscious observers (that would be us) who themselves do not actually reside within this universe and are, in a manner of speaking, spiritual, rather than physical beings. Later in this book this subject will be explored in greater detail. Belief in the supernatural makes it much easier for me to believe in a supernatural, immaterial, creator God.

The testimony of people who have experienced near death experiences (NDE's), past-life memories, past-life and between-lives hypnotic regressions, and other forms of communications from the dead, provide proof that God exists, and also give us valuable insights into the reality of an after life in Heaven, which we will all experience after death. The evidence for the reality and genuineness of these experiences is in my view irrefutable, and will be covered in more detail in a later chapter of this book.

Various polls have revealed that the vast majority of people on earth share my belief in the existence of God, but most do not believe in the divine inspiration of the Christian Scriptures. And that brings us to the second part of this essay. Are the Christian Scriptures divinely inspired by God, and do we find within their pages reliable information about God's nature and how we may relate to Him.

Before I present my case, however, I would like to address a related issue. Many reject the Christian Scriptures due to misconceptions they have about what those Scriptures teach. They reject the Scriptures because they reject the popular view of God as having two irreconcilable aspects to His nature. The God of the Bible is viewed as both loving and hateful, who rewards those who believe with everlasting joy in Heaven, and condemns those who do not believe to everlasting torments in Hell. They cannot accept the teaching that God, who is supposedly a God of love, would banish most of the human race to everlasting Hell. This teaching is contained in the official creeds and doctrinal statements of most Christian denominations and is believed by most professing Christians today. Please understand that this is not what the Scriptures teach. God, who is infinitely greater than any of us, is also infinitely more loving and kind than any of us, and the Scriptures definitely support this view. One of the main reasons I wrote this book is to address this issue.

My belief in the truth of the Christian Bible has been reinforced throughout my life by my own experiences of God working in my life and the lives of those around me, but the foundation of my belief includes both scientific and historical evidence. From a scientific perspective one would expect that the Bible might at least be more scientifically accurate than the scriptures of other religions. Not only does the Bible stand the test, but there is no other scripture that even comes close. For example, there is not a single other religion whose scriptures correctly describe the creation of the universe and the exact order of creation of the Earth and its various life forms. The Bible, on the other hand, correctly describes the "Big Bang" when it describes the creation of the heavens and the Earth out of nothing. In Genesis 1, the exact order of creation is accurately described. The following is taken from an article by Dr. Hugh Ross titled *"Summary of Reasons to Believe's Testable Creation Model:"*

1. *Creation, by fiat miracle, of the entire physical universe (space-time dimensions, matter, energy, galaxies, stars, planets, etc.)*
2. *Planet Earth singled out for a sequence of creation miracles. At its beginning, Earth is empty of life and unfit for life; interplanetary debris and Earth's primordial atmosphere prevent the light of the sun, moon, and stars from reaching the planet's surface*
3. *Clearing of the interplanetary debris and partial transformation of the earth's atmosphere so that light from the heavenly bodies now penetrates to the surface of Earth's ocean*
4. *Formation of water vapor in the troposphere under conditions that establish a stable water cycle*
5. *Formation of continental land masses and ocean basins*

   Production of plants on the continental land masses
6. *Transformation of the atmosphere from translucent to occasionally transparent. Sun, Moon, planets, and stars now can be seen from the vantage point of Earth's surface*

7. *Production of swarms of small sea animals.*
8. *Creation of sea mammals and birds*
9. *Creation of three specialized kinds of land mammals: a) short-legged land mammals, b) long-legged land mammals that are easy to tame, and c) long-legged land mammals that are difficult to tame—all three specifically designed to cohabit with humans*
10. *Creation of the human species*

One of the main obstacles to the acceptance of the Bible as scientifically accurate is the insistence of many proponents of literal inerrancy that the six creation days described in Genesis are literal 24-hour days. The truth is that the literal translation of the word used for "day" in Genesis can mean a 24-hour day, or an unspecified period of time, or an age. Another obstacle is a misinterpretation of the fossil record, which shows an "evolution" of life forms in the various geological strata, from simple forms of life in the oldest strata to higher life forms in the newer strata. The truth is that the literal 24-hour day model cannot possibly explain the indisputable fact that these strata were laid down over millions of years. The theory of Darwinian Evolution by means of natural selection alone also cannot possibly explain the evolutionary process. There are almost no transitional life forms between the various species, which appear suddenly in the fossil record. No mechanism has been discovered by which natural selection can account for such dramatic changes in such short intervals of time. *The "Old Earth, Day-Age Creation Model,"* however, perfectly describes the process, and this model is in full agreement with the Genesis account. According to this model, God created all of the species in successive waves of creation corresponding to the various geologic ages, with the process of natural selection accounting for minor adaptations to changing local environments. For a complete, well-documented, discussion of the Bible and Science I refer you to Dr. Hugh Ross's website: www.reasons.org.

In addition to scientific evidences, a powerful case for the truth of the Christian Scriptures can be made from historical evidence. In a court of law the guilt or innocence of the person on trial is supported by historical evidence. Known historical facts are corroborated by eye witnesses to "prove" the case. In the case of the Scriptures, there are many historical events which are universally accepted even by skeptics. We know that most of the original apostles, and many of their closest followers, suffered intense persecution and martyrdom for what they believed to be the truth of the resurrection, of which they were actual eye witnesses. It is much easier for me to believe the truth of their claims than to believe that they deliberately lied about it for personal advantage.

While I don't believe in the inerrancy of the Christian Scriptures, I do believe they were divinely inspired. Much of the Bible consists of stories, legends, sayings, and actual historical events that were handed down verbally for many years, and in some cases centuries, before they were written down. And even after taking written form they were subject to later additions and embellishments by well-meaning redactionists who exercised a form of poetic license with respect to the literal truth, in order to teach theological truths from their unique perspectives in history. This in my view doesn't make the Scriptures less true from a theological standpoint. It does, however, create problems when we base certain aspects of our theology on a literal interpretation of passages which might not accurate in the objective historical sense. For example, It may well be that the writers and editors of the Genesis accounts believed that the creation of the cosmos, including all mankind, occurred over a period of six literal 24-hour days. It is not necessary for us today to believe this in order to accept the underlying truth that God is, after all, still the creator of everything. At the same time, I would be careful not to develop a doctrine of original sin and/or the moral and spiritual depravity of mankind solely on a literal interpretation of the Genesis account, or to blame everything on Satan, who took the form of a serpent in the mythical Garden of Eden. In a later chapter of this book I will discuss this issue in greater detail.

Another historical argument for the truth of the Scriptures, and the New Testament in particular, would be that there is no other good explanation for the influence of Christianity on subsequent human history. The following is an adaptation taken from a sermon by Dr. James Allan Francis in "The Real Jesus and Other Sermons," c. 1926, by the Judson Press of Philadelphia (pp 123-124 titled "Arise Sir Knight!"):

One Solitary Life

Here is a man who was born in an obscure village, the child of a peasant woman. He grew up in another village. He worked in a carpenter shop until He was thirty. Then for three years He was an itinerant preacher.

He never owned a home. He never wrote a book. He never held an office. He never had a family. He never went to college. He never put His foot inside a big city. He never traveled two hundred miles from the place He was born. He never did one of the things that usually accompany greatness. He had no credentials but Himself...

While still a young man, the tide of popular opinion turned against him. His friends ran away. One of them denied Him. He was turned over to His enemies. He went through the mockery of a trial. He was nailed upon a cross between two thieves. While He was dying His executioners gambled for the only piece of property He had on earth – His coat. When He was dead, He was laid in a borrowed grave through the pity of a friend.

Nineteen long centuries have come and gone, and today He is a centerpiece of the human race and leader of the column of progress.

I am far within the mark when I say that all the armies that ever marched, all the navies that were ever built; all the parliaments that ever sat and all the kings that ever reigned, put together, have not affected the life of man upon this earth as powerfully as has that one solitary life.

Another type of historical evidence for the validity of the Scriptures would be the application of common sense and logic to the testimony of Jesus Christ himself and his followers. Even unbelievers regard Jesus as a great moral teacher, probably the greatest of all time. But if Jesus were only a great moral teacher, and not really the Messiah and the Son of God He claimed to be, He would have been very deceitful or a lunatic, hardly the description of a man who forever changed the course of history and has been worshipped by billions of people since his death. In the words of C.S. Lewis (from his book, *Mere Christianity)*, *"A man who was merely a man and said the sort of things Jesus said would not be a great moral teacher. He would either be a lunatic-on the level with the man who says he is a poached egg-or else he would be the Devil of Hell. You must make your choice. Either this man was, and is, the Son of God: or else a madman or something worse."*

Another reason I believe in the truth of the Christian Scriptures is that in actual practice Christianity works amazingly well for those who devote their lives to its teachings. Christian prayer has the power to dramatically transform and improve our lives, and many who convert to Christianity are rescued from the bondage of fear, unhappiness, and self-destructive lifestyles.

Finally, I believe in the Christian Scriptures because in them I find the absolute highest expression of human ideals, the noblest of which is unconditional, sacrificial love for all mankind, which is embodied in the God of the Bible through the life, teachings, and character of Jesus Christ.

Chapter 4

Is the Bible Literally True and/or Inerrant?

There is a difference between literal truth and inerrancy. The Bible may be considered inerrant, while at the same time make use of symbolic imagery and metaphors for purposes of illustration. The question of inerrancy has more to do with theological, scientific, and historical truth. So, a better way to rephrase the title of this chapter might be this. Is the Bible the inerrant word of God? Or is it the God-inspired words of fallible men, and not true and inerrant in every respect? If the Bible is not completely inerrant, does this negate the parts that are true? If not, how does one decide which parts to believe and which parts to reject? Orthodox Christians can be sharply divided on this issue, while at the same time sharing similar "theological" beliefs and subscribing to nearly identical doctrinal statements and creeds.

Here's my take on this issue. In the pages of the Bible you will find totally reliable information regarding the true character of God and how you may establish a relationship with Him. Please understand, however, that not even the most hard-core Christian fundamentalist believes that every Bible passage is literally true. Some passages are obviously figurative in nature. For example, in Psalm 96:12 we learn that when the Lord comes to judge the earth all the trees of the forest will sing for joy. Most of the parables of Jesus were fictional stories which illustrate spiritual truths. The apocalyptic passages in Daniel, Ezekiel, Revelation, and so on, speak of future events in symbolic terms. Up to this point, proponents of both sides of the inerrancy issue would be in agreement. Beyond this point, however, the issues become clouded.

The issue of inerrancy is complicated by the fact that many of the truths expressed in the Bible are understood, even by proponents of inerrancy, as being generally true, but not in every specific instance. For example, in Ephesians 6:2 children are admonished to honor their fathers and mothers so that everything will go well with them and that they may enjoy long life on the earth. In Proverbs 22:6, we are admonished to *"train a child in the way he should go, and when he is old he will not turn from it."* Obviously, not all obedient children live long lives and not all children who are raised in devoutly Christian homes make the right choices later in life.

Another related issue is the difficulty of separating the words of God from the words of man in the Scriptures. The writers of the Bible, although inspired by God, still expressed their own points of view, which were often contrary to God's truth. The entire books of Job and Ecclesiastes are illustrative of this. Job was under the mistaken notion that God always rewards the righteous and punishes the wicked in this life, and he was unable to understand why he was being punished. His friends were no help. They insisted that Job had committed some grievous sin and was justly suffering God's wrath. Despite all the give and take between Job and his friends, the issue was never clearly resolved. In the end, Job resigned himself to the fact that he should honor God despite, in his opinion, being unfairly treated. Eventually his health and possessions were restored, but one gets the feeling that this ending was added to satisfy those who could not accept the fact that life is not always fair. Was Job an actual historical character, or was the book intended to be understood as a parable illustrating man's inability to understand the ways of God?

In the case of Ecclesiastes, the writer begins with these words, *"Meaningless! Meaningless!"* says the teacher. *"Utterly meaningless! Everything is meaningless."* He goes on to explain how futile life is because, in the end (see Eccl. Chap. 9) all share a common destiny—*"the righteous and the wicked, the good and the bad, the clean and the unclean, those who offer sacrifices and those who do not . . . For the living know that they will die, but the dead know nothing; they have no further reward, and even the memory of them is forgotten."* At the end of the book, the writer hints that it is still worthwhile to keep the commandments of God, *"for God will bring every deed into judgment, including every hidden thing, whether it is good or evil."*

In Jesus' day different parts of the Scriptures were assigned varying degrees of authority, with the Torah, also called the Law, being given the highest level of inspiration. The Torah was comprised of the first five books of the Bible and at the heart of the Torah were the laws given by God through Moses. Second to the Torah was the portion of Scriptures referred to as the Prophets. The books with the lowest level of inspiration and authority were the Writings, which included the historical and poetic works. Moses was regarded as the greatest of the prophets. Therefore his writings were assigned the greatest authority. The books ascribed to the other prophets of God were given greater authority than the "Writings" because the prophets were more directly connected to God than the writers of the other books. For example, one would hardly consider Solomon to be closer to God than Isaiah or any of the prophets. David, who wrote many of the Psalms, although very close to God at times, was also a great sinner.

The same principle of inspiration was applied in the development of the New Testament canon. Greater authority was given to those works which were written by Jesus' disciples and those who derived their information directly from them. There were many gospels written about the life of Christ, and perhaps hundreds of letters circulated in the early church, but only 27 of these documents were eventually included in the official canon. There were basically two criteria used in their selection, the authority of the author's themselves and the degree to which they were used and accepted in the Christian community. Nowhere in the Old Testament or the New Testament is it stated that every word of the Bible is to be taken as true and inerrant. Even if the Bible did make such statements, by what authority would we be able to accept those statements as true? According to II Timothy 3:16, *"All Scripture is God-breathed* (inspired by God) *and is useful for teaching, rebuking, correcting and training in righteousness."* Here, Paul was referring only to the Old Testament, as the New Testament canon had not yet been formulated.

Although Jesus had great respect for the Scriptures, he also took liberties when interpreting them and rendered many of their teachings obsolete by supplanting them with newer doctrines. In Matthew 5, the Sermon on the Mount, Jesus emphasized the importance of the Law and the Prophets, and tells us that *"until heaven and earth disappear, not the smallest letter, not the least stroke of a pen, will by any means disappear from the Law until everything is accomplished,"* and warns us not to break even the least of these commandments. However, He then went on to amplify and change six of these commandments. In the cases of murder, adultery, divorce, oaths, revenge, and hatred of enemies, he made the rules much stricter. Even strict Biblical literalists understand that individual Scriptures must be interpreted in light of the historical context in which they were given. In Old Testament times, due to the "hardness of peoples' hearts," God's laws were more lenient than the standards which he now holds us to.

I personally have come to believe that God's revelations to us through the inspired writers of the Bible are progressive in nature. Over time God has progressively revealed more of his truth. The fact that Solomon and Job were ignorant of an afterlife does not mean that their written works were not inspired by God. They were truthfully expressing what God had revealed to them. If we insist that all Scriptures are inerrant we fail to take into account the progressive nature of God's revelation. The writers of the Bible wrote in different historical contexts and with different purposes in mind. They were inspired by God, but they were not perfect, and their knowledge of spiritual and historical truths was not perfect.

Some believers in Scriptural inerrancy subscribe to a kind of dictation theory of inspiration whereby the words of the Bible are literally the words of God Himself and were perhaps unconsciously dictated to the Bible's writers as they wrote. If this were the case wouldn't you expect the Bible to be a bit easier to understand and a lot less ambiguous and apparently contradictory in nature? If God is perfect one would assume that He is capable of expressing Himself in clear, precise and easy-to-understand terms. If it were God's purpose in writing the Bible to create a perfect work why is it so difficult to understand? Why is there so much disagreement among Bible scholars over its teachings?

Apparently God's idea of perfection is not the same as ours. God's treasures are housed in *"earthen vessels."* The Bible is perfect in the sense that it is perfectly suited for God's purposes. It perfectly expresses what God wants us to hear. If it does not reveal everything we want to know about God, then we must assume that it suits God's purposes for us not to know everything. Later in this book, I will be elaborating on the fact that man's idea of a perfect world is vastly different from what God has actually created. Yet God is perfect. He makes no mistakes. God has chosen to accomplish his purposes mostly through human agency and to a far lesser extent through direct intervention. Assuming this to be true, one would also have to assume that the Bible, because it was created through human agency, would also contain imperfections. It is not God's directly dictated and transcribed words. God's words come to us through the imperfect filter of human understanding and experience. Jesus Christ, the *Logos*, is God's living Word. He is the one who has inspired the writers of the Bible.

Please understand that whether you believe in Scriptural inerrancy or not the fact remains that the Bible must be interpreted by examining a particular verse or passage in light of the historical context in which it was written, and other Scriptures dealing directly or indirectly with the same topic must also be examined. Any given Scripture, no matter how clear the interpretation may seem at first glance, is subject to a variety of interpretations. It may be regarded as figurative or symbolic in nature; it may be regarded as applying only to a particular period in Biblical history, only to be supplanted with other commands given at a later date; it may be regarded as the opinion of the writer, but not necessarily the words of God Himself, and so on. Individual verses and passages of Scripture must be viewed and interpreted in light of the totality of the Scriptures. The teachings of the New Testament shed light on the meaning and intended purpose of various passages in the Old Testament. In some cases the teachings of Christ supplant Old Testament teachings. In other cases New Testament teachings reveal hidden meanings in various Old Testament passages. In most cases, when faced with multiple possible interpretations of a given Bible passage, the intended meaning becomes clear only when other passages are examined which deal with the same topic.

For example, in Matthew 17, Jesus took his disciples aside and admonished them for their lack of faith. He told them that if they had faith even as small as a mustard seed they could move a mountain from here to there and nothing would be impossible to them. Other passages imply that we can have whatever we ask in Jesus' name, and so on (See Matt. 21:22; Jn. 16:24; Mk. 11:24). One could take a "literal" view of these passages and assume that if we just have enough faith we can get from God whatever we want. When other Bible passages are examined, however, we realize that "getting what we want" is not what prayer is all about. James tells us (4:3) that we don't get what we ask for because we ask with the wrong motives and pray selfishly. James also tells us (5:16) that the prayer of a righteous man is powerful and effective. We only become righteous when we abide in Christ and become clothed in his righteousness. When we are able to share the mind of Christ in this way, then what we want will be the same as what God wants and our prayers will indeed become very powerful. A guaranteed "yes" answer to prayer is not simply a matter of asking for whatever you may want at any given moment. When Jesus prayed in Gethsemane, He did not get what He wanted. He did get what He prayed for, however, because His prayer ended with these words, *"not my will, but thine be done."*

A very difficult issue for me personally to resolve was how far I could safely depart from the popular view of Scriptural inerrancy and still maintain my confidence in the Bible as a reliable source of spiritual truth. Today I am able to accept most of the findings of "historical criticism" of the Bible, including source criticism, form criticism, redaction criticism, tradition criticism, canonical criticism, and so on, and still maintain my faith in the Gospel of Christ. Because my study of the Bible is not restricted or confined to a rigid view of inerrancy I am able to more honestly and accurately assess the development of thought throughout Bible history, as God has progressively revealed His truths to us. There is not space in this book to provide an exhaustive treatment of this subject. My main purpose in writing this chapter is to give you a basic understanding of my views regarding Bible inspiration and inerrancy. In subsequent chapters I will be providing Scriptural support for my views on a variety of topics. The ways in which I use Scripture to support those views will amply illustrate how I deal with the questions of inerrancy and progressive revelation when interpreting the Bible and uncovering underlying foundational truths about God and the Gospel of Christ.

I believe the best way to understand and interpret the Bible is to approach it with attitude of submission to Jesus Christ as the Lord of one's life. He is God's living Word to us. As you read the words of the Bible, which have come to you through the imperfect filter of human understanding and experience, trust Jesus Christ, who is Himself perfect, to guide you by His Holy Spirit.

I would like to mention at this point that the main theological positions I have taken in this book are totally supported by the Scriptures, no matter which view of inspiration one might hold. Many who would strongly agree with me doctrinally would also strongly believe in the inerrancy of the Scriptures. Support for my views can also be found among those who hold to a more "liberal" view of Bible inspiration, similar to my own.

Chapter 5

The Jesus of History, the Christ of Faith, and the Synoptic Problem

God speaks to us through the Scriptures, but the Scriptures themselves are not inerrant. God's truths come to us progressively over time through the filter of imperfect human understanding. Sometimes I wish this weren't the case, and that God would communicate to us in clear and unmistakable ways, but I must assume that God is a lot smarter than I and knows what He is doing.

What we find in the Scriptures is a progression of thought, as the nation of Israel learns, through a process of trial and error, the true nature of God and how they should be interacting with Him. I believe that this learning process did not culminate during the earthly life of Christ, but instead after Jesus' resurrection, as Jesus communicated additional truths to us through the Apostles and their followers. I believe that God does have a plan for the ages and continues to reveal new truths to us today, truths which "enhance," but do not necessarily "conflict with" what was taught to Jesus' Apostles 2,000 years ago.

There has been much said about the quest for the historical Jesus. The idea is that by the time the books of the New Testament were written most of the original disciples were gone. Rather than the direct testimony of actual eye witnesses, what we have are second and third-hand accounts that were finally put into writing anywhere from 20 to 70 years after the time of Christ. We all know what can happen when a story is repeated strictly by word of mouth in just a single day, let alone over a period of many years. There are serious factual discrepancies among the Gospels regarding many details of Jesus' life and sayings. This is sometimes referred to as the "Synoptic Problem." The synoptic problem is a sticky one. Some of us would place greater emphasis on the synoptic Gospels (ie. Matthew, Mark and Luke), while others are influenced more by the Gospel of John, which was probably written much later, and which emphasizes the "deity" of Christ.

Then there are the writings of the Apostle Paul. His writings largely predate the synoptic gospels. He was a Jew whose ministry was primarily, but not exclusively, to the Greeks. So are we to base our theology largely on the sayings of the historical Jesus which many feel are best reflected in the synoptic gospels, or on the writings of Paul and John who seem to have written from the perspective of the post-resurrection Jesus. During the first two or three centuries, those who over emphasized the latter tended toward Gnosticism and the view that Jesus was more divine than human. Those who overemphasized sayings of Jesus, as found in the synoptic Gospels, tended toward the idea that Jesus was more human than divine.

The Synoptic Problem is compounded by the fact that there are significant discrepancies in the Gospels regarding the exact wording of the sayings of Jesus, the chronology of events of Jesus' life, and many of the historical details. For example, the accounts relating to the discovery of Jesus' empty tomb, and His post-resurrection appearances, have led some theologians to seriously doubt that Jesus actually rose bodily from the grave. The resurrection narratives are found in Matthew 28, Mark 16, Luke 24, and John 20-21, and they disagree in nearly every detail. Skeptic, Bart Ehrman, in his book, *"How Jesus Became God: The Exaltation of a Jewish Preacher from Galilee,"* summarizes these discrepancies very nicely:

"Read through the accounts and ask yourself some basic questions: Who was the first person to go to the tomb? Was it Mary Magdalene by herself (John)? Or Mary along with another Mary and Salome (Mark)? Or Mary, Mary, Joanna, and a number of other women (Luke)? Was the stone already rolled away when they arrived at the tomb (Mark, Luke, and John), or explicitly not (Matthew)? Whom did they see there? An angel (Matthew), a man (Mark), or two men (Luke)? Did they immediately go and tell some of the disciples what they had seen (John), or not (Matthew, Mark, and Luke)? What did the person or people at the tomb tell the women to do? To tell the disciples that Jesus would meet them in Galilee (Matthew and Mark)? Or to remember what Jesus had told them earlier when he had been in Galilee (Luke)? Did the women then go tell the disciples what they were told to tell them (Matthew and Luke), or not (Mark)? Did the disciples see Jesus (Matthew, Luke, and John), or not (Mark)? Where did they see him? – only in Galilee (Matthew, or only in Jerusalem (Luke)?"

While it is possible to resolve these discrepancies using work-a-rounds and interpretive gymnastics, I remain unconvinced. If these where the only factual and historical discrepancies found in the Bible, I would be more favorably inclined to bend a little with regard to those work-a-rounds. Actually, there are hundreds of such discrepancies throughout the Bible. If you don't believe me, just Google "Bible contradictions" and see what comes up.

So who was the historical Jesus, really? Was he a human being, no different in kind from any of us, who was subsequently "deified" by his followers many years after his death? Did he really say most of the words attributed to him in the Gospels? The Gospel of John, as well as some of the letters attributed to the Apostle Paul, where quite possibly not actually written by them. This was, of course, a well-intentioned and very common literary device back then. I believe that many of the Old Testament books were pseudepigraphical (falsely entitled) as well.

Does this all mean that the New Testament is not a reliable source of information about the person and work of Jesus Christ? I don't think so. Despite the problems given above, and despite the utter impossibility of separating the authentic sayings of Jesus from sayings that were put into his mouth by well-intentioned followers years after the fact, all the "basic and necessary" truths are still there. It doesn't matter to me whether Jesus communicated these truths before or after His death and resurrection. If it is true that Christ was genuinely "interacting" with His followers after the Resurrection, I would assume that the information they received at that time would be just as valid as the information they received prior to the resurrection. This was clearly the case with the Apostle Paul, who received his Gospel message by direct revelation in Arabia during a three-year period immediately after his conversion, prior to the beginning of His ministry. (See Galatians 1:15-18)

The teachings of Jesus were so incredibly insightful, profound and life-changing that He drew large crowds during His earthly ministry. While on earth, He was definitely a very extraordinary man of God. Nevertheless, He was, after all, fully human, and not omniscient. I believe He was a product of His culture and may have started His ministry believing that, as the Messiah, He would be used by God to inaugurate an earthly kingdom. It may have been relatively late in His ministry when He learned that the path He was on would lead to an agonizing death on the Cross of Calvary. In the Garden of Gethsemane He agonized over this and prayed that God would take this "cup" of suffering from Him. Perhaps it was only at the very end of His earthly walk that He began to fully realize and accept the fact that His kingdom would not be "of this world." If this were the case, then after His resurrection there would have been a need to fill in the blanks and clarify these matters with His followers. Obviously, many of His followers were reluctant to believe this, and for many years they continued to preach the apocalyptic message that Jesus would be coming again soon to establish an earthly kingdom.

Eventually hope faded, and Christians began to realize that the inauguration of Kingdom of God earth was going to be an ages-long process. The destruction of Jerusalem in A.D. 70 was in my view the nail in the coffin that finally drove this point home for many Christians. We see evidence of the spiritualization of Christ's message in the Gospel of John, which was definitely written from a post-resurrection perspective. This is clearly expressed in John 18:36, *"Jesus said, 'My kingdom is not of this world. If it were, my servants would fight to prevent my arrest by the Jewish leaders. But now my kingdom is from another place.'"* Especially in the Gospel of John we see evidence that some of these post-resurrection teachings were put into the mouth of Jesus during His earthly ministry. The fact that Jesus may not have actually uttered some of those words while on earth does not make them any less true, in my view.

How important is it really that we separate the Jesus of History from the Christ of faith who continues to speak to us today? Jesus continued to communicate with His followers after His death. He did, after all, rise from the dead. I can easily see how some of those truths could become to some degree amalgamated into the sayings of the historical Jesus. The New Testament was written mostly by those who heard the stories by word of mouth from first, second, and even third-hand sources. You would expect that because of this the New Testament would be filled with blatant contradictions and errors. What I have found instead, is a remarkably consistent and coherent message. Yes, some of the historical details may have gotten jumbled up, and sometimes it is difficult to ferret out truths that are both enhanced and obscured by symbolism and metaphorical imagery. It has been my experience, however, that if I am careful to compare each scripture with all other related scriptures, most of the important truths harmonize very nicely.

So, is it necessary that we are able to distinguish what Jesus actually said during His Earthly ministry from what He has communicated to us after His resurrection? I don't think so. And that is a good thing, because it would be an impossible task.

Chapter 6

Popular Misconceptions about the Nature and Purpose of "Hell"

For most of my life I have been perplexed and, frankly, stumped by apparent incongruities in the Bible concerning the nature of God, especially the BIG question that we have all asked ourselves. How can a God of love send the majority of the human race to eternal torment in Hell, most of whom are really pretty decent folks, at least by human standards? Most evangelical Christians struggle with this question, and the answers most of us have come up with are not all that satisfying. This is probably the single greatest theological issue confronting Christian evangelicals.

Most Christians are greatly disturbed by the doctrine of Hell. There is no avoiding the issue, as the concept of Hell is derived from the New Testament, with some of the most disturbing passages coming from the lips of Christ Himself. Hell is pictured by most Christians as a place of everlasting torment, and the imagery most commonly used is that of a fiery judgment, from which there is no escape.

In general, Christian evangelicals are among the kindest, most forgiving and loving people on the planet, so the doctrine of Hell is not something they are comfortable with. The idea is that you can't just pick and choose what parts of the Bible you want to believe. You have to accept the bad parts along with the good, because if the bad parts aren't true what basis do we have for believing the good parts? As a result, this doctrine is reluctantly accepted, but almost never mentioned from the pulpits and in the Sunday Schools and Bible studies. In the healthiest and fastest-growing congregations the emphasis is placed on the positive aspects of the Gospel and on issues related to successful Christian living.

In an effort to mitigate the negative aspects of this teaching many Christians tend to rationalize to some extent and interpret the "flames" as symbolic of some sort of mental, rather than physical, torture. It also helps some to know that people who go to Hell will be there as a result of their own choices in life. Although very few people would deliberately choose to go to Hell, they nevertheless choose Hell by default when they decide not to follow Christ. Another mitigating factor would be the fact that there apparently are "degrees" of punishment in Hell, just as there are degrees of reward in Heaven. There are a few passages in the New Testament that seem to support this (See Matt. 11:20-22; 2 Cor. 9:6; 5:9-10). And on the positive side the gift of God is eternal life. One should be grateful that any are saved at all, since all are sinners and the wages of sin is death,* according to Romans 6:23. *(*In evangelical Christian circles the "death" penalty for sin is equated with eternal banishment to Hell.)*

Many Christians, despite the above mitigating facts, are very uncomfortable with the notion of Hell and prefer not to think about it. Although most Christians believe in Hell with their intellects, it appears that they don't really believe in it with their hearts. In other words, they act as though they don't believe in it. Most are only mildly disturbed that many of their friends and neighbors, not to mention close family members or relatives, might be headed to Hell after they die.

The situation is further exacerbated by the fact that the life-saving Gospel message does not reach everyone and some are predisposed not to believe it because of very strong religious and cultural biases against Christianity. Not all evangelicals believe this. Some have a more "inclusive" theology and believe that it is possible for non-Christians to become saved without hearing the Gospel message, under certain circumstances, which are not very clearly understood or articulated.

Before expressing my views on this issue I would like to emphasize again that I regard myself to be an evangelical Christian and I believe that my views are entirely consistent with the teachings of Scripture. The major difference between my beliefs and those of the majority of evangelical Christians today is that Jesus could not possibly have paid the penalty for the sins of all mankind on the cross of Calvary if the penalty is everlasting torment in Hell. After all, He only spent two and a half days in the grave and today He is alive and well. I believe that the penalty for sin is spiritual death, or estrangement from God, and this is not a permanent condition. I also believe that Christ made atonement on the cross of Calvary for everyone's sins, and the price only had to be paid once for all. (see Heb. 10:10 and Rom. 6:10) Because of this no one is any longer subject to that penalty. Everyone was technically "saved" from the penalty of sin on the Cross of Calvary, and because of this everyone will be going to Heaven when they die. I realize that some strict Calvinists believe that Christ made atonement at Calvary only for the sins of the elect. However, I believe that the concept of a "limited atonement" is not taught anywhere in Scripture. According to 1 John

2:2, *"He Himself is the propitiation for our sins; and not for ours only, but also for those of the whole world."* According to 1 Timothy 4:10, *"God is the Savior of all men, and especially of those who believe."*

I do need to qualify my statement in the previous paragraph about everyone going to Heaven. Based on the testimony of millions of people who have had near death experiences (NDE's), most of whom where clinically dead during those experiences, virtually everyone goes to the spirit world (ie. heavenly places) when they die. A small minority do find themselves in a "Hell" of their own making. Their negative thoughts carry over with them and they remain trapped in a negative place, a self-inflicted purely subjective reality. I believe that all people were technically saved on Calvary and are indwelt by the Spirit of Christ. The problem is that that most of us are unaware of this and do not experience this salvation in their conscious awareness. Sometimes people who after death find themselves in their own personal version of Hell call out for help and are instantly rescued from their blindness. Others might remain in this condition for extended periods of time, perhaps even centuries by our earthly standards, although time as we know it does not exist in the heavenly realms. The same thing occurs during our earthly existence. The lost condition of mankind is only an illusion and is temporary. No one remains in a lost condition forever. Although we may wander from God in our conscious awareness God never leaves us. Later in this book I will provide a more complete discussion of the validity of NDE's. I believe that what we learn from these testimonies are in complete harmony with the Scriptures.

The popular view of Hell is based on several misconceptions:

The first misconception about Hell is that punishment in Hell lasts forever. Most people assume that the words "everlasting" and "eternal" are accurate translations of the original Hebrew and Greek words in the Bible. Actually, there is no word in Greek or Hebrew that means everlasting or never ending in the sense that most of us understand it. The words which are translated as "eternal," "everlasting," and "forever" are all variants of the Hebrew word *"olam"* and its New Testament Greek counterpart *"aion."* Sometimes the singular version is used; sometimes the plural, and sometimes the adjective. In each case, the reference is to a period of time with a definite beginning and end, which is the exact opposite of the meaning of "eternal" and "everlasting." Sometimes phrases like *"into the ages"* or *"the ages of the ages"* are used to denote several distinct epochs or periods of time in succession to one another. It could be argued that the writers of the Bible, although they had no word for "unending," still intended that meaning. However, the words do not have to be interpreted that way. They can also be interpreted to mean exactly what they meant in the Greek and Hebrew culture, with each age having a beginning and an end. This would be consistent with the New and Old Testament teaching that eventually, after time as we know it comes to an end, and the "ages" come to an end, God will "reconcile" all creation, including all created beings, to Christ. (See 1 Cor. 15:22-28)

The most common argument against this line of reasoning is that if the Greek words which are mistranslated as "eternal" don't really mean "unending" with respect to Hell, wouldn't that mean that they also don't meant "eternal" when used to describe eternal life in Christ? My answer to that question is, "Yes, you would be exactly right about that." *"Aionian"* life, often mistranslated "eternal" life, does not refer to the "duration," but instead to the quality of our life in Christ. The Greek term *"Aionian"* literally means belonging to or pertaining to an age or ages. It means exactly the opposite of eternal and everlasting. Nowhere in the Bible does it refer to an infinite, unending period of time. When Jesus gives us *aionian* life, the life He gives us is Himself. He is the *"way, the truth, and the life."* Everyone will live eternally, both Christians and non-Christians alike. All people continue to live after death in the sense that their conscious existence will never come to an end. *Aionian* life does not refer to never ending conscious existence. Even those who believe in everlasting punishments of the wicked in Hell will acknowledge that the wicked possess everlasting conscious existence. Instead, *aionian* life refers to our quality of existence IN CHRIST (See Rom: 3:24; 6:3-4; 8:1-2, 1-11; 1 Cor. 1:30; 2 Cor. 5:17; 15:22; Eph. 1:1-9; Col. 3:4; 2 Tim. 1:1; 2:19).

If *aionian* life referred to the length of our life the meaning of the phrase would be completely lost. The emphasis should not be placed on the word *aionian*, but instead on the word "life." What distinguishes the Christian from the non-Christian is not the length of his life, but the nature of it. Bible passages which refer to *aionian* life are referring to spiritual life vs. spiritual death, not physical life and death. As Christians, we experience spiritual life in our present walk in this world and during the eons, or ages, to come. To have *aionian* life is to be alive spiritually in Christ. Those who do not have *aionian* life are dead spiritually and separated from Christ in this life, a condition which sometimes, but not always, continues after death. Technically Christ still resides within all of us, but not all are consciously aware of this and as a result are not able to experience *"aionian"* life.

A second misconception about Hell is that the purpose of God's judgments (ie. the "Hells" of our own making) on the unsaved are retribution for the sins they have committed. Actually, God took care of that at Calvary for the sins of all mankind. Sin's death penalty has already been paid. We do need to keep in mind, however, that this did not remove the temporal consequences of our sinful behavior in this world and sometimes the next. Because He loves us we often find ourselves on the receiving end of God's "tough love." To a great extent God has created a self-adjusting universe. The judgments of our Lord do not usually come directly from His hand. They mostly result from the natural laws which He has set in motion, by which *we "reap what we sow."* (See Galatians 6:7) The purpose of God's chastisement is not retribution, but correction. It has the purpose of teaching us valuable life lessons, bringing us to repentance, and restoring us to a loving relationship with Himself through Christ. Conversely, goodness and love create their own rewards. Those rewards which we receive in this life and the next are not things, but instead are the joy and satisfaction of knowing that we have made progress in pleasing God and becoming more like Christ.

A third misconception about Hell is that it is a place of physical torture and torment for everyone there. Although many New Testament passages teach that there will be suffering in Hell, not all will suffer in the same degree. It is conceivable that for some the punishments (ie. God's corrective actions) will be relatively mild when compared to the fate of others. The Hebrew justice system was based on fairness and the punishments fit the crimes exactly, as specified in Leviticus 24:19-21: *"Anyone who injures their neighbor is to be injured in the same manner: fracture for fracture, eye for eye, tooth for tooth. The one who has inflicted the injury must suffer the same injury."*

In Matthew 5:38-48, Jesus took this law of reciprocity to a whole new level by asking us to return good for evil. *"You have heard that it was said, 'Eye for eye, and tooth for tooth.' But I tell you, do not resist an evil person. If anyone slaps you on the right cheek, turn to them the other cheek also. And if anyone wants to sue you and take your shirt, hand over your coat as well. If anyone forces you to go one mile, go with them two miles. Give to the one who asks you, and do not turn away from the one who wants to borrow from you. You have heard that it was said, 'Love your neighbor and hate your enemy.' But I tell you, love your enemies and pray for those who persecute you, that you may be children of your Father in heaven. He causes his sun to rise on the evil and the good, and sends rain on the righteous and the unrighteous. If you love those who love you, what reward will you get? Are not even the tax collectors doing that? And if you greet only your own people, what are you doing more than others? Do not even pagans do that? Be perfect, therefore, as your heavenly Father is perfect."*

Not only is God's justice fair and equitable, with punishments fitting the crimes, but it also includes mercy and forgiveness. Jesus asks us to forgive our enemies so that we might become perfect as God is perfect. In other words, it is the character of God to be loving and forgiving. God's punishments are not disproportionate to the crimes. He doesn't punish temporal sins with infinite punishment in a place called Hell. He doesn't ask us to forgive our enemies, while at the same time refusing to do the same Himself. That would make God the biggest hypocrite of all time. On the Cross of Calvary God cancelled the sin debt of all humanity. Because of this all of God's judgments in this world and the next are for our benefit. They are not punitive in nature. God's judgments are expressions of His love for us.

A fourth misconception about Hell is that the imagery of fire is symbolic of torture and excruciating pain. While most evangelicals believe that the fires of Hell are not literal, they still believe they symbolize extreme suffering, torment and regret. In my view this is only partially true. While a certain amount of pain and regret would be involved in most disciplinary actions, the result is a good one. According to Hebrews 12:11, *"No discipline seems pleasant at the time, but painful. Later on, however, it produces a harvest of righteousness and peace for those who have been trained by it."*

Throughout the Bible the imagery of fire is symbolic of cleansing and purification, not torture. The fires of God's judgment will not be pleasant to endure. Nevertheless, the result will be repentance and purification. According to the prophet Zephaniah, after God's fiery judgment ALL will *"call on the name of the LORD and serve him shoulder to shoulder."*

Zephaniah 3:8-9: *"Therefore wait for me,' declares the LORD, 'for the day I will stand up to testify. I have decided to assemble the nations, to gather the kingdoms and to pour out my wrath on them—all my fierce anger. The whole world will be consumed by the fire of my jealous anger. Then will I purify the lips of the peoples, that all of them may call on the name of the LORD and serve him shoulder to shoulder."*

The prophet Malachi uses the imagery of a refiner's fire or a launderer's soap to describe the day in which the Messiah will bring judgment on Israel.

Malachi 3:1-4: *"See, I will send my messenger, who will prepare the way before me. Then suddenly the Lord you are seeking will come to his temple; the messenger of the covenant, whom you desire, will come," says the LORD Almighty. But who can endure the day of his coming? Who can stand when he appears? For he will be like a refiner's fire or a launderer's soap. He will sit as a refiner and purifier of silver; he will purify the Levites and refine them like gold and silver. Then the LORD will have men who will bring offerings in righteousness, and the offerings of Judah and Jerusalem will be acceptable to the LORD, as in days gone by, as in former years."*

In the above passage fire is used as an instrument of cleansing and purification, and the Levites are refined like gold and silver. In other words, they are purged of their sins and made righteous. This interpretation is in accordance with the New Testament teaching that none of us are righteous and all are in need of cleansing and forgiveness

In Matthew 3:10-12, John the Baptist, the *"Messenger"* mentioned in the above quote from Malachi, uses the same imagery. *"The ax is already at the root of the trees, and every tree that does not produce good fruit will be cut down and thrown into the fire. I baptize you with water for repentance. But after me will come one who is more powerful than I, whose sandals I am not fit to carry. He will baptize you with the Holy Spirit and with fire. His winnowing fork is in his hand, and he will clear his threshing floor, gathering his wheat into the barn and burning up the chaff with unquenchable fire."*

The above passage can be interpreted two ways. The first interpretation is that Jesus will baptize Christians with both the Holy Spirit and with fire. The second interpretation is that Jesus will baptize the Christians with the Holy Spirit and non-Christians with fire. The latter view better fits the context in which John likens this process as one of separating the wheat from the chaff and burning up the chaff with unquenchable fire. It doesn't matter which position you take on this, however, the imagery is still consistent with Malachi's depiction of the fires of God's judgment as a refining process.

According to the Apostle Paul in 1 Cor. 3:11-15, even Christians will experience the refining fires of God's judgment, though perhaps to a lesser degree. *"For no one can lay any foundation other than the one already laid, which is Jesus Christ. If anyone builds on this foundation using gold, silver, costly stones, wood, hay or straw, their work will be shown for what it is, because the Day will bring it to light. It will be revealed with fire, and the fire will test the quality of each person's work. If what has been built survives, the builder will receive a reward. If it is burned up, the builder will suffer loss but yet will be saved—even though only as one escaping through the flames."*

A fifth misconception about Hell is that only God's elect or chosen ones may avoid it. Many students of the Bible believe that the purpose of our election is that God has chosen or elected us for salvation, to the exclusion of everyone who is not of the elect. This is the same mistake that the Hebrew nation made in Old Testament times. They assumed that they where a nation chosen by God for special favor and privilege, when in reality they were chosen for service and were supposed to be a light to the Gentiles and were to become the vehicle through whom God would bless all nations. We Christians are a royal priesthood chosen by God to be a light to the unsaved and reach them for Christ. If God truly is sovereign over His creation and desires that all men be saved, then He is perfectly capable of achieving that end. We Christians must regard ourselves as among the first fruits of God's plan of redemption. We are not privileged, to the exclusion of all others. Instead, we are privileged to be used by God to spread the Gospel to all nations.

The passage of Scripture most often used by Hyper-Calvinists to support their doctrine of double predestination is Romans, Chapters 9-11. Double predestination is the teaching that God predestines only a chosen few, the elect, for salvation, and by default He predestines everyone else to spend eternity in Hell. In this Scripture passage the Apostle Paul teaches exactly the opposite. Here is the sequence of events as Paul describes them in Romans 9-11:

In Romans 9, Paul explains that our salvation is based on God's mercy and not on man's desire or effort. It's completely up to God who gets saved and who remains unsaved (ie. whose hearts are hardened). God hardened Pharoah's heart for the benefit of releasing the Hebrew nation, His chosen people, from slavery and displaying His power in the process.

Romans 9:16-18, *"It does not, therefore, depend on man's desire or effort, but on God's mercy. For the Scripture says to Pharaoh: 'I raised you up for this very purpose, that I might display my power in you and that my name might be proclaimed in all the earth.' Therefore God has mercy on whom he wants to have mercy, and he hardens whom he wants to harden."*

Later in the same chapter Paul explains that it was God's plan to eventually save both Jews and Gentiles. The Gentiles, who were not originally God's chosen people, would one day also be called God's people.

Romans 9:23-24, *"He did this to make the riches of his glory known to the objects of his mercy, even us, whom he also called, not only from the Jews but also from the Gentiles? As he says in Hosea: 'I will call them my people who are not my people; and I will call her my loved one who is not my loved one."*

In Romans 11, Paul explains that only a remnant of the nation of Israel were elected to receive Christ, and the others were hardened.

Romans 11:7-8, *"What then? What Israel sought so earnestly it did not obtain, but the elect did. The others were hardened, as it is written: 'God gave them a spirit of stupor, eyes so that they could not see and ears so that they could not hear, to this very day.'"*

Paul then explains that the nation of Israel did not fall beyond recovery. The transgression of the nation of Israel was the occasion of the Gospel being spread to the Gentiles. He then explains that if the Israel's loss resulted in "riches for the Gentiles" how much greater will be the riches of the nation of Israel when they themselves are restored to *"fullness."*

Romans 11:11-12, *"Again I ask: Did they stumble so as to fall beyond recovery? Not at all! Rather, because of their transgression, salvation has come to the Gentiles to make Israel envious. But if their transgression means riches for the world, and their loss means riches for the gentiles, how much greater riches will their fullness bring!"*

Then Paul tells us that Israel has experienced a hardening only until a full number of the Gentiles have come in. After that, all Israel will be saved.

Romans 11:25-26, *"I do not want you to be ignorant of this mystery, brothers, so that you may not be conceited: Israel has experienced a hardening in part until the full number of the Gentiles has come in. And so all Israel will be saved, as it is written: 'The deliverer will come from Zion; he will turn godlessness away from Jacob. And this is my covenant with them when I take away their sins.'"*

Finally, at the end of Romans 11, Paul sums up the whole matter and drives the message home. He points out that just as we have received mercy as a result of the disobedience of Israel, they will receive mercy as a result of God's mercy to us. God has *"bound all men over to disobedience in order that He may have mercy on all."*

Romans 11:31-32, *"so they too have now become disobedient in order that they too may now receive mercy as a result of God's mercy to you. For God has bound ALL men over to disobedience so that he may have mercy on them ALL."* (The caps are mine)

There is no question in my mind that the Apostle Paul was a universalist.

A sixth misconception about Hell is that it is a physical place or locality. In the Old Testament the word that used to be translated "Hell" is *"Sheol,"* the place of the dead. The literal meaning is simply "unseen." It was not described as a place of suffering and torment. It was a place where everyone went after death and nothing went on there at all. It was just another word for the "grave." If anything did go on there, there was no way of knowing what it was, hence the name "unseen." The ancient Israelites did not believe in life after death. Their views are summarized in Ecclesiastes 9:5-6, *"For the living know that they will die, but the dead know nothing; they have no further reward, and even the memory of them is forgotten, their love, their hate and their jealousy have long since vanished; never again will they have a part in anything that happens under the sun."*

During the Babylonian Captivity the Jews were introduced to the concept of a dualistic conflict between God and Satan, and the additional concepts of rewards and punishments after death in Heaven or Hell. These were taken from the religions of the Babylonians (Mesopotamian myths) and the Persians (Zoroastrianism) during the Captivity. During that period the concept of Satan found its way into the Old Testament, much of which was written during the Babylonian Captivity and thereafter, including the story of Adam and Eve in the Garden of Eden. During the 400-year period between the captivity and the time of Christ, after returning to Palestine, Jewish theology was also influenced by the Greeks, who were in turn had been influenced by the Egyptians, and the doctrine of Hell developed into what is now pictured in some of the apocalyptic and apocryphal literature of the intertestamental period, and eventually found its way into the New Testament as well, particularly in the Book of Revelation. In the New Testament the *"Sheol"* of the Old Testament was transliterated into the Greek word *"Hades,"* which was the "underworld" of Greek mythology.

If you want to believe in this version of Hell you must also believe that it is either an unseen place where nothing at all happens, or a ficry place somewhere under or near the center of the Earth where people are tortured in literal flames. Take your pick.

The other word for Hell in the New Testament is *"Gehenna,"* the garbage dump outside Jerusalem in the Valley of the Son of Hinnom, where in ages past babies were sacrificed to the Canaanite God Molek. In Jesus' day this place was used to burn the garbage from the city and was continually ablaze, and it was full of disgusting worms. Today the garbage dump is gone and I understand that it is quite nice there now, especially in the Spring. In the Synoptic Gospels (Matthew, Mark, and Luke) Gehenna was the word used most often by Jesus, actually eleven times, to describe the fate of those who were not ready for the Kingdom. In the parable of the rich man and poor man, Jesus used the word *"hades."*

Not many evangelicals believe that Hell it is a place of literal fire and torment. Most of them believe that the flames are a metaphor for suffering. I quite agree with this interpretation. I would expand the meaning to include purification as well, as in the case of a crucible or furnace in which gold ore is refined into pure gold. Jesus made frequent use of parables and metaphors to illustrate underlying truths. He used the terms *"Gehenna"* and *"Hades"* because they were well-known and commonly used in the popular culture. I seriously doubt that *"Gehenna"* and *"Hades"* refer to a literal places where people go after they die. Even if this were true there is no reason to assume that the flames are literal or that people will be trapped there for all eternity, without any chance of escape. There is absolutely no Scriptural support for that.

If *"Sheol"* or Hell is a literal fiery place, then the event described in Revelation 20:13-15 makes no sense at all. *"And the sea gave up the dead which were in it, and death and Hades gave up the dead which were in them; and they were judged, every one of them according to their deeds. Then death and Hades were thrown into the lake of fire. This is the second death, the lake of fire. And if anyone's name was not found written in the book of life, he was thrown into the lake of fire."* What would be the point of throwing Hell into Hell? If the Lake of Fire is the second death why throw death into it? Two negatives make a positive. If death and Hell were destroyed, wouldn't the result be the elimination of both? If we rightly assume that death and the fires of Hades are metaphors for God's corrective judgments on sinners, and spiritual separation from God, then destroying them in the Lake of Fire would be a good thing, not a bad thing. Destroying death would make everyone alive. The second death is just the opposite of physical or spiritual death. It actually refers to the elimination of both. It is the "death of death," so to speak. Even Satan was thrown into the Lake of Fire (Rev.20:10), symbolizing the fact that even he will be cleansed and purified in the fires of God's righteous judgments. According to 1 Corinthians 15:26, *"The last enemy to be destroyed is death."* Just a few verses earlier (v. 22), the Apostle Paul pointed that *"as in Adam ALL die, so in Christ ALL will be made alive."* (the caps are mine)

Finally if all sinners at the end of the ages are literally thrown into a Lake of Fire *"for ever and ever,"* prior to the creation of the New Heavens and New Earth, why are all those sinners still hanging around outside the gates of the New Jerusalem? See Rev. 22:14, *"Blessed are those who wash their robes, that they may have the right to the tree of life and may go through the gates into the city. Outside are the dogs, those who practice magic arts, the sexually immoral, the murderers, the idolaters and everyone who loves and practices falsehood."*

The chronology and imagery of the Book Revelation were never meant to be taken literally. The whole thing was a dream or vision, after all. If you try to make literal sense out of it all you end up with are absurdities.

Chapter 7

New Testament Scriptures Which Support the Doctrine of Universal Reconciliation

Luke 6:27-36: *"But I tell you who hear me: Love your enemies, do good to those who hate you, bless those who curse you, pray for those who mistreat you. If someone strikes you on one cheek, turn to him the other also. If someone takes your cloak, do not stop him from taking your tunic. Give to everyone who asks you, and if anyone takes what belongs to you, do not demand it back. Do to others as you would have them do to you." If you love those who love you, what credit is that to you? Even 'sinners' love those who love them. And if you do good to those who are good to you, what credit is that to you? Even 'sinners' do that. And if you lend to those from whom you expect repayment, what credit is that to you? Even 'sinners' lend to 'sinners,' expecting to be repaid in full. But love your enemies, do good to them, and lend to them without expecting to get anything back. Then your reward will be great, and you will be sons of the Most High, because he is kind to the ungrateful and wicked. Be merciful, just as your Father is merciful."* This passage describes not only what God wants us to be like, but also describes the character of God. God wants us to love our enemies and return good for evil. He asks us to be merciful, even as He is merciful. Would God ask us to do something He himself is not willing to do?

Luke 15:4: *"Suppose one of you has a hundred sheep and loses one of them. Does he not leave the ninety-nine in the open country and go after the lost sheep until he finds it?"* Jesus will seek out the lost until he finds them.

John 1:6-7: *"There came a man who was sent from God; his name was John. He came as a witness to testify concerning that light, so that through him ALL men might believe."*

John 1:29: *"The next day John saw Jesus coming toward him and said, 'Look, the Lamb of God, who takes away the sin of the world!'"*

John 3:17: *"For God did not send his Son into the world to condemn the world, but to save the world through him."*

John 3:35, 6:37-39*: "The Father loves the Son and has placed everything in his hands...ALL that the Father gives me will come to me, and whoever comes to me I will never drive away. For I have come down from heaven not to do my will but to do the will of him who sent me. And this is the will of him who sent me, that I shall lose none of ALL that he has given me, but raise them up at the last day."* God the Father gave everything to Jesus and Jesus will LOSE NOTHING that God has given him.

John 6:33: *"For the bread of God is he who comes down from heaven and gives life to the world."* He doesn't just make it available; He actually *gives it to us.*

John 12:32: *"And I, when I am lifted up from the earth, will draw ALL men to myself."* What is it about the word "all" that we don't understand?!!

Revelation 1:18b: *"I [Jesus] hold the keys of death and Hades."* Jesus holds the keys to Death and Hades. The reason He holds the keys is to unlock the doors and release the prisoners.

Revelation 5:13: *"Then I heard every creature in heaven and on earth and under the earth and on the sea, and all that is in them, singing: 'To him who sits on the throne and to the Lamb be praise and honor and glory and power, for ever and ever!'"* This verse refers to EVERY creature, even ALL of those under the earth. This obviously refers to all of the living and the dead.

Ephesians 1:9-10: *"And HE made known to us the mystery of his will according to his good pleasure, which he purposed in Christ, to be put into effect when the times will have reached their fulfillment—to bring all things in heaven and on earth together under one head, even Christ."* All things obviously refers to all people. In verse 12 Paul refers to people who are now Christians as "we who were the first to hope in Christ." Christians are the first fruits, the others will follow.

Acts 3:21 *"He must remain in heaven until the time comes for God to restore everything, as he promised long ago through his holy prophets."*

Romans 5:18: *"Consequently, just as the result of one trespass was condemnation for ALL men, so also the result of one act of righteousness was justification that brings life for ALL men."* Again, what is it about the word "ALL" that we don't seem to understand?

Romans 5:15b: *"For if the many died by the trespass of the one man, how much more did God's grace and the gift that came by the grace of the one man, Jesus Christ, overflow to the many!"* The word "many" obviously means "all." It is contrasted with the same word in the first part of the verse. If "many" does not really mean "all" then it wouldn't mean "all" in the first part of the verse.

Romans 11:25-31: *"I do not want you to be ignorant of this mystery, brothers, so that you may not be conceited: Israel has experienced a hardening in part until the full number of the Gentiles has come in. And so all Israel will be saved, as it is written: 'The deliverer will come from Zion; he will turn godlessness away from Jacob. And this is my covenant with them when I take away their sins.' As far as the gospel is concerned, they are enemies on your account; but as far as election is concerned, they are loved on account of the patriarchs, for God's gifts and his call are irrevocable. Just as you who were at one time disobedient to God have now received mercy as a result of their disobedience, so they too have now become disobedient in order that they too may now receive mercy as a result of God's mercy to you."* This is a very explicit and powerful statement. God hardens the hearts of individuals and nations on a temporary basis in order to accomplish His purposes. He doesn't harden their hearts in order to save only the elect. He does it in order that He might have mercy on all.

Romans 11:36: *"For from him and through him and to him are ALL things. To him be glory forever. Amen."* All things come from God and all things will return back to Him.

Romans 14:11: *"It is written: 'As surely as I live,' says the Lord, 'every knee will bow before me; every tongue will confess to God.'"* A better translation of the word "confess" is "give praise."

1 Corinthians 15:22-28: *"For as in Adam ALL die, so in Christ ALL will be made alive. But each in his own turn: Christ, the first fruits; then, when he comes, those who belong to him. Then the end will come, when he hands over the kingdom to God the Father after he has destroyed all dominion, authority and power. For he must reign until he has put all his enemies under his feet. The last enemy to be destroyed is death. For he 'has put everything under his feet.' Now when it says that "everything" has been put under him, it is clear that this does not include God himself, who put everything under Christ. When he has done this, then the Son himself will be made subject to him who put everything under him, so that God may be ALL in ALL."* Here Paul gives the order in which people will be made alive, first Christ, then those who belong to Christ at His coming, then everyone else after the last of God's enemies have been put into subjection under his feet. The very last enemy to be destroyed is DEATH itself, not dead people. There will be no more death, physical or spiritual. God will be all in all.

Ephesians 1:9-10: *"And he made known to us the mystery of his will according to his good pleasure, which he purposed in Christ, to be put into effect when the times will have reached their fulfillment—to bring ALL things in heaven and on earth together under one head, even Christ."*

Colossians 1:19-20: *"For God was pleased to have all his fullness dwell in him, and through him to reconcile to himself all things, whether things on earth or things in heaven, by making peace through his blood, shed on the cross."*

Philippians 2:10-11: *"that at the name of Jesus every knee should bow, in heaven and on earth and under the earth, and every tongue confess that Jesus Christ is Lord, to the glory of God the Father."* The correct translation of the word "should" is "will." The key phrase is "to the glory of God the Father." This does not describe people in Hell reluctantly and bitterly acknowledging the Lordship of Christ.

1 Timothy 2:3-6: *"This is good, and pleases God our Savior, who wants ALL men to be saved and to come to a knowledge of the truth. For there is one God, and one mediator between God and men, the man Christ Jesus, who gave himself as a ransom for ALL men—the testimony given in its proper time."* If God truly is sovereign over His creation, then certainly He will do exactly what He desires, especially in light of the fact that Jesus Christ already paid the ransom. God wants ALL to be saved. That is why Christ died for ALL, not some.

1 Timothy 4:10: *"(and for this we labor and strive), that we have put our hope in the living God, who is the Savior of ALL men, and especially of those who believe."* The meaning of this verse is so clear. God is the Savior of all, not just those who now believe.

1 Peter 4:6: *"For this is the reason the gospel was preached even to those who are now dead, so that they might be judged according to men in regard to the body, but live according to God in regard to the spirit."* This is a clear indication that people who never heard the gospel during their lifetimes will be given the opportunity of hearing it after death.

2 Peter 3:9: *"The Lord is not slow in keeping his promise, as some understand slowness. He is patient with you, not wanting anyone to perish, but everyone to come to repentance."* God is sovereign. What He wants, He gets. Period.

Hebrews 1:2: *"but in these last days he has spoken to us by his Son, whom he appointed heir of ALL things, and through whom he made the universe."* All things includes ALL of mankind.

Hebrews 2:14-15: *"Since the children have flesh and blood, he too shared in their humanity so that by his death he might destroy him who holds the power of death—that is, the devil— and free those who all their lives were held in slavery by their fear of death."* It is the devil who has the power of death. If the devil is taken out of the picture, then it would follow that all who were subject to the power of death will be delivered from it.

Hebrews 9:26b: *"But now he has appeared once for All at the end of the ages to do away with sin by the sacrifice of himself."* Jesus sacrificed Himself to do away with sin, not just remove the penalty for sin. Eventually all will repent of their sins and worship Christ. At that time there will be no more sin.

Chapter 8

Old Testament Scriptures which Support the Doctrine of Universal Reconciliation

***Genesis 22:18**: "and through your offspring ALL nations on earth will be blessed, because you have obeyed me."* (See also Genesis 12:3; 18:17-18; 26:4 and 28:14)

***2 Samuel 14:14**: "Like water spilled on the ground, which cannot be recovered, so we must die. But God does not take away life; instead, he devises ways so that a banished person may not remain estranged from him."* Those who are "banished" to Hell will not remain there.

***Job 5:17-18**: "Blessed is the man whom God corrects; so do not despise the discipline of the Almighty. For he wounds, but he also binds up; he injures, but his hands also heal."*

***Psalm 13:5**: "But I trust in your unfailing love; my heart rejoices in your salvation."* God's love is unfailing.

Psalm 16:10: *"because you will not abandon me to the grave, nor will you let your Holy One see decay."*

Psalm 30:5: *"For His anger is but for a moment, His favor is for life; weeping may endure for a night, but joy comes in the morning."* God's anger is not eternal. It is only temporary.

Psalm 68:18a: *"When you ascended on high, you led captives in your train;"* This prophecy refers to Jesus leading captives out of Sheol.

***Psalm 72:17-20**: "May his name endure forever; may it continue as long as the sun. All nations will be blessed through him, and they will call him blessed. Praise be to the LORD God, the God of Israel, who alone does marvelous deeds. Praise be to his glorious name forever; may the whole earth be filled with his glory. Amen and Amen. This concludes the prayers of David son of Jesse."* The nation of Israel was chosen, or elected, for the purpose of being used by God to bless all nations.

Psalm 86:9: *"All the nations you have made will come and worship before you, O Lord; they will bring glory to your name."* In the Old Testament, when the term "all nations" is used, the reference is really to "all people."

Psalm 102:19-20: *"The LORD looked down from his sanctuary on high, from heaven he viewed the earth, to hear the groans of the prisoners and release those condemned to death."*

Psalm 119:75: *"I know, O LORD, that your laws are righteous, and in faithfulness you have afflicted me."* God has a redemptive purpose in everything He does. God's punishments are not punitive, but remedial in nature.

Psalm 139:8: *"If I go up to the heavens, you are there; if I make my bed in the depths, you are there."* God is omnipresent. He even resides in the depths of Sheol. The main reason those in Hell remain "separated" from God is that they are unaware of His presence or are unwilling to submit to Him. One day that will all change.

Psalm 145:3-17: *"Great is the LORD and most worthy of praise; his greatness no one can fathom. One generation will commend your works to another; they will tell of your mighty acts. They will speak of the glorious splendor of your majesty, and I will meditate on your wonderful works. They will tell of the power of your awesome works, and I will proclaim your great deeds. They will celebrate your abundant goodness and joyfully sing of your righteousness. The LORD is gracious and compassionate, slow to anger and rich in love. The LORD is good to ALL; he has compassion on ALL he has made. ALL you have made will praise you, O LORD; your saints will extol you. They will tell of the glory of your kingdom and speak of your might, so that ALL men may know of your mighty acts and the glorious splendor of your kingdom. Your kingdom is an everlasting kingdom, and your dominion endures through all generations. The LORD is faithful to all his promises and loving toward ALL he has made. The LORD upholds ALL those who fall and lifts up ALL who are bowed down. The eyes of ALL look to you, and you give them their food at the proper time. You open your hand and satisfy the desires of EVERY living thing. The LORD is righteous in all his ways and loving toward ALL he has made."* Wow! This passage says it ALL! God has compassion on ALL he has made. He is loving toward ALL He has made. He upholds ALL who fall.

Isaiah 14:24, 27: *"The LORD Almighty has sworn, 'Surely, as I have planned, so it will be, and as I have purposed, so it will stand.'... For the LORD Almighty has purposed, and who can thwart him? His* *hand is stretched out, and who can turn it back?"* God accomplishes all He purposes to do. No one can thwart Him. If it is His desire that all be saved, nothing can prevent that from happening.

Isaiah 26:9: *"My soul yearns for you in the night; in the morning my spirit longs for you. When your judgments come upon the earth, the people of the world learn righteousness."* The purpose of God's judgments is to teach righteousness. God's judgments are remedial, not punitive, in nature.

Isaiah 46:9-10: *"Remember the former things, those of long ago; I am God, and there is no other; I am God, and there is none like me. I make known the end from the beginning, from ancient times, what is still to come. I say: My purpose will stand, and I will do all that I please."* Again, all that God wants, He gets. What could be plainer than that. If God desires everyone to be saved, He will accomplish just that.

Isaiah 48:10: *"See, I have refined you, though not as silver; I have tested you in the furnace of affliction."* Again, the purpose of God's judgments is to refine and perfect us.

Isaiah 45:22-24: *"Turn to me and be saved, all you ends of the earth; for I am God, and there is no other. By myself I have sworn, my mouth has uttered in all integrity a word that will not be revoked: Before me every knee will bow; by me every tongue will swear. They will say of me, 'In the LORD alone are righteousness and strength.' ALL who have raged against him will come to him and be put to shame."* You just can't get any plainer than this. This is the passage Paul was quoting in Philippians 2:10-11. This passage makes it very clear that those who were bowing down to Jesus and confessing Him as Lord included ALL who have raged against Him.

Isaiah 54:7-8: *"For a brief moment I abandoned you, but with deep compassion I will bring you back. In a surge of anger I hid my face from you for a moment, but with everlasting kindness I will have compassion on you, says the LORD your Redeemer."* God abandons sinners only for a brief moment, in the scheme of things, but his kindness and compassion are everlasting.

Jeremiah 30:23-24: *"See, the storm of the LORD will burst out in wrath, a driving wind swirling down on the heads of the wicked. The fierce anger of the LORD will not turn back until he fully accomplishes the purposes of his heart. In days to come you will understand this."* One day the Lord will be finished with His anger and achieve His heart's desire. His heart's desire is that ALL would come to repentance and be saved.

Lamentations 3:31-33: *"For men are not cast off by the Lord forever. Though he brings grief, he will show compassion, so great is his unfailing love. For he does not willingly bring affliction or grief to the children of men."* The meaning of this passage is so plain it needs no further commentary.

Ezekiel 18:23: *"Do I take any pleasure in the death of the wicked? declares the Sovereign LORD. Rather, am I not pleased when they turn from their ways and live?"*

Ezekiel 33:11: *"Say to them, 'As surely as I live, declares the Sovereign LORD, I take no pleasure in the death of the wicked, but rather that they turn from their ways and live. Turn! Turn from your evil ways! Why will you die, O house of Israel?'"*

Joel 2:28, 3:21*: "And afterward, I will pour out my Spirit on all people. Your sons and daughters will prophesy, your old men will dream dreams, your young men will see visions...Their bloodguilt, which I have not pardoned, I will pardon. The LORD dwells in Zion!"*

Zephaniah 3:8-9*: "Therefore wait for me,' declares the LORD, 'for the day I will stand up to testify. I have decided to assemble the nations, to gather the kingdoms and to pour out my wrath on them—all my fierce anger. The whole world will be consumed by the fire of my jealous anger. Then will I purify the lips of the peoples, that all of them may call on the name of the LORD and serve him shoulder to shoulder."*

Chapter 9

The Word of God vs. the Traditions of Men

Admittedly, the doctrine of universal reconciliation, also referred to as Christian universalism, represents a major departure from current Christian orthodoxy, not to mention centuries of Christian tradition. At the same time, I do maintain that this doctrine is Scriptural and definitely not a departure from the orthodox Christian theology of the first four centuries of the Church's existence.

To be sure, my credentials do not even come close to matching those of the majority of evangelical pastors, seminary professors, and theologians. This deficiency, however, can also be regarded in some respects as an advantage in discovering truth in the Scriptures. Theological errors often arise as a result of approaching the Scriptures with preconceived notions and from the point of view of one who has a vested interest in maintaining the status quo. Jesus had great respect for the Scriptures, but interpreted them in ways which emphasized the spirit rather than the letter of the Law. The Scribes and Pharisees viewed Jesus as a threat to their authority. They were jealous of his popularity. Instead of listening to what Jesus was teaching, and reexamining their views based on this new information, they became defensive and were blinded to the truth.

In 1517, when Martin Luther posted his 95 Theses on the Castle Church door in Wittenberg, Germany, he was expressing a minority opinion. In fact, he may have been the only person in the world at that time who believed many of the doctrines outlined in that document. He believed that Christian doctrine should be based on the authority of the Scriptures alone. When we cede to religious authorities the sole right to interpret the Scriptures and formulate church doctrine, we are in greater danger of falling into heresy than when we are allowed to read and interpret the Scriptures for ourselves.

When Christian doctrine becomes institutionalized in the form of official creeds and formal doctrinal statements, there is a tendency among church and denominational leaders to conform to those teachings out of loyalty to their respective church organizations and in order to maintain their positions of authority. The individual members of those congregations are reluctant to express their honest doubts and questions regarding those official teachings for fear of being criticized or even ostracized. Church members want to be loved and accepted by others in their congregations. As a matter of fact, these psychological and social considerations are often the primary reasons for joining a local church. For many church members these factors are more important than the church's specific doctrinal positions.

Have you ever considered why the majority of individuals in any given Christian denomination all tend to interpret the Scriptures in exactly the same way? Is it because they, by some extremely odd coincidence, all study the Scriptures with an open mind and independently arrive at exactly the same conclusions? Or is it because they cede their right to interpret the Scriptures for themselves, and instead rely upon the interpretations provided to them by their teachers and pastors? This is how Christian theology becomes institutionalized into systems of thought that eventually become "cast in granite" and resistant to change.

I am not saying that we should completely disregard centuries of Christian tradition. Christian pastors, teachers and theologians have served an indispensable purpose over the centuries, and have laid an impressive foundation on which we can build. Ignoring this heritage would be ludicrous. It would be like starting from scratch and trying to build an advanced technological society by throwing out every scrap of scientific research and starting again with the re-invention of the wheel. Pastors, teachers and seminary professors provide an important link to the past and are necessary for guiding us in our study of the Scriptures. It is important to remember, however, that Luke commended the Christians in Berea for examining the Scriptures to verify that what Paul was teaching them was indeed the truth (Acts17:11).

When we are presented with new information from an outside source or from our own individual study of the Scriptures we should be open to fresh revelations from God. We should never be afraid to question traditionally held beliefs. We should never be afraid to ask honest questions and express honest doubts. We should embrace truth, no matter what the source. The truth is always our friend, never our enemy. Jesus is the way, the TRUTH, and the life. In my opinion the truth will lead us to Jesus.

Before the New Testament Scriptures were written and canonized, questions of church doctrine were settled by the Apostles who had been with Christ during His earthly ministry and were directly commissioned by Christ to proclaim the Gospel. Initially, the head of the Church at Jerusalem was Peter, to whom Christ entrusted the *"keys of the Kingdom,"* symbolizing Peter's authority over the Church, presumably in both temporal and doctrinal matters (see Matt. 16:19). The Apostle Paul on many occasions was forced to defend his apostleship, mainly because he did not walk with Christ during Christ's earthly ministry and was not directly commissioned by Christ before Christ's ascension into Heaven. To some, Paul's gospel of salvation by grace apart from works was a departure from what was being taught by the other Apostles. In Galatians 1 & 2, Paul asserted his right to apostleship on the basis of his direct confrontation with Christ on the road to Damascus, and he emphasized the fact that the gospel he preached was taught to him directly by Jesus Christ during his time in the wilderness of Arabia. Nevertheless, Paul felt compelled to go to Jerusalem and share his views with the Apostles there, just to make sure he was preaching the truth and had not been laboring in vain. In Acts 1:12-26 we learn that when a new Apostle was selected as a replacement for Judas, one of the primary qualifications was that the candidate had to have been a disciple of Jesus during His earthly ministry, from John's baptism up to the time of Christ's ascension. The reason there are no more apostles in the Church today is that there are no more living witnesses of the resurrection of Christ who were directly commissioned as Apostles by Christ Himself.

The most accurate testimony we have today of what the apostles taught is the New Testament, which was written by the Apostles themselves or by those who were closely associated with them. As you are aware, members of the Roman Catholic Church, instead of basing doctrine on the teachings of the New Testament alone, also rely on traditions adopted and handed down by a succession of Apostles that continues to this day. Nowhere in the Bible is it taught that the keys of the Kingdom were to be passed to successive generations of Apostles. Proof of this lies in the fact that many doctrines taught in later generations by those apostolic successors are in direct conflict with the original teachings of the Apostles, as recorded in the New Testament.

Although bishops, pastors and teachers were appointed by the Apostles and their successors to oversee the affairs of the church and its doctrines, authority was never given for them to formulate new doctrines. Instead, it was their job to preserve the integrity of what had already been taught to them by the original Apostles. Today, the New Testament is the only reliable source of those teachings. When confronted with "later traditions" which contradict the teachings of the New Testament Scriptures, priority should always be given to the Scriptures themselves.

Interestingly enough, the doctrine of endless punishment in Hell was totally absent from any of the Church's creedal declarations during the first 400 years of Church history. Most of the early Church fathers, including Pantaenus, Clement of Alexandria, Origen, Didymus the Blind, Gregory of Nyssa, Basil the Great, Gregory of Nazianzus, Diodore of Tarsus, Theodore of Mopsuestia, Eusebius of Caesarea, and Theodoret, believed in Universal Restoration. It would be fair to mention that a small minority of the Church Fathers believed in endless punishment, while others believed in the annihilation of the wicked. Some had no definite opinion. The fact remains, however, that as the early creeds were developed, numerous doctrines were fiercely disputed at various Church councils and gatherings, without even a whisper of condemnation of the doctrine of Universal Reconciliation.

With the preceding in mind, which traditions should we conform to? Should we base our doctrines on the traditions of the first four centuries?, or those of the next eleven centuries prior to the Reformation, commonly called the Dark Ages?, or those of the Reformation period?, or those of the Christian Fundamentalist Movement of the late 19th and early 20th Centuries?

Jesus had harsh words for the Pharisees who had substituted their human traditions for the actual commands of God. The Pharisees were extremely self-righteous and they set up many man-made rules which were primarily used as a basis for religious exclusion. In the words of Jesus, they *"have let go of the commands of God and are holding on to human traditions."* (Mark 7:8)

The obvious point I am making here is that rather than trying to conform to the various human traditions, wouldn't it make better sense to allow the Holy Spirit to guide you into truth as you study the Scriptures for yourself? Can God be trusted to guide you correctly and not lead you astray? Of course He can. This does not mean that all of us will arrive at the same set of theological conclusions. We will end up disagreeing on many unimportant doctrinal issues, but we will all be brought closer to Christ Himself and the truths that matter most. The amazing thing about Christianity is that despite huge differences of opinion among its adherents on a variety of issues, it seems to "work" wonderfully for those who seek to establish a personal relationship with God through Christ and apply the teachings of Scripture to their daily lives.

Chapter 10

Understanding the Trinity

A very strong case can be made from Scripture for both the Unitarian and the Trinitarian views. I won't bore you with the details. You can easily learn about the arguments on both sides from other sources. What I will attempt to do is reconcile the two based on simple logic. Many of my comments in this essay are speculative in nature. At the same time, I have tried to remain true to the Scriptures. It is doubtful that most who read this chapter will agree with all of the points I make. Hopefully, my comments will at least provide you with some new and helpful thoughts and insights.

Let's begin with the assumption that the writers of the Bible were inspired and have communicated to us the basic truths of the matter. Most of the Scriptures in support of each view appear to be quite unambiguous and for the most part clearly stated. So I would have to assume that both the Unitarian and Trinitarian views are true and compatible with one another, hence we are dealing with a paradox, not a contradiction.

It is clear from many statements of Christ himself that He and the Father are not one and the same, and that God the Father is greater than the Son (John 14:28). Jesus prayed to the Father (Mark 1:35). He gave God the Father credit for the performance of His miracles (John 14:10). He was not omniscient (Matthew 24:36), and He had to learn about God much in the same way that we do (Luke 2:52). He had to grow in wisdom and favor with both God and Man. He was definitely separated from the Father and wouldn't return to the Father until after His death, burial and resurrection (John 20:17). He even said He was not good and that only the Father in Heaven is good (Luke 18:19). He prayed in Gethsemane for God to remove the *"cup"* of suffering that He was facing, and God turned Him down (Luke 22:42). He referred to Himself as the Son of Man, not the Son of God (Matthew 18:11), and never once directly and unambiguously claimed to be God Himself. He made statements about the oneness He experienced with the Father, but then went on to explain how all of us could experience the same (John 17:21).

On the other hand, He was given the name *"Emmanuel,"* which means *"God with us"* (Matt. 1:23). He did describe Himself with the term *"I AM,"* a designation which refers to God Himself, and that He pre-existed Abraham (Jn. 8:58). He is referred to by the writers of the New Testament as the only begotten Son of God (Jn. 3:16), and as the Alpha and Omega, the beginning and the end (Rev. 22:13), which implies that He existed at the beginning of time and also at the end of time. In other words, He, like God the Father, is co-eternal. He did say, *"I and the Father are one"* (Jn10:27). He allowed Himself to be worshipped by His followers after His resurrection. When Thomas called Him *"my Lord and My God,"* Jesus did not reprimand him (Jn. 20:28). He was worshipped by His followers (Matt. 14:33; 28:9) and at the end of the ages every knee will bow to Him and worship Him (Phil. 2:9-11). His *"equality"* with the Father prior to His incarnation is described in Phil. 2:6.

So how could both of the above descriptions of Christ be true? We won't find a detailed discussion of this issue in the Bible. As a matter of fact, the deity of Christ did not become codified and clearly spelled out in the form of official creeds until centuries after the Bible was written. So, let's get one thing straight from the beginning. Your eternal destiny doesn't depend on which view you take regarding this controversy. If it were that important, I'm sure that the writers of the Bible would have spelled it out much more clearly and talked about it a whole lot more than they did. What they did spell out in no uncertain terms is that Jesus was unique and one of a kind, the *"only begotten"* Son of God (Jn. 3:16), and that He made atonement for the sins of the world on the cross of Calvary (1 Jn. 2:2). He is *the "way, the truth, and the life,"* and all roads to the Father go through Him (Jn. 14:6). There is no other way to the Father except through Jesus Christ. He is the *"door"* through whom we must pass in order to be reconciled to God (Jn. 10:7). The uniqueness of Christ is affirmed not only by Trinitarians but also by many Unitarians. The difference between the two views relates to the question of whether there is only one triune God who exists in three persons, or is there only one God, period, and one or two other spiritual entities (Jesus and the Holy Spirit) who are less than God. In my view, the line of demarcation between these two views is very fine and is mostly semantic in nature.

Now it's time to apply a bit of common sense logic to this question. Let's start by taking everything out of the picture but God Himself. Let's assume that Christ and the Holy Spirit do not yet exist. Let's also assume that the universe in which we live had not yet been created. So we start with God, and no other persons or things. All that exists is God. God is literally *"all-in-all."*

For God Himself to meaningfully exist there would have to be some context in which events and interactions, including divine thoughts, could occur in sequential order. In other words, some sort of time must exist in the mind of God. For this reason I would postulate that God is not a timeless being. He is an infinite being, but not timeless or limited in any way by the forward or reverse direction of time. He is able to experience all past, present and future events simultaneously. From God's point of view everything that ever will happen has already happened. He is able to view His creation(s) from all possible points of reference. God experiences time both sequentially and simultaneously.

I would further speculate that if God is love and loving by nature, as the Bible attests, then for any kind of loving interactions to occur there would need to be at least two or more persons or entities participating in those interactions. It would seem logical to me that God's first act in time would be the creation of one or more persons or entities with whom He could interact. According to the Bible, Christ was the first (Col. 1:15). So Christ did have a beginning in time. Based on my knowledge of quantum mechanics and the conservation of energy (God Himself being made up of pure energy) I do not believe that Christ was created out of nothing. He was created out of or from God's own essence (pure energy). He came from God in the sense that a human baby is made from the body parts of the mother and father. Jesus was *"begotten"* from God in the same sense that human parents beget their children. Jesus was divine in the sense that everything that comes out of God is part of God Himself. He was fashioned form God's DNA, so to speak. He also had a separate and distinct personality with whom God the Father could interact.

I believe there is another reason for Christ's existence. He is the personification of a God who otherwise would be invisible, impersonal, and unknowable. *"No one has ever seen God, but the one and only Son, who is himself God and is in closest relationship with the Father, has made him known."* (John 1:18) In other words, Christ exists for the benefit of all humanity, that we might have a way to know and connect with God, the Father.

That brings us to a discussion of the Holy Spirit, the third person of the Trinity. In the Bible God is described as being a spirit. *"God is spirit, and his worshipers must worship in the Spirit and in truth."* The same is true of Christ. He exists in Heaven today in spiritual form, in a spiritual body, not made of flesh and blood. According to 1 Cor. 15:50, *"flesh and blood cannot inherit the kingdom of God, nor does the perishable inherit the imperishable."*

In addition to being in spirit form, both God the Father and the Son have a spirit. Christians are said to be indwelt by both the Spirit of God and the Spirit of Christ, and the two are used pretty much interchangeably. *"You, however, are not in the realm of the flesh but are in the realm of the Spirit, if indeed the Spirit of God lives in you. And if anyone does not have the Spirit of Christ, they do not belong to Christ."* (1 Cor. 3:16-18).

For me the conclusion of the matter is this. Both God the Father and Jesus Christ are different manifestations on a single divine Godhead. The term "Spirit" simply refers to "what they are made of." As God's only begotten son Christ is made up of "God parts," ie. spirit. Both the Father and Son share the same spirit, but also exist as separate entities. A very literal translation of John 1:1 expresses this connection: *"In the beginning was the Word* (ie. the Christ)*, and what God was, the Word was."* Because both the Father and the Son exist in spirit form they can divide themselves into an infinite number of smaller pieces and focus their attention in many different places at once. Each piece is intimately connected with the whole and knows what all the other pieces are up to. The spirit of God can listen to millions of different prayers at the same time. God is omnipresent. His Spirit and the Spirit of Christ are everywhere. All creation is infused with the Spirit of God and of Christ. Christ is the image of the invisible God and in Christ all things hold together. *"He is the image of the invisible God, the firstborn of all creation. For by Him all things were created, both in the heavens and on earth, visible and invisible, whether thrones or dominions or rulers or authorities – all things have been created through Him and for Him. He is before all things, and in Him all things hold together."*

If you are confused by all this you are not alone. Rather than trying to figure this all out, it might be best to just go with the flow and use biblical descriptions and don't be too bothered by the ambiguities. The deeper things of God are sometimes beyond human comprehension, and may be experienced without being fully understood.

So how do we human beings fit into all this? Are you a spiritual being with a physical body, or are you a physical body that possesses a human spirit, or are you only a physical being with no spirit? According to Romans 8:16, *"The Spirit Himself testifies with our spirit that we are children of God."* Human beings do have a spirit. Another word for the human spirit is the "soul." This is indicated in the parallelism in Luke 1:46-47, *"And Mary said: 'My soul glorifies the Lord and my spirit rejoices in God my savior."* In this passage, the words "soul" and "spirit" are used interchangeably. There is a sense in which the spirit or soul refers to our real or whole self, as opposed to just the material self. In Genesis 2:7, man is described as becoming a *"living soul"* after God breathes into him the breath of life.

Two other sources of truth also confirm the idea that man is a spiritual being, the testimony of science and the testimony of millions of people who have had near death experiences (NDE's).

As I mentioned earlier in this book many scientists, especially theoretical physicists, are coming to realize that we don't actually live in a physical, material world, but a "supernatural" world instead. Their belief in a natural world subject only to the natural laws of Newtonian physics has given way to the idea that the world we observe and experience consists solely of immaterial wave functions that may be described only as probabilities and possibilities, and do not collapse into reality unless observed by conscious observers who themselves do not actually reside within this universe, and are in a manner of speaking spiritual rather than physical beings.

The evidence for the reality and genuineness of the out-of-body near death experience (NDE) is in my view irrefutable. The testimony of millions of people who have had near death experiences, most of whom were clinically dead at the time, confirms the fact that the spirit or soul of man exists quite independently of the physical body and survives after death.

According to the Bible our entire universe, including all the people in it, was created through Christ. Christ is the intermediary through whom God created us. But we were not created out of nothing. Life was breathed into us by the Spirit of God. So you could say that we all share a divine connection with God. Because we were created by Christ we are basically made up of "Christ parts," or spirit. We were created in the image of God, who is spirit. It is also apparent, however, that most of us are not consciously aware of this and feel isolated from God. Most of us view God as a divine being who lives up in Heaven somewhere in a separate place. Of course God Has not separated Himself from us. Instead God has literally breathed Himself into all of us and given to all of us a portion of His Spirit. The difference between those who are saved and those who are not has to do with our awareness and experience of this connection.

When Jesus actually entered into the space-time universe which He created, it was for the purpose of identifying with and communicating with His created beings, who during their time on Earth are incapable of directly communicating with God the Father or with Christ Himself, or the Holy Spirit, for that matter. The immaterial and the material have no way of making direct visible or auditory contact. They exist in two entirely separate planes of existence. We can't see, hear, or touch God with our physical senses. When Christ took human form it was necessary for Him, in order to become fully human, to divest himself of many of His divine attributes. As an actual physical human being, He like the rest of us did not have the ability to see, touch and feel God in the way that He could before His incarnation. He started out from scratch, as it were, and had to learn who He really was and subject Himself to the limitations that all rest of us face. He was no longer omniscient because His mind was no longer connected to God in the way that it once was. He was no longer divine and He was fully human in every respect. When He said that God was greater than He, He was being truthful. He was totally dependent upon God for everything that He accomplished on Earth. He needed to pray for God's help just like the rest of us. He experienced all the human passions and temptations that the rest of us feel, except that He was without sin. The reason for this is that He was full of the Holy Spirit who gave Him the ability to withstand temptation and perform many miracles. When He came to Earth He literally *"emptied"* Himself of His Godhood and became a servant of God, and demonstrated God's love for us by dying on the cross of Calvary for the sins of the world (See Philippians 2:6-11). After the resurrection everything He gave up in order to fulfill His mission on Earth was restored to Him., and He was given a name that would be above all names. Every knee will eventually bow to Him and He will be worshipped as Lord by everyone. Once everyone has learned their life lessons and been formed into the likeness of Christ, they will be presented by Christ to God, faultless before God's throne.

So is there only one God? Yes. Is Jesus God? Yes. I would say that He is a part of God and has all the attributes of God, but at the same time He has a personality that is separate and distinct from God. He is both the object of God's love and the vehicle through whom God expresses His love towards untold billions of His created beings. When on Earth was Jesus fully human? Yes. He came from God, but in His actual conscious awareness He was not God and did not, at least in the beginning, have direct knowledge of who He really was. Like the rest of us, He had to grow in wisdom and stature and favor with both God and man.

To summarize, everything that comes from God or is created by God is technically part of God. God is by nature multi-dimensional in that respect. From our point of view within the confines of the physical bodies in which we temporarily reside we are separated from God. Our personal experiences play out over time, but from God's perspective, they have already occurred and there was never a time that they did not yet occur. Christ was begotten of God, but from God's perspective there was never a time in which Christ did not exist. The Holy Spirit is just another name for God Himself and also of Christ. The Spirit of God is the same as the Spirit of Christ. It is that part of God that connects directly with our human spirit, our real self. One day Christ will gather all of us up in Himself, completely perfected, and present us to the Father, and we will experience complete oneness with God the Father, Son and Holy Spirit, and God will finally be "all in all." (See 1 Cor. 15:22-28 and Jude 1:24-25.

Chapter 11

Understanding the Atonement

Regarding our "sin debt"

My father once told me that whatever He gave to me I owe to my children, not to him. We don't owe God anything. Instead, we owe it all to the rest of God's children. I have been forgiven much, and I need to pass that forward. The purpose of God's so-called punishments is to correct us and lead us to repentance. God has always been, and always will be, our loving heavenly Father. Calvary did not change the way God deals with us and our sinfulness. It changed the way we view God, as a loving Father who gives to us sacrificially without wanting anything more from us than our love and gratitude. He wants this for our benefit, not His. What He wants for us is that we learn to love others as He loves us. When we learn to do this our lives will be wonderfully transformed as we identify with the Christ of Calvary and begin to think and act like Him.

The purpose of animal sacrifices

The system of making animal sacrifices to appease an angry God was inherited by the Hebrews from previous and surrounding cultures. It is not the blood of animal sacrifices that cleanses us from sin. Instead, it is the attitude of repentance that accompanies those sacrifices.

See Isaiah 1:11: *"The multitude of your sacrifices-- what are they to me?" says the LORD. "I have more than enough of burnt offerings, of rams and the fat of fattened animals; I have no pleasure in the blood of bulls and lambs and goats."*

Also see Hosea 6:6: *"For I desire mercy, not sacrifice, and acknowledgment of God rather than burnt offerings."*

The Old Testament sacrifices were a type or symbol of what was to come in the person of Jesus Christ. The "blood" of Christ, I believe, is also a symbol of a deeper truth, that Godly love is sacrificial in nature. *"Agape"* love is by definition sacrificial. It costs you something. In the case of Calvary, the cost was Jesus' life.

So, when the writer of Hebrews says that *"without the shedding of blood there is no remission of sin,"* (Heb. 9:22) he is referring not to the physical act of killing an animal, but to the change of heart that accompanies it. The same is true for Christ's sacrifice on Calvary. It was not the physical shedding of Christ's blood that made atonement for our sins. Instead it was the underling truths that the blood atonement represented. God in the person of His Son, Jesus, identified Himself with our sin and shame and took upon Himself the burden of our sin. When we look to the cross for mercy and forgiveness, we are forgiven and freed from the bondage that sin holds over us.

The Atonement

The cross of Calvary is God's way of identifying with us through an incredible act of humility and submission. This was God's way of demonstrating His love for us. *"But God demonstrates his own love for us in this: While we were still sinners, Christ died for us."* (Rom. 5:8) You don't really understand a person, and cannot fully appreciate that person's pain and suffering, unless you have actually walked in his/her shoes. The real message of Calvary is exactly the opposite of what most evangelicals preach. Instead of a super Holy and separate God requiring the blood of men to appease His anger and satisfy the demands of justice, we instead see God Himself in the person of His Son, Jesus, humbling Himself and literally becoming one with us in our suffering and pain. Not only is God able to look upon sin and abide in the presence of sin, He actually became sin for our benefit, in the person of Jesus Christ. *"God made him who had no sin to be sin for us, so that in him we might become the righteousness of God."* (2 Cor. 5:21)

On Calvary, God has demonstrated to us that literally nothing can separate us from His love. No matter how sinful and unworthy we might think we are, none of us is so bad that God cannot love us and actually live in us. The feelings that we have of isolation from God and abandonment by God are illusions. Christian Salvation may best be regarded as getting rid of the illusion and experiencing God's presence in our lives. We are not saved from the wrath of God, but from our failure to understand how loving and understanding God really is. Our God is indeed a God of wrath, but the object of His wrath is godlessness and wickedness, because these things are harmful to us, the objects of His love. *"The wrath of God is being revealed from heaven against all the godlessness and wickedness of people, who suppress the truth by their wickedness."* (Romans 1:18) God hates sin, not sinners. Rather than separating Himself from us because of our sin, He is present with us through all our sinning, trials and suffering.

The penalty for sin is spiritual death, or estrangement from God. This is not a permanent condition. That which is dead can be made alive again. Christians, who were once dead in their sins, have been made alive in Christ. According to Ephesians 2:4-5, *"because of his great love for us, God, who is rich in mercy, made us alive with Christ even when we were dead in transgressions—it is by grace you have been saved."* (See also Romans 6:1-11)

If the penalty for sin were everlasting torture in a place called Hell, then Jesus could not possibly have paid the price of our sins on Calvary. He rose from the dead less than three days later and is very much alive today in Heaven, not Hell.

Jesus' purpose in coming to Earth was to redeem all mankind from sin and death. *"For God did not send his Son into the world to condemn the world, but to save the world through him."* (John 3:17) On Calvary, Jesus acted as a surrogate for all mankind, when He endured estrangement from God and died both spiritually and physically. According to 1 John 2:2, *"He himself is the propitiation for our sins; and not for ours only, but also for those of the whole world."*

The difference between those of us who are saved and those who are not saved has to do with our awareness and experience of the connection that we all have with God through Christ. God is omni-present and exists everywhere, including in the hearts of all mankind. When we by faith enter into relationship with the Christ of Calvary, we are awakened to this connection and experience God's love, mercy and forgiveness in a personal way.

Chapter 12

Is the Experience of Christian Salvation Instantaneous or a Process?

Between 1900 and 1925, Russell Conwell delivered his famous speech, *"Acres of Diamonds,"* over 5,000 times. In this speech Russell told stories of people who sold their lands and went off in search of riches, only to find out later that great riches were discovered on the lands that they had left. The most prominent story in this lecture is about a Persian by the name of Ali Hafed, who sold his farm and used up all the money from the sale during a world-wide search for diamonds. Eventually he spent all his money, ended up destitute and committed suicide. Afterwards, diamonds were discovered on the property that he had sold, and that farm became the site of the largest diamond mine in the world. That reminds me somewhat of a story that Jesus told of a Prodigal Son who took his inheritance ahead of schedule and left home. After squandering his inheritance he became destitute. Unlike the stories in Russell Conwell's speech, however, this story had a happy ending. The Prodigal Son eventually found true riches, but not until after returning home.

The Kingdom of God is not something a person finds away from home. It may only be found within. I believe with all my heart that all were saved on the Cross of Calvary, because Jesus died for the sins of all humanity. *"He Himself is the propitiation for our sins; and not for ours only, but also for those of the whole world"* (1 John 2:2). *"God is the Savior of all men, and especially of those who believe"* (1 Timothy 4:10). According to 1 Cor. 15:22, *"all will be made alive in Christ."* Not only were we all saved on the Cross of Calvary, but we were at the same time raised up with Christ and seated with Him in the heavenly realms. *"God raised us up with Christ and seated us with him in the heavenly realms in Christ Jesus"* (Ephesians 2:6).

The point I am making here is that Salvation in Christ is something everyone already possesses. The problem is most people are unaware of it and are not able to experience it. The experience of Christian salvation is described in the Bible as a past, present and future event, depending on which aspect of the salvation experience is being referred to. After all, Christ saves us from many different things, and we are saved from these things at different times. Some of the things Christ saves us from have not even occurred yet. In the mind of God, who is able to view the past, present and future as a single event, salvation may be viewed as occurring instantaneously. But from our human perspective, we view and experience our salvation as various stages of a process which plays out over time. In the broadest sense the term "salvation" refers to many different experiences and events, culminating in the final event at the end of the ages when all are completely redeemed and glorified in heaven.

To some, salvation means to have eternal life, which they would define as "unending conscious existence." As I pointed out earlier in this book, that definition of salvation is based on an incorrect translation of the Greek word *"aionian,"* which actually means the opposite of eternal and everlasting. It refers to a limited period of time, or an age, with a beginning and an end. This definition of salvation is also erroneous because the word *"zoe,"* or "life," does not in this context refer to physical or conscious life. Those who receive *"aionian"* life during their earthly existence are already conscious and alive physically. *"Aionian"* life to refers to spiritual life, not physical or conscious life. Although *"aionian"* life may be experienced in the present, it may only be experienced partially. Spiritual life, or fellowship with God, is something that we grow into. For some, this spiritual awakening begins suddenly during dramatic conversion experience. Others grow into relationship with Christ more gradually and are not able to identify a specific point in time when they were converted. Right now we see Christ only through the eyes of faith, as in a mirror darkly, but some day we will meet Him face to face and will know Him fully (1 Cor. 13:12). Most evangelicals would agree that an important component of Christian salvation is being made spiritually alive in Christ during one's earthly existence. The mistake they make is adding an everlasting time component to it. All Christians will indeed live forever, but so won't everyone else. Conscious existence does not end with the death of the physical body.

Another very important component of Christian Salvation has to do with the forgiveness of sin and being saved from the power that sin has over us. No one can be completely saved in this lifetime with respect to gaining victory over the sin in their lives. Believers are admonished in 1 John 1:9 to confess their sins and seek God's cleansing on a regular basis. We still struggle with sin in our lives (see Romans 6-8). *"If we say we have no sin, we deceive ourselves and the truth is not in us."* (1 John

1:8) While it is true that Jesus died for our sins on Calvary, we still suffer the temporal consequences of our sin and still experience the righteous judgments of God in this life and the next. The purpose of our Heavenly Father's chastisement is to refine and purify us and mold us into the image of Christ. This aspect of Christian salvation does not happen instantaneously. It is an ages-long process that continues after death.

The final component of Christian salvation is the experience of the ultimate redemption and glorification of our souls in Heaven. Obviously, none of us are currently saved in this sense. In the following Scripture passage, the Apostle Paul describes this aspect of our salvation as something we experience only partially in this life.

"*I consider that our present sufferings are not worth comparing with the glory that will be revealed in us. For the creation waits in eager expectation for the children of God to be revealed. For the creation was subjected to frustration, not by its own choice, but by the will of the one who subjected it, in hope that the creation itself will be liberated from its bondage to decay and brought into the freedom and glory of the children of God. We know that the whole creation has been groaning as in the pains of childbirth right up to the present time. Not only so, but we ourselves, who have the firstfruits of the Spirit, groan inwardly as we wait eagerly for our adoption to sonship, the redemption of our bodies. For in this hope we were saved. But hope that is seen is no hope at all. Who hopes for what they already have? But if we hope for what we do not yet have, we wait for it patiently.* (Romans 8:18-25)

Chapter 13

The Gospel of Christ Should Not Be Viewed as a "Get-Out-Of Jail-Free Pass"

Both Christians and non-Christians will face judgment in coming ages. On the cross of Calvary, Christ paid for the sins of all and guaranteed the ultimate redemption of all, *"especially"* those who are now Christians (1 Timothy 4:10). However, God continues to lovingly judge our sins and correct and chastise us for good reason (Hebrews 2:6). What loving father wouldn't? If we just substitute the word "judgment" for "hell," we can begin to understand how God, to one degree or another lovingly judges every one. In the coming ages, those who were Christians in this present age will most certainly find themselves on the receiving end of Christ's judgment (Heb. 9:27).

Many Christians think that when they became Christians they received some kind of get-out-of-jail-free pass that exempts them from any future judgments of God after they die. If, instead of equating God's fiery judgments with retribution in Hell, we view them as a purifying and refining process (Isaiah 48:10), it is easy to understand that in varying degrees, God will be judging both Christians and non-Christians alike. Paul warns Christians about this judgment of their works by fire (1 Corinthians 3:12-14). James warns Christians that faith alone, apart from works, will not exempt them from God's judgments (James 2:12-18). The law of sowing and reaping applies equally to both Christians and non-Christians (2 Cor. 9:6 and Gal. 6:7-8). Many Christians view the parable of the separation of the sheep and the goats as not applying to them, because they are saved by grace, not works (Matt. 25:31-46). But Jesus clearly indicated that many of those who are turned away believed in Him and thought they knew him (Matt. 7:22-23). Many Christians think that the parable of the rich man who was being punished in Hades and the poor man who was being comforted in the bosom of Abram does not apply to Christians. Most of us identify with the poor man, when maybe we should view ourselves as similar in many ways to the rich man, instead. Some of us might mistakenly be relying on our correct theology to exempt us from God's judgments, a modern day form of Phariseeism.

No one believes and appreciates the doctrine of Salvation by grace, apart from works, more than I. Because of God's wonderful gift to us at Calvary, there are no barriers at all to our establishing a relationship with Him. When we come to Him repenting of our sins, He freely forgives us. If, however, we willfully continue in sin, He lovingly judges, and chastises and corrects us. This is true for Christians and non-Christians alike. Nowadays, many born-again Christians have been misled into thinking that most of the teachings of Jesus do not apply to them, because they think that somehow the rules have changed after Pentecost and that the new law of grace somehow trumps the law of sowing and reaping that Jesus taught in so many ways.

I believe that we are saved by grace, not of ourselves. It is important to remember, however, that the born again experience does not result in the instantaneous achievement of perfection. Rather it should be viewed as the beginning of a wonderful process of transformation which is accomplished in the heart of every believer by God's Holy Spirit. Because of Calvary, the spiritual death penalty of sin has been removed and death has been defeated. But Christ's death on Calvary did not remove the need for God to lovingly guide, chastise and correct His children in order to mold them into the image of Christ (Romans 12:1,2). This process of transformation continues into the next life and the ages to come. One day, at the conclusion of the ages, Jesus will finally present every last one of us faultless, and with great joy, before the glorious throne of God the Father (Jude 1:24).

Chapter 14

Does the Salvation Process Continue Into the Next Life?

Romans 8:29: *"For those whom He foreknew, He also predestined to become conformed to the image of His Son."*

God's ultimate goal is to transform each of us into the image of Christ. I believe this refers not only to giving us spiritual bodies like Christ, but the shaping of our characters as well. This being the case, I would assume that God will not be finished with us immediately after we die, when we receive our spiritual bodies.

Paul referred to some of the Christians in Corinth as *mere "babes in Christ"* (1 Cor. 3:1), and some of them were sick and dying because of their sin (1 Cor. 11:30). It is obvious from these passages, and from simple observation, that Christians do not enter life after death with fully reformed characters. Some, perhaps most, Christians think that our basic character will be instantly changed at the rapture, when our bodies are transformed, but is this really the case? If God were to change our characters instantly in this way, the only way He could do it would be to reprogram our brains, as with a computer or robot. Would the result be an authentic change in character, or the loss of genuine character, instead? Only through real and genuine life experiences can we develop genuine qualities of character, especially that of *Agape* love which involves by definition sacrifice and selfless acts of kindness. Also, an important facet of genuine love is empathy, or the ability to feel what others are feeling and identify with the sufferings of others. This can only be genuinely learned from actual human experience.

If God were to instantly create these attitudes, feelings and qualities of character, without exposing us to the actual living conditions under which they are authentically produced, they would not be real, in my view. That is why, when he created us, he placed us in a flawed world and gave us the freedom to make both right and wrong choices, suffer the consequences of those decisions, and in the process develop genuine qualities of character. One of my favorite Scripture passages that describes this process is found in the book of James:

James 1:2-3 *"Consider it pure joy, my brothers whenever you face trials of many kinds, because you know that the testing of your faith develops perseverance. Perseverance must finish its work so that you may be mature and complete, not lacking anything."*

According to the above passage, *"perseverance must finish its work."* If this work has not been finished by the time you die, then it may logically be assumed that more time will be required after death. If we view salvation as a process, rather than an instantaneous event, then the warning that James gives in Chapter two of his epistle regarding the relationship between faith and works would apply to Christians, even after death. We are saved by faith, not of works, but our salvation is an ages-long process and will not be complete until our character fully conforms to that of Christ.

Sometimes the Bible expresses truths from a positional point of view, from the viewpoint of our position in Christ. Positionally, according to Ephesians 2:6, we have already been seated with Christ in the heavenly places. From God's point of view, who can view the events of history from a timeless perspective, the process of our transformation into the likeness of Christ has already been accomplished. He views us *"in Christ"* through the cross of Calvary. But in our human experience, we view this transformation as a process that occurs over time. Especially in the writings of Paul, many of these truths about our relationship with Christ are expressed as positional truth, while at other times they are expressed as experiential truth. These conflicting views of our salvation may be easily resolved if you view salvation as a continuing process from our human experiential perspective, but a completed process from God's perspective.

Chapter 15

What is "Saving Faith" and Where Does God Draw the Line?

In the evangelical Christian community there is much confusion over the issue of faith and works. The problem arises when one or the other of these is viewed as a necessary qualification for salvation. Questions arise regarding the amount and type of faith that is required, or what specific doctrines about Christ must be included in one's confession of faith. If faith must be accompanied by works, as validation of the authenticity of one's faith, how many and what kind of works would be sufficient? How does God draw the line between who is saved and who is not? How is a believer to know for sure on which side of that dividing line he or she stands?

Does saving faith have to be absolute, or is there some room for doubt? Common sense would tell you that faith is almost never an all-or-nothing proposition. Some believe strongly, while some believe weakly, with many doubts and reservations. Where does God draw the line? If acknowledging Jesus as Lord of one's life is a necessary requirement, just exactly how submissive must one be to Jesus in order for it to be considered truly repentant? Must one repent of every single sin and completely change the course of one's life, or is this something one grows into?

If you view salvation as an either-or proposition and view it as something that occurs at a single point in time, then you have the impossible task of determining the point at which an individual can say for sure that he or she is saved. It's not as easy as you might think to draw a line between those who are saved and those who are not.

Let's suppose you line up all the people who have ever lived. At one end of the line would be people who are obviously not saved. Those would be the Hitlers, mass murders and God-haters of the world. At the other end would be believers who have absolutely no doubts at all, who are absolutely 100% committed to Christ as Lord. Let's assume there are several billion people in that line? On a scale of total saving faith at one end to no faith at all at the other end, where does God draw the line?

Assuming your assumptions are true regarding people as being either saved or not saved, how much difference would there be between the two individuals who are standing in the place where God supposedly draws the line? Logically, there would be virtually no measurable difference between the faith of the two individuals on either side of that line. To make matters even worse, people on both sides of that precise dividing line would be continually changing places as their attitudes fluctuate from moment to moment. Yet, according to the above assumptions, the individual on the correct side of that dividing line would be saved and spend eternity in Heaven, and the person on the other side would be condemned to everlasting torment in Hell. How would you reconcile this with your view of God as both loving and just?

If we view salvation as not limited to a single conversion event, but as a process or series of events, then we are better able to resolve the difficulty described above. If you believe in the doctrine of universal reconciliation, that eventually everyone will become fully reconciled to Christ, then you don't have to worry about some line of demarcation that God supposedly draws between the saved and the unsaved.

Rather than agonizing over whether you are genuinely saved or not, wouldn't it be better to understand that everyone, including you, has already been redeemed by the blood of Christ, and Christ is in the process of seeking out those who have lost their way and will eventually bring them all to Himself. The individual who is looking for certainty regarding his or her relationship with God is not going to find it by trying to stay on the right side of some imaginary dividing line that God supposedly draws between those who are saved and those who are not. Assurance of salvation is best achieved by realizing that God loves us all unconditionally and that all are in the process of becoming more fully saved.

Chapter 16

Still Not Convinced? Take the Test!

According to Ephesians 2:8-9, *"it is by Grace you have been saved, through faith – and this not from yourselves, it is the gift of God – not by works, so that no one can boast."* Aside from John 3:16 and Psalms 23, this is probably the most often quoted passage of Scripture in the Bible, and it represents the heart of the Gospel. Unfortunately it has also been one of the most misunderstood of all Bible passages.

No matter how much credit we would like to give to God for our salvation, we still resist giving God ALL the credit. We still want to reserve some of the credit for ourselves. Although the passage clearly states that our salvation is *"not from ourselves,"* we still insist that there is something we must do to make ourselves eligible for salvation. Most evangelical Christians believe that there are "preconditions" that must be met in order to become saved. Although there is disagreement about how these preconditions relate to one another, there is general agreement that they must be evident in the life of the true believer.

One precondition is belief or faith in Christ and His atoning death and resurrection.

Another precondition of salvation is repentance. Both John the Baptist and Christ Himself preached a gospel of repentance. Repentance is a change of attitude toward sin, a turning from sin, and a turning towards Christ for salvation.

Although not a precondition of salvation, good works always accompany salvation. The Bible clearly teaches that although no one is justified by works, saving faith is always accompanied by works. Good works are the proof that the faith is real.

In order for you to determine whether or not you have satisfactorily met the supposed necessary preconditions for salvation, I invite you to take the following test:

On a scale of one-to-ten, rate the strength and quality of your belief or faith in the deity of Christ and His atoning death and resurrection at Calvary:

1. I absolutely believe it, without ever the slightest trace of doubt.
2. I believe it very strongly, but on rare occasions I might experience doubts in moments of weakness.
3. I believe it very strongly most of the time, but sometimes wonder if it's really true.
4. I believe it is probably true, but I could be wrong.
5. I would give it about a 50/50 chance of being true.
6. It might be true, but I have no way of knowing for sure if it really is.
7. It's probably not true, but I would like it to be true.
8. It's probably not true, and I don't much care about it one way or the other.
9. I know it's not true, and I doubt that I am wrong about it.
10. I am absolutely certain that it's not true.

On a scale of one-to-ten, rate the degree of your repentance from sin and desire to turn from it:

1. My attitude toward the sin totally changed since I became a Christian, and I have turned away from every known sin in my life. I haven't looked back since.
2. I have repented of all the sin in my life, but do struggle from time to time with some minor sins.
3. I repented of my sins and asked forgiveness for them, but there still remain major areas of sin in my life which I am struggling with.
4. I have asked Jesus to forgive my sins, but I have to admit that there are many areas of sin I am still holding back on.
5. I have been growing in my walk with Christ. I am making progress with the sin in my life, but still have a very long ways to go.

6. I have repented of some of the sins in my life, but there are still many sins that I am not yet willing to let go of.
7. I have had a conversion experience, but not much has changed with respect to my attitude toward major sins in my life.
8. I have lots of sin in my life, but I don't think it's really that big a deal.
9. I love the sins in my life and couldn't care less about what God thinks about them.
10. I live my life without any guilt at all for my sins, and I wish you would leave me alone.

Finally, on a scale of one to ten, rate yourself on the amount and quality of the good deeds which you are producing in your life as evidence of your salvation:

1. I devote almost every waking moment of my life to the Lord's service, and I give away almost all of my money to the Lord's work and to charitable causes.
2. Although I am not perfect in this regard, I must say that I produce more good works than at least 90% of the Christians I know.
3. I consider myself to be above average in this respect, and I desire to produce an increasing amount of good works as I grow in Christ.
4. I am about average, compared to other Christians I know.
5. I am below average, when compared with other Christians, but significantly above the level of the average Joe on the street.
6. I have to admit. I'm pretty selfish and don't share very much of my time, talent and money with others.
7. I mostly look out for number one, but am respectful of the rights of others.
8. I mostly take from others.
9. I am downright mean towards others, and I lie and cheat without any remorse at all.
10. I am downright evil and delight in the misery of others.

Now that you have completed the above self-evaluation, let's take a look at your score. A total of three points is the best you can score. A score of 30 is the worst. Where do you think God draws the line when deciding who is qualified to be saved or not? If you believe that salvation is an all-or-nothing proposition, then it is impossible for you to know for sure that you are saved. If you believe, on the other hand, that God's gift of salvation is an act of pure grace, completely apart from anything that you can take credit for, then you can know for sure that you are at least in the process of becoming saved. No one is completely saved. Even a perfect score on the above test would not qualify anyone for complete salvation. In order to be completely saved you would have to be completely and totally united with Christ and perfected in Heaven. In this present life we are only saved to the degree that we abide in Christ.

Faith should not be regarded as a prerequisite for salvation. It is simply a word used to describe the means by which we enter into relationship with Christ. It is trusting Christ to save us, not on the basis of any qualification or merit on our part, but solely on the basis of His shed blood on Calvary for our sins. It is not our faith that qualifies us for salvation. As a matter of fact, the word faith is used because there is always an element of doubt present.

Rather than thinking of faith as some sort of requirement for salvation, why not think of it as a door instead? God has given a measure of faith to everyone, and Jesus stands behind that "door" of faith and *"knocks."* (Rev. 3:20) He invites you to enter into a relationship with Him. Simply open the door and invite Him into your life. There are no preconditions. You come as you are. You have nothing to commend yourself to Him, except His shed blood at Calvary.

It is Jesus who produces the evidence of your salvation. Apart from Christ you can produce nothing of lasting value. When you open the door and enter into relationship with Him, wonderful things begin to happen.

You can take no pride in the degree to which you experience God's salvation in Christ. God is the sole initiator of your salvation. It is He who sought you out. Any faith that you exhibit, or good works that are manifested in your life, are completely a result of God's initiatives. Because Christ paid the penalty for the sins of all mankind, eventually all mankind will come to full repentance and be reconciled to Christ. While it is true that Christians today are among the first fruits of God's plan of redemption, we were warned by Jesus not be prideful and not to think ourselves as deserving of greater rewards than those who are last to be saved. In the end, all will be rewarded. I suspect that the rewards will not take the form of things, but instead the utter joy that we will experience when completely united with Christ. I believe that in the end all will receive the same reward. Jesus illustrates this truth in the Parable of the Vineyard in Matthew 20.

Chapter 17

"What Must I Do To Inherit Eternal Life?

After listening to a very excellent sermon on the parable of the Good Samaritan, it occurred to me that this parable conflicts with the popular teaching among some Christian evangelicals that an individual becomes saved at the instantaneous moment in time when he or she confesses Christ as Savior. The born again experience is incorrectly viewed by many of us as a once-in-a-lifetime single event. As you read the Scripture passage below, ask yourself if you have ever satisfied Jesus' requirement at any single point in time in your life.

Luke 10:25-37 **(The Parable of the Good Samaritan)**

25 On one occasion an expert in the law stood up to test Jesus.
"Teacher," he asked, "what must I do to inherit eternal life?" 26 "What is
written in the Law?" he replied. "How do you read it?" 27 He answered:
" 'Love the Lord your God with all your heart and with all your soul and
with all your strength and with all your mind'; and, 'Love your neighbor
as yourself.'" 28 "You have answered correctly," Jesus replied. "Do this
and you will live." 29 But he wanted to justify himself, so he asked Jesus,
"And who is my neighbor?" 30 In reply Jesus said: "A man was going
down from Jerusalem to Jericho, when he fell into the hands of robbers.
They stripped him of his clothes, beat him and went away, leaving him
half dead. 31 A priest happened to be going down the same road, and
when he saw the man, he passed by on the other side. 32 So too, a Levite,
when he came to the place and saw him, passed by on the other side. 33
But a Samaritan, as he traveled, came where the man was; and when he
saw him, he took pity on him. 34 He went to him and bandaged his
wounds, pouring on oil and wine. Then he put the man on his own
donkey, took him to an inn and took care of him. 35 The next day he took
out two silver coins and gave them to the innkeeper. 'Look after him,' he
said, 'and when I return, I will reimburse you for any extra expense you
may have.' 36 "Which of these three do you think was a neighbor to the
man who fell into the hands of robbers?" 37 The expert in the law

replied, "The one who had mercy on him." Jesus told him, "Go and do likewise."

I was raised in the Christian evangelical tradition and was taught repeatedly that in order to become saved you need to believe in the deity of Jesus, confess your sins, and ask Him into your heart. When you do this, you will be instantaneously born again and receive life eternal. You instantly pass from death to life. The problem with this is that it does not square with the answer that Jesus gave to the expert in the law in answer to the question, *"what must I do to inherit eternal life?"* I don't believe Jesus viewed the born again experience as something that happens instantaneously, based on a doctrinal confession of faith and a one-time act of repentance. When the teacher of the Law asked Jesus what he must do to inherit eternal life, Jesus did not say, "bow down to me as Lord and repent of your sins." Instead he laid down a requirement that is impossible for anyone to achieve at any instantaneous moment in time. Who of us is ever able to arrive at a state of mind in this lifetime where we can honestly say that we love God with all our heart, soul, strength and mind? Who of us even comes close? Who of us even comes close to the ideal of loving one's neighbor as oneself?

The requirement given by Jesus for inheriting "*aionian*" life was something that we are only able to partially achieve in this lifetime and something that we grow into as we walk with Christ. When we enter into relationship with God through faith in Jesus, we begin a process of becoming more and more saved. We don't start by loving God with all our hearts and our neighbor as ourselves. Instead, we come to Christ "as we are," sinners becoming saved by grace. Our salvation was initiated by Christ, and, through the indwelling of the Holy Spirit, He begins a process of transformation which will not be complete until the end of the ages.

The requirements for inheriting "*aionian*" life, which were given by Jesus to the teacher of the law, are fulfilled by the Holy Spirit at work in our lives. We begin by establishing a love relationship with God. This increases our ability to love others, as the love of God flows through us. Our salvation experience began before the world was created when God decided to redeem His creation. The end result, the salvation of all mankind, was assured at Calvary when the ransom was fully paid for everyone's redemption. A major step in our personal salvation occurred when Christ sought us out and drew us into a relationship with Himself. For some of us this was a single, dramatic event. For others, it was took the form of a more gradual awakening of faith. For some, it will not occur until after death. In Adam all died. In Christ all will be made alive

(1 Cor. 15:22). The process of being made alive in Christ does not occur instantaneously for anyone.

Jesus, in his answer to the teacher of the law, laid out the requirements for inheriting *"aionian"* life, but he did not specify exactly when this would occur and he never said it would occur instantaneously. He never said that we could achieve salvation through our own efforts. As a matter of fact, He set the standard so high as to be humanly impossible. In another place, He said that *"with men it is impossible," but with God "all things are possible."* (Matthew 19:26).

Chapter 18

Theological Correctness and Christian Salvation

Theological correctness refers to the insistence of many religious conservatives upon the profession of certain theological beliefs as a necessary condition of Christian salvation and inclusion in the family of God. For many Christian conservatives the Gospel of Jesus Christ is good news, it would seem, only for those who are fortunate enough to be exposed to this belief system and subscribe to it. It doesn't matter how religious, moral, or otherwise deserving an individual might be, salvation and entrance into God's heavenly kingdom is only available to those who subscribe to a very detailed system of theological beliefs about the work and person of Jesus Christ. In other words, in order to be saved one must not only be spiritually, morally and ethically correct, but theologically correct as well.

Just how detailed is this system of necessary and required beliefs? Well, in the view of many Christian evangelicals it is more detailed than you might think. For example, it is not enough to be a follower of Jesus Christ and seek to obey his religious and ethical teachings. There are certain specific teachings about his person and ministry that you must also subscribe to. You must believe that He is not only the Son of God, but is uniquely the "*only begotten*" son of God and at the same time He is also God Himself. Additionally, you must believe in the atonement, and not just any definition or theory of the atonement will do. You must believe in what is referred to as the substitutionary atonement, that Jesus on the cross of Calvary took upon himself the sins of all mankind, and paid the penalty for your sins. In order to be saved you must receive Christ as your personal Savior and Lord and ask forgiveness for your sins based on Jesus shed blood on the cross of Calvary. In other words, it is not enough just to believe that Jesus is the unique son of God, and is actually God himself, the third person of the Trinity, and that He died for the sins of mankind, but you must also believe that he rose bodily from the dead and is alive today, and you must enter into a personal relationship with him and ask him to forgive your sins based on his shed blood on Calvary. And you need to be sincere about it! Hypocrites and unbelievers will definitely not be admitted into Heaven. Exactly how strong or perfect your belief or faith must be is never been made clear. Just to be sure, it would help to produce a sufficient amount of follow-through and good works as evidence that your faith is genuine.

Naturally the above level of theological correctness would pretty much rule out 99 percent of the people on earth as candidates for salvation. Most Roman Catholics wouldn't make it, because they rely mostly on their good works for salvation and have little understanding of the principle of salvation by *"grace apart from works,"* whatever that really means. Mormons are excluded because although they believe that Jesus is the Son of God they don't believe he is the unique Son of God and that He is actually God Himself. And of course, Mormons don't really believe in the Christian God, because they believe that God was once a man and that it is possible for men to actually become gods. Boy, talk about theological incorrectness! Jehovah's witnesses are excluded because they don't believe in the Trinity or that Jesus was the unique son of God, and they rely mostly on their own good works for their salvation. Many, if not most, Christian liberals are excluded because they don't believe in the deity of Christ or the resurrection of Christ or the substitutionary atonement. Even though many of those Christian liberals are deeply devoted to God and seek to follow the teachings of Christ, they are not technically born again or saved. Of course, if most professing Christians are not theologically correct enough to enter Heaven, what chance is there for the Hindu, Moslem, Buddhist, Atheist, or the starving beggar on the streets of Calcutta who doesn't have even the slightest clue that God loves and cares about him.

Nevertheless, the Bible does teach that theological correctness is an important part of the salvation process. The issue I have with those who insist on theological correctness as a condition of salvation concerns the timing of it. Becoming saved and experiencing Christian salvation is a process that does not occur at any one instantaneous point in time. None of us are completely saved yet. The converse is also true. No one is completely lost. I believe that Christ made provision on Calvary for the salvation of everyone, and everyone is in the process of becoming fully saved. God is at work in our lives before, during and after our profession of theologically correct beliefs about Jesus Christ. In my view, religiously devout individuals who are genuinely seeking to please God, though misinformed on many important theological points of doctrine, may be closer to God, and farther along in the salvation process, than individuals who subscribe to all the correct doctrines but are not seeking to please God in many important aspects of their lives. Filling the gaps in our theological understanding is something that God will do for all of us sooner or later. For most, this will not occur until after death.

Chapter 19

Experiencing Christ

Many Christians place enormous importance on the necessity of belief or faith in Jesus Christ as a prerequisite for receiving God's gift of salvation and eternal life. Many would add an additional requirement of correctly believing in a variety of specific doctrines about Christ, as well, including the Deity of Christ, His virgin birth, His atoning sacrifice on the Cross of Calvary for the sins of the world, and His literal resurrection from the dead three days later. As part of my research for a thesis which I wrote in college, I surveyed the beliefs of a variety of Christian denominations. I developed a doctrinal questionnaire and administered it to the entire congregations of several Christian churches. One of the questions listed several "fundamental" Christian doctrines which included the following: Belief in the Deity of Christ; the Substitutionary Atonement; the Virgin Birth of Christ; the Resurrection of Christ from the Dead; acknowledgment of Christ as Lord of one's life; repentance from sin; the literal, verbal inerrancy of the Scriptures; and a few others. The question was, *"Which of the items on the list are absolutely necessary for salvation?"* As one might expect, members of the more liberal denominations checked fewer items on the list than members of the more conservative denominations. Many members of very conservative fundamentalist congregations checked every single item on the list.

The conditions for salvation are further complicated by the difficulty of establishing exactly how much belief or faith would be required. Belief, or faith, is characterized in many Bible passages as being strong or weak in various circumstances and from one individual to the next. How would one distinguish between saving faith and faith which doesn't quite cut it? This is not an easy question to answer.

In the case of the prerequisite of repentance from sin and acknowledging Jesus Christ as Lord of one's life, how is it possible to know for sure just how much repentance is required or to what degree a person must yield to the Lordship of Christ in his or her life?

The problem resolves itself, however, if you define a Christian to be a person who has a personal relationship with Christ, rather than a person who merely subscribes to a system of beliefs. As you know after reading this far into this book, I believe that everyone is in the process of becoming saved. I believe that one day all creation will become fully reconciled to Christ. I believe that Christ died for the sins of all mankind, and because of this all mankind will eventually become saved. Because Christ paid the penalty for sin, once for all, and for all time, there is no good reason that anyone should not be able to establish a personal relationship with God through Christ. We come to Christ "as we are" with all of our sinful baggage and with woefully inadequate faith and doctrinal understanding. He turns none of us away (see John 6:37). He loves every one of us with infinite, *"agape,"* love and sees us not only as we are, but also as we will become.

Our salvation is *"in Christ"* (see Rom. 3:24; 8:1; 1 Cor. 1:30; 15:22; 2 Cor. 5:19; 2 Tim. 1:1; 2:10). What that means is that our salvation is in our relationship with Christ. The degree to which we experience Christ in our lives is the degree to which we have become saved. The Gospel of Christ is good news. It is not a set of intellectual, doctrinal, and behavioral barriers which we must overcome in order to be accepted by God.

By regarding Christian salvation as something one experiences, rather than something one acquires at a specific point in time, most of the difficult doctrinal issues resolve themselves. One no longer needs to wonder, "Am I saved or not?" The religious elite of Jesus' day were harshly criticized by Christ for their hypocritical and self-righteous attitudes. On the other hand, Jesus was welcoming and kind to those who were regarded by the religious elite as the least worthy, such as the woman caught in adultery, the poor widow who only had one small coin to donate, the tax collector, the despised Samaritan, the Roman Centurion, lepers, outcasts of society, and especially children who knew little or nothing about religious doctrine.

If we regard the Bible not as God's direct words to us in the objective sense, but instead as a testimonial record of man's genuine encounters with God, then it would follow that in order to fully understand what the writers were trying to communicate we must experience God for ourselves. No one ever got saved by knowing or believing something about God (see James, Chapter 2). We experience God's salvation only as we experience Christ himself. Some view the salvation experience as inviting Christ to forgive your sins and asking Christ to come and live inside your heart. If that's as far as it ever goes, however, it cannot be said that you have become fully saved. You may have taken a very important first step, but you may only be regarded as a *"babe in Christ"* (see 1 Cor. 3:1). If you invite Christ into your life, but don't allow Him to control various aspects of your life, then He is not really living inside you. Christ is omnipresent. Technically He lives everywhere. He exists inside and outside of everyone. When the Bible refers to Christ as abiding or living inside of you, it is not talking about Christ merely taking up space. When Paul said, *"for to me to live is Christ" (Phil. 1:21),* he was saying that he was allowing Jesus to control every aspect of his life. Paul yielded up his body, his hands, his feet, his mind, and allowed Christ to use them as instruments for carrying out the ministry of spreading the gospel. Paul so completely identified with Christ that he could honestly say, *"I no longer live, but Christ lives in me" (Gal. 2:20)*

The essence of the Gospel and the Christian experience as communicated in the New Testament is that God was in Christ reconciling the world to Himself (2 Cor. 5:19). The power that sin and death held over mankind was defeated at Calvary and there now remains no obstacle preventing us from knowing God intimately and experiencing a truly abundant life in Christ.

So, exactly how does one go about experiencing Christ, as described above? The key to achieving this is to focus on the relationship with Christ and not on acts of obedience and the avoidance of sin. Remember that your salvation experience was initiated by God and that every sinful act (or failure to act) or attitude that you could ever possibly become guilty of has already been covered by the blood of Christ at Calvary. God loves and accepts you just as you are. There is nothing you can do to be worthy of God's love or in any way be deserving of the salvation He offers to you in Christ. Salvation is a gift that God offers to all. There are no preconditions that must be met. All that remains for you to do is to experience it. All you need to do is allow Christ into your life and get to know Him. Thank Him for everything He has done for you and ask for His help and guidance with every important decision you need to make in life. Share with Him all your burdens, heartaches, disappointments, worries and cares. Ask Him to intercede in your life and the lives of those whom you love and those whom you ought to love. Ask Him to help you develop qualities of Godly character and experience the fruit of the Spirit, such as love, joy, peace, patience, kindness, goodness, faithfulness, gentleness and self-control. When you stumble, ask Him to pick you up. When you think wrong thoughts or act in selfish ways or commit wrongful acts, ask God to forgive you. Ask God to forgive you for sins which you are not yet willing to give up. It's OK. He understands. Rome wasn't built in a day. Your salvation experience is an ages-long journey that begins with just a few halting steps.

Paul admonishes us to *"pray without ceasing"* (1 Thes. 5:17). Talk to God throughout the day, every day. In the beginning you may only remember to talk with Him once or twice a day, or once or twice a week. That's OK. He is always by your side anyway. He will never leave you nor forsake you. It's hard to discipline yourself to spend hours on your knees each day in fervent prayer, as is the habit of some (not many). I myself prefer a more casual approach. Brother Lawrence, a medieval monk, described his experience with Christ as *"practicing the presence of God."* It was simply a matter of continually reminding himself that God was present in his life and cared about every daily activity of life. Brother Lawrence played a very humble role in the monastery. He worked mostly in the kitchen and referred to God as *"the God of the pots and pans."* Even in the most mundane aspects of daily living, Brother Lawrence enjoyed the presence of God.

God's perfect standards of behavior are impossible for anyone to attain in this life. You will never measure up to those standards. The harder you try to please God by measuring up to those impossible standards the more defeated and frustrated you will become in your daily walk with Christ. Most likely, you will give up trying altogether. The secret to making progress in your Christian walk is to not try so hard. Keep the lines of communication open between Christ and yourself. Transfer the load onto the back of Christ and allow him to carry it for you (see Matt. 11:28-29). He wants to live His life through you. When you transfer the burdens of daily living and Christian service to Him, then it becomes His problem and not yours. He is more than capable of doing what you cannot possibly do in your own strength.

Is it really that easy, you might ask? What about passages in the Bible that indicate the necessity of self-denial and sacrifice as a condition of salvation and following Christ? Did not Christ say that if you did not love Him even more than your own family you were not worthy of Him? Did He not say that in order to follow Him you would have to deny yourself, take up a cross of suffering daily? Did He not say that if your righteousness did not exceed that of the Scribes and Pharisees you could not enter the Kingdom of Heaven? Did He not say that you cannot serve two masters and that you had to choose between serving the "world" and serving Him? Did not the Apostle Paul say in Romans that a true Christian is one who has yielded himself to Christ as an obedient servant?

Here's my answer. In response to one of those harsh sayings of Jesus, his disciples asked, *"How then can anyone be saved?"* Jesus answer was that with God all things are possible (see Matt. 19:16-27).

The process of becoming a Christian and becoming saved is not instantaneous. A Chinese philosopher once said that a journey of a thousand miles begins with a single step. The salvation process involves identifying with Christ and getting to know Him on a more and more personal level as time goes on. It involves substituting the righteousness of Christ for your own. It involves substituting the work of Christ for your own. It involves depending on Christ to accomplish every positive good deed in your life through you and on your behalf. Apart from Christ we can accomplish nothing of lasting value (John 15:5). The Christian walk is characterized as a process of letting go, rather than trying harder. It involves stepping aside and allowing Christ to step in. Salvation is a gift, not a result of good works. There is no room for boasting. Christian baptism pictures our salvation as a process of identifying with Christ in His death, burial and resurrection. We die to our old way of life and rise up with Christ in newness of life. We shed the old and put on the new. In the words of Paul, *"old things pass away and all things become new"* (2 Cor. 5:17). The key to all this is our relationship with and our identification with Christ. Our salvation is *"in Christ."* We are only saved to the extent that we abide in Christ.

One day we will become completely saved, and our final redemption will result not from our own efforts but from the work of Christ in our hearts and minds. It is He who is able to keep us safe until that day and eventually present us faultless before the throne of God (Jude 1:24).

So, relax, and quit worrying about not being able to measure up. Practice the presence of Christ in your life with every step you take. Be aware of His presence and closeness to you. Bring every care and concern to Him and ask Him to handle it for you. Ask Him for His strength to carry on when faced with difficult, even impossible circumstances. Thank Him continually for the bountiful blessings in your life. The closer you walk with Christ, the more like Him you will become. The more you experience Christ Himself, the more you will experience the fruit of His Spirit in your life. This fruit includes not only the benefits of love, joy, and peace, but also the development of Godly character, which includes traits such as patience, kindness, goodness, faithfulness, gentleness and self- control.

Self-denial is a part of that package, but what you receive in return makes everything else pale by comparison. If you want your dog to let go of the dirty old bone he dug up in the back yard present him with a nice juicy steak. That is what God does for you. He wants you to give up your old way of life, but the new life He gives you in return is infinitely better than the one you are leaving behind.

Chapter 20

Abba, Father
Assurance of Salvation

Years ago, while helping out at a children's church camp, I witnessed an interesting phenomenon. About 100 children in grades 4-6 were gathered around a campfire in a small outdoor amphitheater under the pines, listening to an evangelistic message given by the camp speaker. At the conclusion of the message the speaker invited those who wanted to receive Jesus as their Savior and Lord to come to the front. Nearly all the children in the audience came forward and repeated the "sinner's prayer" and asked Jesus to come into their hearts, forgive their sins, and give them eternal life. Camp leaders rejoiced to see so many children become saved on that occasion. I didn't share their enthusiasm. It was my opinion at that time in my life that the commitment required for a true and genuine conversion experience was beyond the comprehension of young children.

At that time in my life I believed that in order to become genuinely saved a person must not only receive Christ as Savior, but also as Lord. My belief was that although salvation was undeserved and not earned by doing good works, the sincere intention to follow through with good works was a necessary ingredient of "saving" faith. I believed that in order to become a Christian one needed to genuinely repent of one's sins and acknowledge Christ as Lord of one's life (Romans 10:9,10). I didn't believe that the children who went forward to receive Christ at that church camp could possibly understand what it really meant to repent of sin and commit their lives to Christ as Lord. While it was true that they were at some level entering into a relationship with Jesus, I believed that their commitment to follow Christ was superficial at best. I now admit that I did not fully understand the import of what Jesus was saying when He told His disciples to allow the little children to come to Him and don't hinder them for the Kingdom of Heaven belongs to such as them (Matt. 19:14). In another place, He said that anyone who will not receive the Kingdom of God like a little child will never enter it (Luke 18:17).

What I didn't fully realize was that the follow through of righteous living is a natural outgrowth of a right relationship with Christ, not a result of self-generated good works. To be in right relationship with Christ one must approach Him with an attitude of child-like helplessness, trust and dependence.

The Apostle Paul, in Romans 8:13-16, warns us that those who live according to the sinful nature will die, and only those who are led by the Spirit of God are the true sons of God. In Romans 6, 7 & 8, Paul reacts to a form of "easy believerism" that results from a misunderstanding of what Paul meant by salvation by grace apart from works. Some in the Church understood that to mean that since we are saved by grace, and not by works, it is not necessary to follow Christ's commands and avoid sin. In these three chapters Paul went to great pains to point out that a life of good works and the avoidance of sin was the natural outflow of a genuine conversion experience. When one is in right relationship with Christ, the Holy Spirit guides and motivates the believer to live a life which is pleasing to God. It is the Holy Spirit, not the believer, who produces the changed life. In the Scripture passage cited at the beginning of this paragraph (Rom. 8:13-16), Paul explains that we don't produce good works out of fear. The Holy Spirit is not a spirit of fear, but of sonship, whereby we cry *"abba"* (daddy or da da), Father. It is God's Holy Spirit who testifies with our human spirit that we are God's children. The Apostle Paul in all of his letters continually urged believers to live up to their calling in Christ and he expressed hope and confidence in their ability to do so (see Romans 8:1-4). The writers of the other New Testament letters universally reacted against what I would call "easy believerism." They made it very plain that a changed life was the inevitable result of a genuine conversion experience. It is interesting to note that despite repeated warnings about the dangers associated with falling away from faith and falling into sin, the writers expressed confidence that this would not happen to true believers.

Some of the most unsettling passages of Scripture regarding the security of the believer come from Hebrews. In Hebrews 3:12-14 the writer warns the readers not to have unbelieving hearts that turn away from God. He further warns, *"We have come to share in Christ if we hold firmly till the end the confidence we had at first."* Later, in Hebrews 6:4-6, the writer notes that it is impossible to restore to repentance those who *"fall away,"* after having tasted the *"goodness of the word of God and the powers of the coming age."* In Hebrews 10:26-27, he gives a further warning: *"If we deliberately keep on sinning after we have received the knowledge of the truth, no sacrifice for sins is left, but only a fearful expectation of judgment and of raging fire that will consume the enemies of God."* The above passages are often quoted out of context to prove that people can lose their salvation if they don't continue doing good works and holding onto your faith till the end.

If you carefully read the context in which those above verses were written, however, you will realize that they were written to encourage, not discourage, the readers. The whole point of the book of Hebrews was to explain how Christ's perfect sacrifice on the cross of Calvary could do what animal sacrifices could not. The animal sacrifices offered only a temporary covering of sin and had to be repeated over and over. Christ's sacrifice, on the other hand, only had to happen once for all time and for all the sins of mankind. If the blood of Christ is not sufficient to permanently cleanse us from sin, then no other sacrifice remains that can do the job.

The writer of Hebrews expresses confidence that the warnings really do not apply to the audience to whom he is writing. In Hebrews 6:9, the writer tells the readers that he is confident of *"better things"* of them, *"things that accompany salvation."* He urges them to *"show diligence to the end in order to make your hope sure."* According to Hebrews 10:39, *"we are not of those who shrink back and are destroyed, but of those who believe and are saved."* If we have been saved, there is never a danger of losing our salvation. I believe in the saying "once saved, always saved. When we "fall away" we do not lose our salvation. We only lose our confidence in and assurance of salvation. For assurance of salvation we must be currently walking in right relationship with Christ.

The salvation experience is a two-part process. The first part is cleansing from sin. The second part is the infilling of the Holy Spirit who gives us the power to overcome sin in our daily living. We don't become instantly perfect, but with God's help we do make progress in our Christian walk, and the end result, which is our ultimate redemption in Heaven, is guaranteed. According to Ephesians 1:11-13, we who were chosen in Christ (i.e. those of us who have entered into a saving relationship with Christ) were *"sealed"* by the Holy Spirit, whom God has given to us as an advance deposit or guarantee of our inheritance until our final redemption. The Holy Spirit guarantees our redemption and produces the evidence of our salvation and enables us to make progress in our Christian walk.

In the three letters of John, and also in 1 & 2 Timothy, Titus, and 2 Peter, readers are warned that all true Christians do not willfully and habitually practice sin. These were not warnings to Christians about the danger of losing their salvation. Instead, they were a response to a serious heresy that had gained a foothold in many churches of the day.

There were heretical teachers in many local congregations, some of whom traveled from church to church, who taught what is believed to be an early form of Gnosticism. These teachers denied the incarnation of Christ and taught that only the spirit is good and the body is evil. Therefore, Christ never truly became flesh and died for our sins. They believed that the Spirit of Christ only temporarily inhabited the body of Jesus, and then departed before Jesus was crucified. They reasoned that since the body is evil it doesn't matter what you do with it. Therefore, all things done in the body, including sexual immorality and the breaking of God's laws, were permissible. Obviously those who espoused this form of Gnosticism never had a saving relationship with Christ. Some of them feigned a form of godliness in order to gain the trust of the church members, but eventually many of them abandoned the charade, showed their true colors, and left the church, hence the statement by John in 1 John 2:18: "*They went out from us, but they did not really belong to us, for if they had belonged to us, they would have remained with us.*"

Listen to the words of assurance that John gives to those of us who really do know Christ: *"And this is the testimony: God has given us eternal life, and this life is in his Son. He who has the Son has life; he who does not have the Son of God does not have life. I write these things to you who believe in the name of the son of God so that you may know that you have eternal life"* (1 John 5:11-13).

It is important to understand that we do not rely on our good deeds and acts of righteousness in order to remain qualified for salvation. Instead, good deeds should be regarded as indicators of God's Holy Spirit at work in our lives. Becoming a Christian is so easy a child can do it. The follow through after our decision to receive Christ into our lives, although difficult at times, can be made much easier if we yield to the leading of the Holy Spirit and allow Jesus to carry some of the load.

John 10:28-29: *"And I give unto them eternal life; and they shall never perish, neither shall any man pluck them out of my hand. My Father, which gave them me, is greater than all; and no man is able to pluck them out of my Father's hand."*

Chapter 21

Predestination and Free-Will

Calvinism

Years ago, when I was first exposed to an extreme form of Calvinism, I was shocked to learn that the doctrine of predestination was still alive and well. It hadn't died out in the era of Jonathan Edwards as I had thought. The idea that God would arbitrarily decide in advance who would be saved and who would spend eternity in Hell, without giving anyone a say in the matter, simply repulsed me. Not only was this doctrine alive and well, but it was, and still is, the predominant view in many mainline protestant denominations and even in the Baptist church, of which I was a member.

According to an extreme form of this system of thought, sometimes called hyper-Calvinism, Jesus only died for the Elect (limited atonement), and God only loves the Elect, and it is impossible to become saved by one's own volition, because God decides in advance who is going to desire to be saved and who is not. When God calls you to be saved His grace is irresistible. If He does not call you then it would be impossible for you to come to repentance and be saved. The idea is that man is totally depraved and unless God intervenes and awakens in him a desire to become saved, the result is a hardened heart that cannot be changed.

One of the main themes of this system of thought is the sovereignty of God. The idea is that God is all-powerful and completely sovereign over His creation and will absolutely accomplish all that He sets out to do. Because God is sovereign and does not save everyone, it must be assumed that God does not want everyone to be saved. Not all Calvinists are this extreme in their beliefs. Many do not believe in the limited atonement and many believe that God really does love everyone. He just loves the elect in a different way than those who are not of the elect.

All Calvinists teach that human freedom is an illusion. It only seems real because God allows us to make our own choices in life, sometimes referred to as free-agency, to distinguish it from free-will. The idea is that we are free to do what we want, but what we want is not determined by us, but by God. So we don't really possess free-will, only free-agency.

Of course, there are many Scriptures that refute these teachings, but there is also much Scriptural support for some of them.

Arminianism

Arminianism came about as a reaction against Calvinism. Arminians believe that Jesus did indeed die for everyone and that we are all genuinely free to make our own choices in life. While it is true that God decides in advance (elects, chooses, predestinates) who will become saved, His choices are based on His foreknowledge of who would be predisposed to receive the Gospel and who would not. According to Arminianism, human freedom is real and God's grace is offered freely to all.

The Arminian arguments seem sound enough at first glance, and there is much Scriptural support for this system of thought. However, as I pondered their arguments I came to a very disturbing realization. Human freedom must be an illusion, even if the Arminians are right and the Calvinists are wrong. If God doesn't determine our desire to be saved or not, what does? Can any of our choices in life actually be self-caused? While it is true that we are free to make our own choices in life, we are not free to determine what our desires will be. All of our thoughts have an antecedent cause. The choices we desire to make in life, if not directly determined by God, are at least indirectly determined by Him. After all, it was God who created the universe and set in motion random processes which resulted in our birth, genetic, social, societal, and psychological make-up and environment. We didn't choose where we would be born or in what kind of family or social environment we would be raised. All of these factors combine to make each one of us unique and different.

The reason my choices in life are different from yours is that I am different from you. Did I cause myself to be different? Not really. So, whether you believe that your uniqueness was caused by God or by random processes, it is still not self-caused. If you choose to become saved and I do not, who is to blame? Ultimately, we must "blame" God for all the choices we make in life. God is the one who started it all, knowing full-well what the result would be and how each individual life would be affected.

So, it doesn't matter whether you take the Calvinist position or the Arminian position, God is still ultimately responsible for all that happens.

God's Foreknowledge and Human Freedom

It has been correctly argued that if God has a perfect knowledge of all future events then those events must be immutable, and all human actions leading up to those events must also be immutable and not subject to change. If this is the case, then human freedom must be an illusion. If all our future actions are known by God they cannot be changed, or else what is known by God is not accurate. The arguments relating to the incompatibility of God's foreknowledge and human freedom lie at the center of the Calvinism vs. Arminianism debate. The major thrust of the Arminian argument is that God knows in advance what choices man will freely make. But if those choices are known in advance, counters the Calvinist, then they cannot possibly be changed and human freedom must be an illusion. All of man's future actions must be cast in granite, and man is not really free to change or alter that course. Even before you were born, your eternal destiny was sealed and it cannot be changed. The Calvinist concludes that your eternal destiny was predetermined by God, since God set in motion a sequence of events which cannot be altered, knowing in advance that the result would be the eternal damnation of some and eternal life in Heaven for only the Elect. The Arminian would argue that although the future cannot be changed, your future is the result of choices which are freely made, and that your actions, although foreknown by God, are not predetermined by God. But this argument only begs the question. None of man's choices are freely made if they are the result of events set in motion at the beginning of time and not subject to alteration. Your choices in life, if not determined by direct intervention or orchestration of God, are at the very least indirectly determined by God because God set everything in motion, knowing the result of His actions in advance.

A third point of view, which is really a variant of Arminianism, is the idea that God does not have exhaustive and detailed, knowledge of the future because even God cannot know what does not exist. This is sometimes referred to as Open Theism. The word "open" refers to the openness of God to change His mind in response to new information and change His behaviors, resulting in an altered future. Since future events technically do not exist until they actually happen, it can be argued that God can still be omniscient and not know the future in every detail. In other words, even an omniscient God cannot know what is unknowable. This is true of both past, present and future events. God cannot know that an event in the past, present, or future has occurred if it has not actually occurred. God cannot know that something is true when it actually is not.

For example, God only knows that four plus four equals eight. He cannot know that it equals nine, or any other number besides eight. According Open Theism, God, based on His exhaustive knowledge of the present, can only know what the most likely future outcomes will be and the ways He intends to shape future events as He interacts with His creative beings in response to their choices in life that for the most part are not directly coerced by God.

For me, Open Theism at first seemed to be an attractive alternative to the traditional Calvinistic and Arminian positions, and it harmonized beautifully with the way the Scriptures picture God's interactions with his created beings. In the Bible, God is often "surprised" or disappointed by man's moral and ethical choices and He changes His behavior in response to those choices. Examples of this kind of interaction are countless. The story of the Genesis Flood, for example, pictures God as being grieved that He had made man, and then decided to start over again. Many of the prophecies of the Old Testament were conditioned upon human responses and behavior. Even the most hard-core Calvinist must acknowledge that if God's knowledge of the future is exhaustive and complete, God certainly does not behave as though this were true. In response to man's choices God decides what He is going to do next. The whole idea of prayer and supplication is to ask God to do something He would not otherwise do.

However, there are two major arguments against the notion of Open Theism. One is the testimony of the Scriptures themselves, and the other relates to science and logic.

Regarding the testimony of Scripture. Many of the Bible's predictive prophecies may be understood to be contingent upon man's response, and consequently subject to change. Other prophecies, however, are not so easily explained in this way. For example, how could Jesus know in advance that Peter would be tested three times, and deny knowing him three times, before the cock would crow the next morning? I'm sure you are well aware of many other similar examples.

Regarding my understanding of science and logic, it has been pretty well established that space and time as we know it are interrelated and only have relevance within the bounds of the physical universe which God created. For God to have created the universe would it not be logical to assume that He would not be subject to its limitations? Wouldn't God have to exist in other dimensions which transcend our space-time continuum, and most probably be able to view His creation from all spatial and temporal points of reference?

Again the question arises, if God is able to view the future in every detail from a vantage point outside our space-time continuum would not the future then be unchangeable and human freedom an illusion? The Armenian would argue that even when viewed from outside the boundaries of our universe the only future God can see is the one that currently exists, one that will happen if God does not interfere. After all, even an omnipotent God cannot know something that does not exist. However, as God interacts with humanity the future changes. Hence, as man interacts with God he changes his destiny. Thus the future that God sees sometimes happens, and sometimes not, depending on how present circumstances change in response to God's initiatives. The Calvinist would then counter with the argument that the future that "currently exists" includes God's future interventions, hence we come right back to the same problem of the future that God sees being immutable.

What if, however, God deliberately chooses to see the future from only one perspective in time, the present, for the sake of preserving human freedom? In other words, what if God chooses to only view our space-time universe from within? Just as *He "emptied"* himself of certain Godly characteristics when He incarnated Himself as Jesus Christ, would not the same principle hold true as He "enters" human history at various times in order to interact with humanity. May we regard any act of God whereby He communicates directly with humanity as a form of incarnation? This would not necessarily prevent God from seeing the future, but the future that God sees would have to consist entirely of extrapolations based on current events. Of course this would not explain examples of predictive prophecy in the Bible such as Peter's denials. In order to make accurate, immutable predictions such as this Jesus would have had to rely on information from an "outside source," hence his dependence on God the Father through prayer. Only God the Father could view things from this vantage point. I know this is speculative, but could this not possibly explain the need for God's triune nature? Let's assume that God's ability to see the future is limited when He views it from within our current space-time continuum, but when He views it from outside He sees the final result, which definitely would be fixed and immutable. Would this negate human freedom? Not necessarily. The future that God sees from outside the universe would be the result of man's ongoing interactions with a God who truly cannot see the future. In other words, God would be behaving in this world as though the future were not fixed. Man's choices would be free in the practical and functional sense, yet they would still be fixed and immutable from God's external perspective.

Freedom of Will vs. Freedom of Choice

Many Christians resist the Calvinistic teaching that man does not possess free will and that God is truly sovereign over His creation, and that all human events are caused by God in accordance with His perfect will.

There are two main reasons why they resist this teaching.

First, they resist it because they believe that God is both loving and just, and they don't think God should be blamed for unjustly condemning the majority of the human race to an everlasting Hell. In their view, God's decision to condemn individuals to Hell should be based on their freely made choices in life, which are not predestined or coerced by God.

Secondly, they resist it because they don't clearly understand the difference between Freedom of Will (Free Will) and Freedom of Choice (Free Agency). Clearly, God allows us to make our own religious and moral decisions. Not only are we given this freedom of choice, but we are indeed held accountable by God for our choices. We are punished for making the wrong choices and rewarded for making the right choices.

At first glance that all seems quite fair. A serious problem arises, however, when we delve a bit deeper and ask the question, "Why do we make these choices?" Why does one individual freely choose to become saved and another individual freely choose otherwise? What is it that makes the one individual different from the other in that respect?

Some would answer in this way. An individual chooses to become saved because he desires or wants or wills to be saved. In other words, our moral and spiritual choices in life are based on what we desire, want, or will to do.

We are free to make whatever moral and spiritual choices in life that we desire to make. The Calvinist would refer to this freedom of choice as Free Agency in order to distinguish it from Free Will, which would be the freedom to choose what our desires would be in the first place. The Calvinist would agree that God allows us to freely choose to do good or evil. On the other hand, they would argue that we do not possess free will. In other words, we do not freely choose our wants and desires.

Let me illustrate this in another way. My wife likes broccoli and I don't. We both may freely choose to eat it or not. But we don't choose whether or not we like the taste of it or would desire to eat it. If God were to perform a miracle (and indeed that would be quite a miracle) and cause me to like the taste of broccoli, then I would most certainly freely choose to eat it. If God did not perform this miracle, then I most certainly would freely choose not to eat it. So you see, it is very easy for God to influence the choices we make in life by altering the conditions of our lives which determine our attitudes and motivations.

Free will is not a Biblical term. Although the Bible clearly teaches that we are to be held accountable for the choices we make, it nowhere teaches that we made ourselves. We were all created unique and different. We did not choose our parents or our physical, mental and emotional capacities. We did not choose the bewildering variety of human events which have uniquely shaped our thought processes. Our wants and desires (our "wills") have been uniquely shaped, predetermined if you will, by our DNA and the various external events and circumstances of our existence. None of us has freely chosen who we are. We did not freely choose our own uniqueness.

It could be argued, correctly in my view, that God did not directly cause us to accept or reject His offer of salvation. It could also be correctly argued that God is indirectly the cause of everything. He created the universe and everything in it and set in motion a sequence of events that resulted in your existence and everything that is unique about you. Most would agree that when God set in motion this chain of events He foreknew what the result would be. He knew in advance what your choices would be. Apparently He was OK with this result, or He most certainly would have changed it. God is omnipotent and completely sovereign over His creation. He is more than capable of changing the outcome of all human events, should He so desire.

According to Ephesians 2:8-9, we have been saved by grace. Our salvation is "*a gift of God, not of ourselves, lest anyone should boast.*" Because our salvation is not a result of anything meritorious on our part, the converse must also be true, that those who are lost remain so due to no fault of their own. Both conditions are the result of God's choice.

It has been argued that Universalism must be false because for God to eventually save everyone He would have to violate their free will and force them to receive Christ against their wills. It makes better sense that God would save only those who want to be saved, and allow others to freely choose not to be saved.

Here is my answer.

It is a fallacy to assume that in the interest of preserving mankind's freedom of choice God limits what He is able or willing to do. This line of thinking is fallacious in more ways than one.

First, it is nowhere taught in the Bible. The terms “free will” and “freedom of choice” are not found in the Bible. You will find the terms “will” and “choose” in many places, but these terms are never discussed or used in connection with the term “freedom.” And nowhere does the Bible indicate that God has placed limits of any kind on His power or ability to accomplish whatever He sets out to do. As a matter of fact, you will find many verses and passages that indicate exactly the opposite (see Isaiah 14:24, 27 and 46:9-10).

Part of the fallacy of assuming that God somehow limits Himself by giving mankind freedom of choice is the assumption that this is some kind of trade off that God makes. It is nowhere taught in the Bible that God allows bad things to happen, mainly sin and suffering, in order to preserve human freedom. The truth is that God created a flawed world on purpose and with loving intent. He gives us the freedom to fall into sin and experience both good and evil in our lives because this is necessary for our spiritual growth. It is impossible to develop good or positive traits in isolation from their evil and negative counterparts. God does not allow or permit things to happen which are not in accordance with his perfect will. When an omniscient and all-powerful God permits something to happen, it's because He wants it to happen.

Another fallacy related to the above is the false notion that God is unable to influence our behavior without restricting our freedom of choice. God can easily cause us to freely make the right choices, simply by shaping our thoughts and desires. This in no way violates our freedom to choose. He does this in a variety of ways that are amply illustrated in the Scriptures.

Here are some examples:

The Holy Spirit convicts (or convinces) us of our sinfulness (John 16:8). God works in our hearts to convince us that we are sinners in need of a Savior. Through the Holy Spirit He opens our spiritual eyes and enables us to see the truth, not only about our sin, but also about our need for God's remedy, Jesus Christ.

The converse is also true. When it suits His purpose God also can (temporarily) harden our hearts and blind us to the truth. There are numerous references to this in the Bible, the most famous of which is the hardening of Pharaoh's heart prior to leading the Israelites out of bondage in Egypt (Exodus 9:12).

Similarly, God in New Testament times hardened the hearts of His own chosen people in order that the Gospel might be more easily spread to the Gentiles. Please carefully read Romans 11:25-32. Here we learn that Israel's blindness was only temporary, until the *"fullness of the Gentiles has come in."* Afterwards, *"all Israel will be saved."*

Paul's conversion in Acts, Chapter 9, is an example of God's direct, dramatic, and miraculous intervention to convince Saul, a persecutor of Christians, that His views regarding Jesus were completely erroneous. It suited God's purposes to hurry up the process of Paul's conversion and make it as dramatic as possible because a lot was at stake regarding the propagation of the Gospel to the Gentiles. Paul was one of those Israelites who were temporarily "blinded" to the truth. God used this occasion to open his eyes.

There would be no point to intercessory prayer if we did not believe that God is able to change people's hearts and draw them to Christ. It was Paul's heart's desire and prayer that Israel be saved (Romans 10:1). When God gave us freedom of choice, He did not totally relinquish control over our lives. God does not make our decisions for us, but He is fully capable of influencing our thoughts and attitudes of heart which comprise the motivation for the decisions that we make.

Evangelism and preaching of the word are also necessary for this process to occur. In addition to correct attitudes of heart, information is also needed. We cannot possibly freely choose to receive Christ as our Savior and Lord if we have never heard of Him or if the information we have about Him is erroneous. So, a very important tool God uses to influence our decision to receive Christ is the sending out of messengers, armed with Gospel information. See Romans 10:14-15.

Rewards and punishments in this life and the next are another way God influences the moral and spiritual decisions that we make. In Matthew 6:19-21, God motivates us to live righteous lives in order to lay up for ourselves. *"treasures in Heaven"* The converse to positive motivation is the negative kind, which takes the form of various punishments and chastisement in this life and also in the next.

Technically, free agency is not the same as free will. This I have made clear, but for God's purposes it accomplishes the same thing. Free agency allows us the perception and experience of having free will and allows us to make right and wrong decisions and bear the consequences of those decisions. As a result of these subjective experiences we learn first-hand about good and evil and experience spiritual growth. Free will is technically an illusion, but a very useful one from God's perspective.

A good analogy would be setting up a military training exercise in an artificial setting. For the participant, the experience seems very real and the result is pretty much the same, as if the learning took place under actual combat situations. God actually takes this a bit further and does not actually inform the participants that they are only experiencing a simulation which is taking place under very controlled circumstances. That makes the experience even more "real" for the participant. The nice thing about this training exercise that we call life is that God remains in control and does not permit matters to get out of hand, as might be the case if He granted us genuine free will and took away all the restraints, as in the case of an actual combat situation.

For our wills to be completely free God would have to completely restrain Himself from intervening into our lives to influence our decisions. The extent to which God intervenes and influences our decisions is the extent to which our freedom of will is restricted. I suppose one could argue that the actual truth of the matter lies somewhere in the middle, that God allows us some measure of free will, but with restrictions. The interesting thing about all this is that recent discoveries relating to general relativity and quantum mechanics seem to support the idea that the universe is not actually real. I discuss this in more detail in a later chapter of this book. The only genuine reality is our subjective experience and perception of it.

The conclusion of the matter is this. By allowing the freedom to choose God in no way limits Himself. He is still fully capable of eventually bringing us all to repentance by influencing our wills by the various means noted above. This, I believe, defeats the argument that God's doing so would somehow violate man's "freedom to choose."

Universal Restoration

The obvious resolution to the Calvinism vs. Arminianism debate is the doctrine of Universal Restoration which in my view is plainly taught throughout the Scriptures. It doesn't really matter if our choices in life are "freely" made or not. God has already decided that eventually all will come to Christ, each in his own turn, some sooner, some later. All will receive the same reward in the end. Since God is the ultimate cause of all our decisions, it fitting that He gets ALL the credit.

Ephesians 2:8-9: *"For it is by grace you have been saved, through faith--and this is not from yourselves, it is the gift of God--not by works, so that no one can boast."*

I love the Parable of the Vineyard. It beautifully illustrates the above principle.

Matthew 20:1-16: *"For the kingdom of heaven is like a landowner who went out early in the morning to hire men to work in his vineyard. He agreed to pay them a denarius for the day and sent them into his vineyard. About the third hour he went out and saw others standing in the marketplace doing nothing. He told them, 'You also go and work in my vineyard, and I will pay you whatever is right.' So they went. He went out again about the sixth hour and the ninth hour and did the same thing. About the eleventh hour, he went out and found still others standing around. He asked them, 'Why have you been standing here all day long doing nothing?' 'Because no one has hired us,' they answered. He said to them, 'You also go and work in my vineyard.' When evening came, the owner of the vineyard said to his foreman, 'Call the workers and pay them their wages, beginning with the last ones hired and going on to the first.' The workers who were hired about the eleventh hour came and each received a denarius. So when those came who were hired first, they expected to receive more. But each one of them also received a denarius. When they received it, they began to grumble against the landowner. 'These men who were hired last worked only one hour,' they said, 'and you have made them equal to us who have borne the burden of the work and the heat of the day.' But he answered one of them, 'Friend, I am not being unfair to you. Didn't you agree to work for a denarius? Take your pay and go. I want to give the man who was hired last the same as I gave you. Don't I have the right to do what I want with my own money? Or are you envious because I am generous?' So the last will be first, and the first will be last."*

Chapter 22

How both Good and Evil Serve God's Purposes

Have you ever wondered why God isn't at least as smart as you? Honestly, if you were God and had a chance to create your own world, would your world be different from the one God actually created? What is your idealized vision of a perfect world? At one time or another haven't you wished that you could live in a world that wasn't so deeply flawed by suffering and sin? Have you ever wondered why God seems to hide Himself from public view, making it difficult for so many to believe in Him? Have you ever wondered why God doesn't intervene more often into human affairs to set things back in order? Wouldn't you just love to have a crack at playing God and be able to create world peace, bring instant retribution (or instant rehabilitation) upon all the bad guys, and eliminate all hunger, poverty and disease? Wouldn't you just love to be able to show yourself to the world, instead of remaining invisible, and make it easy for everyone to believe in you? And why make people wait for heaven? Why not just send everyone there right now, or why not just create a heavenly utopia right here on earth?

What would that heavenly utopia of yours be like? Would everyone be rich? If so, then who would serve them? Or would they all be like witches and just wrinkle their noses to make everything happen instantly without the need for any kind of work? If you were God would you force everyone to love you and respect you, or would you let them all do as they pleased, so long as they didn't hurt anyone else in the process? Would it be OK for them to just thumb their noses at you and go on with their lives as though you didn't even exist? Would you be a loving God or an indifferent God? Would it matter to you whether or not people loved you back? Would there be losers as well as winners at sports, business, and other endeavors? Would you have to work and train hard to win at sports, or would we all just be able to run like the wind, with no effort at all?

How would you deal with those who did harmful and hurtful things to others? Would you provide instant retribution, or rehabilitate them on the spot? What about the injured parties? Would you heal their wounds or would you just not allow bad people to hurt them in the first place? How would you control people's actions? Would you force them to think only good thoughts and make it impossible for them to think bad thoughts and do bad things? How would you accomplish that? Would you somehow program their brains to only behave in certain ways? If you programmed them to only make wise and correct choices, then how could they take pride in making those choices? How would they develop any feelings of self worth and experience the exhilaration of success, if success came easy and required no effort?

Would people be allowed to experience sorrow and defeat? Would you create a race of robots, or would you create a race of people with free will and allow them to make both right and wrong choices? Would you instantly correct them when they make mistakes, especially mistakes that might be harmful to others, or would you allow them to learn from their mistakes and improve their qualities of character in the process?

Would you want your presence to be visible and known to all? Or would you want people to sometimes wonder about and question your existence? If you were to impose your presence on everyone, in unmistakable, visible form, do you think that might have an inhibiting effect on their actions? Do you think they might be inclined to behave because you're sitting right there in front of them, rather than because they really want to do the right thing? In other words, do you want them do good because they are intimidated by your presence or because they have become genuinely good people? If they are to make free moral choices for the right reason, do you think it might be necessary for them to be equally free to make the wrong choices?

Would you want everyone to be good looking, or would you prefer that they develop the qualities of character to the point where outward appearance would be irrelevant to them? How would you go about making them beautiful on the inside? What qualities of inner character would you want them to develop? Would you want them to be loving, kind, generous, thoughtful, brave, resourceful, grateful, satisfied, happy, ambitious, motivated, strong willed, purposeful, energetic, helpful, self-sacrificing, humble, obedient, and so on? If so, how would you go about helping them to develop those qualities? Would you just snap your finger and instantly program their brains to think that way? What would be the difference between those programmed creatures and robots or computers? Or would you prefer to create a race of authentically human individuals with the freedom to make right and wrong choices, who would in the process of making those choices and experiencing the natural consequences of such develop genuine qualities of character?

If self-sacrificing love were your chief characteristic how would that affect the way you interact with your created beings? Would you want them to be capable of responding to you in kind? By definition, self-sacrificing (*agape*) love involves putting another's needs ahead of one's own. Is self-sacrifice even possible in a utopian world where sadness, failure, disease, and evil do not even exist? If there were nothing but good in the world, nothing but success and happiness, then there would never be a need for sacrifice. The kind of love that is appreciated the most, the kind that costs you something, would be completely absent in such a world.

How would you create joy in the hearts of your subjects, if they were never to experience sorrow? How would they even be able to know that they are happy?

The truth is that every single character quality you, as God, would desire to see in your created beings can only be defined and made possible by the existence of an opposite negative quality. God cannot create light unless he also creates darkness because one is defined by the other. He cannot create love without hate. He cannot create justice without injustice. He cannot create joy without sorrow. He cannot create patience without trials. Positive qualities cannot develop in isolation from their negative counterparts.

A perfect world is not possible without built-in imperfections. Makes you wonder what Heaven is like, doesn't it? And, would it make any sense at all to create a Heaven without a Hell?

Chapter 23

Life Isn't Supposed to Be Fair

At various times in our lives we have all felt unfairly victimized by the actions of others or by negative circumstances of life. When so called "bad things" happen to us, one thing is certain. We are not being punished by God in order to "even the score." Because of Calvary, the trials and negative experiences in our lives must always be regarded as a form of guidance or correction. When God allows "bad" things to happen to us there is always a good purpose. The specific purpose varies depending on our needs. Sometimes we need correction when there is sin in our lives which needs to be dealt with. Heavenly "spankings" may be painful, but in the end the positive fruits of righteous living far outweigh the pain (Heb. 12:11). In other cases, so-called "negative" circumstances may be a form of guidance whereby God seeks to change the course or direction of our lives. By closing doors in this way God opens up other doors to more productive opportunities. Sometimes negative circumstances are God's way of helping us to identify with those who need our help. These negative experiences increase our ability to relate to and empathize with those in need.

Not all bad things that happen to us are directly caused by God. While God is sovereign over His creation and will eventually cause everything to come out all right in the end, He mostly achieves His purposes through human free agency. In order for our choices to be freely made there must be only minimal direct coercion on the part of God, so He set in motion many random processes. He does not directly orchestrate every event in human history. God primarily influences the course of history through human agency. In 1 Corinthians 12, Paul uses the analogy of the Church acting in this world as Christ's body. We are the hands and feet God uses to achieve His goals.

The world that God created is filled with imperfections, but perfectly suited for what God wants to accomplish in our lives. The imperfections which include sin, suffering, difficulties, obstacles, and challenges of every kind act like the abrasive surface of the sandpaper which He uses to smooth our rough edges. They may also be likened to the tool the diamond cutter uses to create the perfect finished diamond, or the pruning shears of the farmer who cuts off certain branches of the tree so it will bear more fruit.

There is the example in the Bible (see John 9:1-3) where one of Jesus' disciples asked whether a man's blindness from birth was a result of his own sin or the sins of his father. Jesus' response was that the blindness was not a punishment for sin but that God would be glorified when he was healed.

We are often tempted to blame God for allowing tragedies to occur in our lives and in the lives of others. Children die in infancy and tragic accidents occur all the time. Millions die from starvation, natural disasters, war and injustice every day. Why does God allow all these terrible things to happen? How can we reconcile this with God's loving nature? The only way we can do this is to understand that God knows what He is doing and in the end we will all be the better for it.

To relegate the final solution to God alone, however, is to miss the entire point of the Scriptures and completely misunderstand the reason for our existence here on Earth. That is not the way God works. He gives us the honor and privilege of being His agents of mercy. We are the hands and feet God uses to alleviate human suffering and achieve the ultimate redemption of all mankind. When tempted to complain about our own misfortunes we would all be well advised look on the positive side of things and take full advantage of the opportunities God gives us serve our brethren on His behalf and develop Christ like qualities of character in the process.

One more thought. Because there is a randomness to many of the events in our lives, we cannot say that each event has a distinct purpose, as though God put it there for a special reason. In a broad sense there is a reason God allows these events to occur, and in the long term God will see to it that His ultimate redemptive purposes are achieved. But in the short term what gives purpose to the events in our lives is the way we respond to them. No single event should be regarded as good or bad in and of itself. *"We know that in all things God works for the good of those who love him, who have been called according to his purpose."* (Romans 8:28) The events of our lives have the potential to produce positive or negative results. If we love God and seek His purposes in our lives, then there will be a good result. If not, then the opposite may be true. Events which we may generally regard as good, in and of themselves, may in reality cause much harm to ourselves and others, while many so-called negative events may be blessings in disguise. For example, too much money can be good or bad for us, depending on our attitude. Physical disabilities have the potential of bringing out the best or the worst in people. No hardship, trial or misfortune may be considered bad for us if viewed from a Godly perspective.

No matter how difficult our lives may seem in the present moment, we must understand that God can use these difficulties for good and that eventually relief will come. God's judgments are pictured in the Bible as a refining process whereby we are purified and made righteous. If we respond correctly to adverse situations in the crucible of this present life we may avoid much greater pain in the next. According to 1 Corinthians 11:31, *"if we would judge ourselves, we would not be judged."*

When we respond positively to negative circumstance we are blessed by God and develop wonderful qualities of Godly character, such as the fruit of the Spirit listed in Galatians 5, which include love, joy, peace, patience, kindness, goodness, faithfulness, gentleness, and self-control. In the midst of suffering and trials we simultaneously experience love, joy and peace.

I leave you with one of my favorite Scriptures, from James 1:2-4: *"Consider it pure joy, my brothers, whenever you face trials of many kinds, because you know that the testing of your faith develops perseverance. Perseverance must finish its work so that you may be mature and complete, not lacking anything."*

Chapter 24

The Twinkie Defense

The expression "Twinkie Defense" derives from the trial in 1979 of Dan White who was accused of killing San Francisco Mayor George Moscone and Supervisor Harvey Milk. His defense team argued that because Dan White had been consuming large quantities of Twinkies and Coca-Cola, he should not be held responsible for his actions in those killings. A noted psychiatrist argued that White was suffering from extreme depression at the time of the killings; he had become lazy and had quit his job and shunned his wife. He had previously been very clean cut and a fitness and health food fanatic. It was argued that the sugary diet worsened his mood swings to the point that he was on some kind of automatic pilot when he exploded uncontrollably and committed the two murders. The defense lawyers successfully argued for a ruling of "diminished capacity," and instead of receiving a murder conviction Dan White was only convicted of voluntary manslaughter. This unpopular verdict resulted in riots on the streets of San Francisco.

Although the Twinkie Defense may seem somewhat ludicrous to many of you, the defense lawyers' arguments do have some merit. As a matter of fact, they could have made their case even stronger by arguing that no one should ever be held responsible for anything they do, because it cannot be proved that any one's actions are self-caused. Ultimately all of our actions are determined by circumstances which are external to us. If you think about it for just a minute you will realize that I am right about this. Pick any human action and ask yourself, why was it done? Yes, the perpetrator freely chose to commit the sinful act, but his desire to commit the act resulted from external circumstances including genetic make-up, psychological, societal, and familial influences, over which he had no direct control.

Let's take the example of the drunk driver who is convicted of manslaughter in the deaths of innocent parties in another car. Why manslaughter and not murder? The reason is that the drunk driver was operating his car in a condition of diminished capacity and his judgment was impaired. He was guilty of driving while intoxicated, but not murder. If you take the argument further, you might ask, why should he even be convicted of manslaughter and driving under the influence? It could be argued that when he first got into the car he was operating in a condition of diminished capacity due to the fact that he was drunk. So, how could you hold him accountable for getting into the car? Let's back it up even further. Should he even be held responsible for drinking too much? After all, the fact that he even drinks alcoholic beverages at all is due to the fact that those beverages were made available to him by grocery clerks who sold them to him in first place. Or, why not blame instead the manufacturer of the booze, or the drunk driver's parents who might have failed to warn him of the dangers of drinking alcoholic beverages and or failed to set the proper example?

Was he operating in any kind of diminished capacity when he first decided to drink alcohol? My answer is, yes. He was not able to correctly anticipate the long term consequences of this seemingly innocent activity of social drinking. Is it his fault that God gave him a brain that works differently from that of the guy who chose not to drink and drive? Not really.

There is a sense in which all of us could make a valid case for diminished capacity with respect to our sinful natures. According to the Apostle Paul, none of us has the capacity to live a righteous life apart from the power of God's Holy Spirit within us. We are all born with sinful natures and cannot help ourselves.

In Romans 7:14-25, Paul explains the nature of this diminished capacity: "*We know that the law is spiritual; but I am unspiritual, sold as a slave to sin. I do not understand what I do. For what I want to do I do not do, but what I hate I do. And if I do what I do not want to do, I agree that the law is good. As it is, it is no longer I myself who do it, but it is sin living in me. For I know that good itself does not dwell in me, that is, in my sinful nature. For I have the desire to do what is good, but I cannot carry it out. For I do not do the good I want to do, but the evil I do not want to do—this I keep on doing. Now if I do what I do not want to do, it is no longer I who do it, but it is sin living in me that does it. So I find this law at work: Although I want to do good, evil is right there with me. For in my inner being I delight in God's law; but I see another law at work in me, waging war against the law of my mind and making me a prisoner of the law of sin at work within me. What a wretched man I am! Who will rescue me from this body that is subject to death? Thanks be to God, who delivers me through Jesus Christ our Lord!*

So why does God hold us accountable for our sins? The answer is that regardless of how diminished our capacity might be we are still sinners and our sins negatively impact not only our lives, but the lives of others. Therefore, it is for our benefit, and the benefit of those whose lives we touch, that we abstain from sin and obey the commandments of God. If we are unable to abstain from sin, due to our diminished capacity, then God needs to take corrective action.

For example, a convicted murder could have been severely mistreated as a child and taught from birth that violence is an acceptable way of dealing with problems. He might even be mentally ill or prone to violence due to defective brain chemistry or wiring. It doesn't really matter what the reason is. If society allows him to go without punishment and does not restrain his behavior in any way, then many others will be harmed.

According to the Bible, the penalty for sin is spiritual death, which could be described as a kind of prison or banishment from God's Kingdom. It is God's plan to eventually redeem everyone from this prison, which we call spiritual death, and eventually grant them all admission into the Kingdom, but not until they are fully rehabilitated. His plan is two-fold. First, on the Cross of Calvary, in the person of his Son, Jesus Christ, He paid the penalty himself on our behalf. Secondly, and equally important, through various corrective actions and the influence of the Holy Spirit God eventually causes all human beings to repent of their sins and learn to live Godly lives so that that they might become fit for entrance into the Kingdom.

This is why God still holds us accountable for our sins, despite our "diminished capacities."

Chapter 25

Understanding the Will of God

According to Romans 12:1-2, God's will for us is that we present our bodies to Him as living sacrifices and transform our thinking into patterns which conform to His will, rather than generally accepted thought patterns of the society in which we live. Because God's will for our lives conflicts with generally accepted patterns of behavior, discovering God's specific will for us is for the most part a counterintuitive process. The Bible is full of truths that directly contradict the natural thought processes of those who are uninformed by Scripture and who are not sensitive to the leading of the Holy Spirit. For example, we are told in Scripture that in order to become alive in Christ we must first die. We are told to return good for evil and bless those who curse us.

In our efforts to obey the will of God in our lives we must learn to think differently from mainstream society. I once heard a motivational speaker say that if you never want to make a major mistake in life just observe what the vast majority of people do in various situations and then do just the opposite. Jesus said the way that leads to eternal life is narrow and there are few that find it, but the way that leads to destruction is broad and easy. God's will more often than not leads through closed doors, rather than open ones. It more often than not represents the difficult way, not the easy way.

External circumstances of life are unreliable indicators of God's will for our lives. Sometimes our good deeds are rewarded in this life with pain and sorrow. Sometimes defeat, rather than victory, is God's chosen path for us. Ultimately everything will be set right, but in our earthly walk with God He asks us to take the least chosen path. It is a mistake to assume that when bad things happen in our lives we have not been obedient to God's will, or when good things happen we are being rewarded for obeying God's will. To be certain, the spiritual and moral choices we make in life definitely affect our temporal circumstances, but those affects may not be relied upon for confirmation that we are obeying the will of God.

What God cares about most is how we relate to Him and others, regardless of the short term results. God's primary focus is on our eternal destiny. The fruit of the Spirit in our lives are qualities of character which are quite independent of outward circumstances (Galatians 5:22-23). Traits such as love, joy, peace, patience, kindness, goodness, faithfulness, gentleness and self-control are best developed as we respond in God-approved ways to the challenges of daily living, especially adverse circumstances. These qualities are all that we will be able to take with us when we die, and they are the best indicators that we are living our lives in harmony with God's will. They are also the key to ascertaining the will of God for us when making choices in specific life situations.

Some aspects of God's will are easily understood by those who are willing to thoughtfully and carefully read the Scriptures, because they apply equally to all believers. The general commandments of Scripture, although subject to some differences in interpretation, are pretty plain to most of us. Difficulties in understanding the will of God most generally arise when seeking God's will in specific and unique situations. Examples include making career decisions, choosing a mate, deciding how do divide our time among various activities of daily living, making financial decisions, deciding which specific ministries we should engage in, and so on. We are all very different and totally unique with respect to our spiritual gifts and abilities, social and ethnic backgrounds, living circumstances, personal desires and natural tendencies, family and church upbringing, and so on. Because of this, obeying the will of God takes us in many different directions. Discerning the will of God for us in these highly specific and unique situations is not always easy. Also, keep in mind that in many situations God may not have a preference and may be perfectly content to give you the freedom to choose from a number of equally acceptable alternatives. For example, does God really care what color shirt you put on each morning? There is no indication in Scripture that God desires to directly control every small detail of our lives.

This same reasoning can be extended to other choices we make in life, such as career choices, which church we join, which organizations we support, or which sports or hobbies we engage in. When making these choices it is helpful for me to understand that as long as I seek first God's Kingdom and acknowledge Him in all my ways I can trust Him to direct my paths. (See Matt. 6:33 and Prov. 3:5-6) God allows each of us to make our own choices in life. The more closely we align our thinking to that of Christ, the more likely we are to make choices which are in harmony with God's purposes for our lives. I believe that when faced with more than one choice in a given situation, neither of which is in direct conflict with a specific or implied command of God in Scripture, there may quite possibly be more than one choice that would be acceptable to God. He is fully capable, in His divine providence, of effecting the proper outcome in every circumstance. Augustine summed the matter up very succinctly when he said, *"Love God and do as you please."*

Chapter 26

Thank God for Narrow-Minded People

Most of us like to think of ourselves as being relatively tolerant, broadminded individuals, preferring to give the benefit of the doubt whenever possible to those who differ from us. No one wants to be thought of as a know-it-all, or a narrow-minded bigot. Our society in recent years has become increasingly diverse and pluralistic, and traditionally held religious and moral beliefs are no longer widely held in the popular culture. Those who resist the growing secularization of governmental, educational, and even religious institutions are labeled as intolerant religious extremists who wish to impose their narrow-minded beliefs on society.

The truth is, however, that there is no virtue in being broad-minded. What is there to admire in a person who has no convictions or firmly held beliefs? Extremists of all kinds pose a great danger to our society, but the greatest danger by far comes from those who lack strong convictions of any kind. If our culture ultimately collapses and falls into total moral and spiritual chaos, it will be the well-intentioned middle-of-the road, live-and-let-live, tolerant, broad-minded, majority who are the most to blame.

And what is true at the societal level is equally true at the personal level. It seems that most Christians in our country today have grown very comfortable and affluent. While it disturbs them to witness the slow disintegration of the political, social, religious, and moral fabric of the society at large, they for the most part are willing to let things slide because it is all happening so gradually. It's like the frog that is placed in a pan of cold water and gradually allows itself to be cooked to death as the water slowly heats to a boil. What we as individuals fail to realize is that we are being gradually conditioned and changed by the mores of the society at large, and our personal convictions are being compromised in the name of broad-mindedness and tolerance. As a result, we increasingly find ourselves reflecting in our own personal lives the non-Christian values of the popular culture. We can see it happening everywhere. Traditional beliefs and convictions are gradually giving way not only in the society at large, but also in the Christian community. You can name just about any sin, and it will be almost as prevalent in the Church today as in the society at large, such as premarital sex, alcoholism, drug addition, marital infidelity and divorce, materialism, anger, hatred, envy, selfishness, greed, and so on.

It is painful for me to admit this, but I myself have not been immune to this process. Although I have avoided some of the more egregious sins, I have grown more materialistic over the years and far less committed to Christian causes than in my youth. I need to recognize what has happened to me, repent of it, and purpose in my heart to become less broad-minded, narrow my focus, and renew that "first love" that I had for Christ. It's never too late to start over. I don't want to be like that frog that didn't wake up in time to jump out of the pan and avoid being boiled to death.

Because this process of moral and spiritual capitulation in the life of many Christians takes place gradually over many years, radical solutions may be required. Addictions to illicit sex, drugs, alcohol, cigarettes, and pornography all require drastic action, and so do addictions to other sins that develop and worsen over time. The Bible makes it plain that it is a radical step to become a Christian. It is compared with dying and being born again. Christians are described as *"new creatures,"* no longer slaves of sin, but of Christ instead. Christ prayed that we, though in the world, would not be of the world (John 17:14-16). We are not to conform to the patterns of this world, but be transformed instead. We are supposed to stick out like sore thumbs (Romans 12:2). If the worst that happens is that we are labeled as narrow-minded bigots, we would be getting off easy. In some ways the church today faces a more difficult challenge than in the first century or in areas of the world where Christians are persecuted. During times of persecution when the society at large is intolerant of Christians, the battle lines are clearly drawn and there is little room for compromise. Today the battle lines are blurred, and the enemy wears the same uniform as we do, so to speak. We all look the same. We all behave the same. We intermix socially and intermarry. We depend on one another for our jobs, the education of our children, our civil services, our national defense, and so on. For the most part, we watch the same TV programs, the same movies, even the "R" rated ones. We listen to the same music, and wear the same fashions.

One or two hundred years ago, the problem was not nearly as great because the religious and moral values of the church were more closely reflected in the general culture. If the church had managed to strictly maintain those standards to the present day, we would indeed be sticking out like sore thumbs and would be labeled by society as extremely narrow-minded. Try to imagine how Christians from the past would react if they were suddenly thrust into our modern society. Imagine asking one of them to accompany you on all of your daily activities for a week or so. Would they be offended and embarrassed at some of the things you see and hear on a daily basis? Now try to imagine taking Christ with you in the same way. We're supposed to be doing that anyway, aren't we? But for the most part we don't, and that is the reason our consciences have become dull in so many areas. I wonder how broad-minded Christ is when it comes to the spiritual and moral compromises we make on a daily basis? There is not much we can do as individuals to change the overall condition of the society at large, but imagine the impact we would have on the individual lives of people we know if we were to make fewer compromises in our activities of daily living and focus on pleasing Christ instead.

Chapter 27

Christian Service How Much Is Enough?

It's very difficult, actually impossible, to know where to draw the line with regard to how much Christian service is enough and how much sin we should tolerate in our lives. How does one decide how many people to pray for each day? How much of one's income should be given to the church, the needy, and to missionary causes? How much of one's free time should be devoted to the Lord's work? No matter how much we do for the Lord, there is always more we could have done. When measured by God's highest standards, the heart of man is *"desperately wicked,"* and *"none are righteous, no not one, and our righteousness is as filthy rags"* (See Jer. 17:9 and Isa. 64:6). How do we effectively deal with sin in our lives? Where do we draw the line regarding the amount of sin we are willing to tolerate?

As Christians, we know that because of Calvary we owe no sin debt to God (Heb. 10:14). We also know that from God's eternal perspective, we are already perfected and seated with Christ in the heavenly places (Eph. 1:3 and 2:6). God has substituted the righteousness of Christ for our own (Phil. 3:9). He has not only forgiven our sins, but He has cast them into the sea and does not even remember them (Micah 7:19; Psalms 103:12; Jeremiah 31:34). When I have been justified by Christ, it really is "just-as-if-I'd" never sinned, from God's eternal and timeless point of view.

From our human perspective, however, God's grace and forgiveness are viewed and experienced as a process that occurs over time. So we are told to *"work out our salvation with fear and trembling"* (Phil. 2:12) and seek forgiveness for the sins we commit, on a continuing basis (1 John 1:9). Our salvation will not be complete until Christ finally presents us faultless before the throne of God in Heaven at the end of the ages. Although our sins are covered by the blood of Christ, we still experience the practical consequences of sin in our daily lives. Those consequences include guilt, shame, sorrow for the harm done to others, and regrets due to lost opportunities. The closer our walk with God, the more sensitive we become to our failures and shortcomings and the greater our perceived need to seek daily cleansing and spiritual renewal.

Now, let's get back to the question of where to draw the line when it comes to how much sin we should be willing to tolerate in our lives. Regarding sins of *"commission,"* or wrongful thoughts and acts, it is important that we not only ask God's forgiveness, but just as important that we purpose in our hearts not to repeat these sins and that we make restitution whenever possible to the persons who may have been harmed by our wrongful acts. If we do not do this, then the inevitable result will be feelings of guilt, shame and sorrow, not to mention lost spiritual blessings.

With regard to sins of *"omission,"* (things we should be doing but aren't) how much is enough? Does God want me to give away every last dime I have to the poor and Christian causes, to the point where my family and I are barely able to subsist? Does God want me to never stop praying, to the extent that every waking thought is directed towards God? Does God want me to share the love of Christ with virtually everyone I meet? Does God want me to spend every waking moment in some kind of Christian service? Is it a sin of omission to reserve any time at all for the satisfaction of my personal desires? Is it sinful to take even brief vacations from Christian service? Does God want me to take up a cross daily and deny myself to the point of complete exhaustion? Does He want me to sacrifice for the benefit of others to the extent that I totally neglect my own needs?

Now we are getting to the crux of the problem. Somehow we have come to think that the closer we approach God's perfect standards of behavior the more arduous, difficult and miserable our lives might become. It's bad enough that God denies us sinful pleasures, but to make matters worse, does God also expect us to devote every waking moment to unselfish causes? Is it sinful to fall short of such seemingly impossible standards? The answer is, "yes." But I am not at all sure that the achievement of such a state of sinless perfection would make you all that miserable. Of course, we have no scientific experimental data on which to base my judgment in this matter, because there are no observable examples of individuals who have even approached such a state of perfection and lived to tell about it. It appears to me, however, that Christians who have most closely approached that sinless ideal are definitely much happier and more joyful than those who haven't.

It is very clever deception that self-indulgence brings pleasure, and abstinence from sin causes much pain. Although this often happens in the short term, the long-term result is exactly the opposite. God's truth may be easily demonstrated in this regard. Just take the ten most self-indulgent people you know and compare them with the 10 Godliest people you know. Which group is the most joyful? Which group is the least joyful? Case closed!

Now, let's ask the question again. Where should you draw the line regarding the level of sin you will permit in your life? How would you achieve an acceptable balance in this regard?

A better question to ask is this. How much do you want to be blessed by God?

Since writing this essay, I have been asked, *"What is wrong with trying to achieve balance in life?"* Is it not possible to take things too far in one's spiritual walk and become so spiritual that one is of no earthly good? Wouldn't it be all wrong to spend all one's waking hours serving God to the point where one neglects family obligations and takes no pleasure in the fruits of one's labors? Is it wrong to enjoy well-deserved material blessings of life that come from hard work? Did not God put us on earth to enjoy it? Doesn't He want us to live balanced, productive lives?

To compartmentalize our lives in this way, I believe, is a serious mistake. Maximum service and devotion to God should not prevent us from enjoying the material fruits of our labors or cause us to neglect our families or cause us to exhibit extreme, fanatical forms of behavior. The Apostle Paul admonishes us do everything *"as unto the Lord."* Material possessions, in and of themselves, are spiritually neutral. They are neither good nor bad. We should be grateful to God for His bounty towards us and regard these possessions as ultimately belonging to God, not us. He has placed us on earth to be wise stewards over his creation and all material blessings derived there from. God loves to give good things to His children. If in our hearts we are totally submissive to God, He loves to shower us with blessings. I don't think God makes a distinction between "spiritual" and "material" blessings, however. All blessings should be regarded as "spiritual" blessings. We should view them all as gifts from God. He gives them to us for our personal enjoyment and also to enhance our spiritual walk and provide us with resources to help those in need. Paul was able to find peace and contentment and joy in all circumstances, whether in want or plenty.

The most extreme form of spiritual devotion is not to live a monastic life where one gives all one's possessions away, and live a cloistered existence in isolation from society. Even medieval monks did not have this view. Although they withdrew into monasteries, they remained relevant to the society around them. They preserved and copied the Scriptures; they worked hard at raising crops and animals and at various secular endeavors; they gave to the poor and provided sanctuary to the oppressed, and so on. It was their calling to serve God in a cloistered fashion. I remember reading a small pamphlet describing the life of a humble monk, named Brother Lawrence. He referred to God as a *"God of the pots and pans,"* because he found opportunity to enjoy and practice the presence of God in all aspects of his life, even while doing mundane tasks such as cooking and washing the pots and pans. To *"pray without ceasing"* does not mean to withdraw to one's prayer closet every chance one gets and withdraw from life. It means to enjoy and practice the presence of God in every act of life. It doesn't mean that every waking thought should be directed towards God. It does mean that everything we think and do is in harmony with God's purposes in our lives and we should be grateful to God for all of His gifts to us.

In summary, to serve God in an extreme fashion does not result in misery but joy. Self-denial, although a prerequisite for discipleship, does not always result in poverty and suffering. If it does, then God will see to it that we are ultimately rewarded with unspeakable joy. The other side of the coin of self-denial, is a positive affirmation of the Lordship of Christ in one's life and the dedication of our lives and possessions to His service. In order to use God's gifts, we must first be in possession of them. While we are asked to give up many of our possessions in the form of tithes and offerings and in service to those in need, we are also asked to be good stewards of the possessions that we keep. There is no easy answer to what kind of balance one must maintain in this regard. That is between you and God. Put God first in your life and ask Him for those answers. He will direct your paths.

Chapter 28

Overcoming Addictions

One of the biggest problems we face in our Christian walk is overcoming addictive behaviors in our own lives and in the lives of those whom we love and want to help. Many addictive behaviors are overtly sinful, while others do not become sinful until they become habitual to the point that they pose a threat to our physical or psychological well-being, or hinder us in our Christian walk and service to others. When speaking of addictions, the ones that most frequently come to mind are those which involve alcohol, drugs, gambling, pornography, and sexual promiscuity. Other activities are less overtly sinful, but can still devastate our physical and psychological well-being, and cause tremendous harm to our Christian walk and our families and loved ones. Examples of these types of activities would include smoking, bad temper, gluttony, compulsive spending, or any other behavior which has the potential of becoming addictive and harmful. Many of these harmful addictions involve activities which are spiritually and socially acceptable when exercised in moderation, but become harmful if overdone.

In Ephesians 5:18, we are advised not to get drunk with wine, but instead be filled with the Holy Spirit. Drinking alcoholic beverages is an example of an activity which when practiced in moderation is not overtly sinful, but which has the potential of developing into harmful, addictive behavior. The simplest way to prevent addiction to alcohol is to totally abstain and never take the first drink. The Bible does not expressly forbid drinking alcoholic beverages. However, in this day and age when non-alcoholic drinks are more readily available than in Jesus' day, why tempt fate? No one who begins to drink in moderation can with any degree of certainty predict that he or she will not eventually become an alcoholic or abuse alcohol in other ways. It has been estimated that about one in ten adults suffers from alcoholism, including many Christians. While it has not been absolutely proven that people can be genetically predisposed to alcoholism, that possibility cannot be ruled out. Others may be predisposed to alcoholism due to psychological make-up or social influences, while still others gradually drift into alcoholism by consciously or unconsciously using alcohol as a method of coping with stresses in their lives.

The surest method of avoiding alcohol addiction is total abstinence. Just don't take the first drink. It is much easier to say "no" to the first drink than it is to undo a drinking habit later on. The same is true for other potentially addictive behaviors, such as smoking, fornication, gambling and illicit drugs. In 1 Corinthians 10:23-33, the Apostle Paul makes a compelling case for abstinence. In verse 23, he points out that though many activities may be permissible, not all are necessary or constructive. Paul made the personal choice to avoid eating meat sacrificed to idols, even though there was nothing inherently wrong with this practice. But for the sake of the *"weaker brethren,"* who believed this practice to be wrong, Paul abstained from eating this meat. Paul did not want by his example to influence others to engage in a practice which they thought sinful, thereby wounding their consciences and *"causing them to stumble."* Although there is not a direct correlation between addictive behavior and eating meat sacrificed to idols, Paul teaches us a principle here which does apply. It is perfectly OK for me to drink alcohol in moderation, so long as I can control my behavior and not drink to excess. But I need to understand that by doing so I may cause a Christian brother to stumble, if because of my example he begins to drink in moderation and eventually becomes an alcoholic. It might be that he is genetically or psychologically predisposed to alcoholism, or he may not have the same ability as I to cope with the stresses of life that can in some cases lead to alcoholism. This principle especially applies to us as parents. Our children are very strongly influenced by our behavior. If we drink alcohol our children are likely to do so as well. The same holds true for other potentially addictive behaviors, such as smoking, gambling, and drugs, none of which are expressly forbidden in the scriptures. Total abstinence, therefore, represents the first line of defense in overcoming harmful addictions in the individual lives of Christians and in the lives of those for whom they become centers of influence, such as family members, friends and acquaintances, and church brethren.

Other addictions, however, are not so easily prevented. It is impossible to completely abstain from many activities which have the potential of becoming harmfully addictive. Examples include gluttony, harmful gossip, bad temper, a critical spirit, compulsive spending, and so on. Almost any behavior, whether biblically acceptable or not, has the potential of becoming harmfully addictive. Obesity, for example, has become a major health problem in our country today, but we all have to eat. Overeating cannot be prevented by abstinence. Most of us at times have problems controlling various potentially addictive behaviors. It is impossible to abstain completely from these things. In areas where complete abstinence is impossible, or in areas where it is too late for abstinence, we face two challenges. The first is to prevent the behavior from escalating to the point of harmful addiction, and the second is to overcome an addiction that has already developed.

The key to successfully dealing with both of these challenges is given to us in Ephesians 5:18, where we are admonished not to get drunk with wine, but instead be filled with the Holy Spirit. The main point of this verse is that the best defense is a good offense. If you want to prevent or avoid a bad behavior, replace it with a different and beneficial behavior. Ever try to take a bone out of the mouth of a dog? The harder you pull, the more tenaciously the dog clings to the bone. But if you were to offer the dog a big, fat, juicy steak, he would drop that dirty old bone in a heartbeat. If we are not able to replace negative behaviors with positive ones, we have no hope at all of preventing or overcoming many harmful addictions. If we have no desire to be filled with the Spirit of God and allow God to control our lives, then we are doomed to failure. Even if we were able to prevent or overcome some of our addictions due to sheer force of willpower or some secular intervention or counseling program, what would be the point? Sooner or later our lives would end up in the toilet anyway. The whole point of our existence is to know and serve God and experience the abundant life that can only be found in Him.

The first step you must take in dealing with harmful addictive behaviors in your life is to acknowledge your utter dependence on God. And you must believe that although the addictive behaviors in your life may bring you temporary relief and pleasure, the new behaviors that God wants you to replace them with will bring you far greater joy and rewards. Here's an example of how this principle can be applied to a common addiction, over eating and eating too much of the wrong kinds of food. How does one go about replacing harmful activities with beneficial activities in this area? First, seek the infilling of the Holy Spirit and ask God to take control of this area of your life and all other areas as well. Don't just ask for help with your problem of obesity. Yield every area of your life to His control. *"An idle mind is the Devil's workshop."* If our time is not filled with beneficial activities, we tend to fall prey to our negative cravings. When I am busy, I tend not to think about food. But when I have nothing to do and get a little bored, eating a snack or going out for a bite to eat gives me something to do. For people who over eat, food is often used as a substitute to fill emotional and psychological voids in their lives. People often over eat to compensate for loneliness, unrequited love, feelings of rejection, boredom, feelings of inadequacy, and so on. Dedicating your life to God's service and involving yourself in Bible study, church activities, and Christian service to others can not only fill your time with beneficial activity, but also go a long way toward filling many of your emotional, psychological and social needs. Remembering the lesson of the dog and the dirty old bone, empty your house of all foods that are bad for you and fill your cupboards with foods that are good for you. Instead of denying yourself by dieting, eat all you want, but eat only foods that are good for you. Eat tons of vegetables, lean meats, fish, and complex carbohydrates.

And for goodness sake, go on the offense. Don't just do a token or minimum amount of daily exercise, do it passionately. Do three, four, five times as much as what is recommended. Don't just do it three or four days a week, for 20 minutes or so each time. Exercise for at least an hour each day, and do something you can learn to love and enjoy. See how good you can become at it. Get passionate about your weight. Your goal should not be to just lose weight. Your goal should be to become as physically fit as possible. Major addictions are not problems which are going to go away if you just dabble at them. Keep track of your progress on a daily basis. Keep score. Keep track of your weight loss and the amount of daily exercise you do each day. Take pride in yourself and what you expect to accomplish. Find a partner or group of partners who can work with you and help you. Don't just associate yourself with people who have the same problem as you. Involve yourself with people you admire and respect.

Most of our negative addictive behaviors are a result of emotional, psychological and spiritual voids in our lives. If you don't fill your life with challenging, purposeful activities, you become vulnerable to a host of negative, self-destructive behaviors. Big problems require big solutions. Major changes must be made in every area of your life, not just in areas that seem to be related to your addiction. Treating only the symptoms will not cure you. The root causes are spiritual, moral, emotional and psychological in nature. To be filled with the Holy Spirit means to turn over control of every area of your life to God. Whatever your addiction, go on the offense, not defense. Attack the problem from every angle. Work on every area of your life. And remember, you serve a mighty and powerful God who loves you and wants nothing but the best for you, both in this life and the life to come. You do not have the abilities or resources to deal with your addictions on your own power. Instead of allowing your addictions to control you, be controlled by the Holy Spirit instead.

Chapter 29

A Little Bit of Faith Is All You Need

More important than the strength of your faith is the faithfulness of the one in whom your faith is placed. It has taken me the better part of a lifetime to completely understand and appreciate this truth. I vividly remember how frustrating it was for me as a child to talk to God. It seemed like my prayers were just bouncing off the walls and ceiling, and it bothered me that God, it seemed, did not even make the slightest attempt to confirm to me that He even existed. I remember one day in my bedroom at the age of seven or eight literally banging my head against the wall after a frustrating attempt to communicate with God in prayer. I never openly discussed the problem of my unbelief with anyone, not my parents, or pastor, or even my closest friends.

All of us tend to live double lives, the life we live publicly for all to see, and the private life within that we seldom reveal to others, not even our most intimate friends. To one degree or another, we tend to be hypocritical in nature, mainly because we have a built in need to be loved and accepted by others. I sometimes wonder if the non-conformist rebel who outwardly expresses his true inner feelings is not in some ways closer to God than the externally religious person who refuses to honestly express his inner doubts and insecurities. I believe that those who are the farthest from God, however, are those who do not have strong feelings about God one way or the other.

The advice I am sharing with you in this chapter is based on three major premises. First, God never intended your path to faith to be easy. Secondly, belief or faith is not the opposite of doubt. Thirdly, God really does want to make Himself known to you, and He wants to bless you abundantly.

It is a generally accepted truth that hard won victories are sweeter than ones that come easy, with no struggle. True self-esteem and personal satisfaction come as a result of achievements based on hard work and sacrifice. We find this principle expressed everywhere in Scripture. Jesus taught that one must deny himself and lose his life in order to save it. The great faith chapter in the Bible, Hebrews 11, clearly teaches that the exercise of faith involves hardship and sacrifice. Abraham by faith left everything and made his home in a strange land, and had to start completely over again in life. By faith he was even willing to sacrifice his only son, Isaac. Joseph remained faithful to God despite being sold into slavery by his brothers and being thrown into prison in Egypt after being falsely accused of adultery. By faith the prophets of God remained true to their calling despite persecution, torture and death. Almost all of Jesus' apostles were eventually martyred for their faith.

It is amazing to me that many who rarely lift a finger to serve God, let alone face persecution and martyrdom, somehow feel abandoned or neglected by God because God doesn't make it easy for them to have faith and believe in Him. Somehow, we've come to believe that our lack of faith is God's fault. If you believe nothing else, please understand and believe that nothing worthwhile in life comes easy, and that is the way it should be.

Another misconception most of us have is that belief and doubt are opposites and cannot happily coexist. The truth is that belief, or faith, is not an all-or-nothing proposition. Absolute total belief without any trace of doubt is a near impossibility. If you get right down to it, you cannot absolutely prove that anything exists outside of your own mind. But that doesn't keep you from exercising faith and acting on what you believe is most probably true. Everything in life, even in the strictest of scientific disciplines, is based on probabilities, not certainties. There is the story of a tight rope walker who strung up a high wire across the Niagara Falls. In front of a large crowd he easily walked across the top of the falls and back, without incident. Then he grabbed a wheel barrow and placed it in front of himself on the wire and his accomplices placed in it a large bag of cement. He turned to the crowd and asked how many of them believed he could safely walk across and back with the wheel barrow. All the hands went up. He then turned to a person in the front row, who had his hand up, and asked, "If you really believe I can do this, then would you be willing to get into the wheel barrow yourself, in place of the cement?"

The true test of one's belief in anything is the willingness to act upon it. Jesus taught that if a person had faith which was only the size of a tiny mustard seed, he could literally move a mountain (Matt. 17:20). What is most significant about this teaching is not that faith can move mountains, but that it takes only a tiny amount of faith. The size and strength of your faith are not nearly as important as the faithfulness of the one in whom you place your faith. If you've got some mountains that need moving in your life, and God feels that you are sufficiently prepared personally and spiritually for them to be moved, he will indeed perform the miracle if you ask. Just as your physical body grows stronger with exercise, so will your faith in God, as you put it to use. There is great virtue in exercising faith in the presence of doubt. Remember Jesus' words to doubting Thomas, who had to touch and feel the wounds in Jesus' hands and side before he would believe. Jesus said that those who believe without the visible proof are the ones who receive the greater blessing (See John 20:24-29).

In addition to the difficulty we face in believing that God exists, we must also believe that He rewards those who seek Him. It's one thing to know and understand that God loves mankind, but it's quite another to believe that He loves you personally and wants to bless you abundantly. Jesus has said in no uncertain terms that all who come to Him He will in no wise cast out (John 6:37). Peter said that all who call upon the name of the Lord will be saved (Acts 2:21). In John 3:16, we read that all who believe in Christ will receive *"aionian"* life. In this verse, the words *"believe in"* refer not to mere intellectual belief, but the pronoun *"in"* implies motion toward the object in the original Greek. The meaning is closer to the word "into" than the word "in." It is more like water being poured "into" a glass from a pitcher than water that is just sitting in the pitcher, going nowhere. It is like the example of the tight rope walker who asked the bystander to get into the wheelbarrow. To get into the wheelbarrow one does not need perfect faith or belief, just enough to enable oneself to get in.

The same is true of our relationship with Christ. Mere intellectual belief, no matter how strong or sincere, will not get us saved. When we act upon our belief, no matter how weak or halting that belief may be, and come to Christ asking for His forgiveness and acceptance, He will never turn us away. After our initial salvation experience, our faith will grow stronger as we exercise it and put it to work by obeying the commands of Christ and serving Him. Just be careful not to confuse the abundant life with the easy life. And remember that God loves you despite the fact that you are a sinner, and He wants to bless you abundantly as you move forward with Him in faith.

Chapter 30

Growing into Christ

It was a liberating experience for me to learn that Christian salvation is not an all-or-nothing event that occurs at only one instantaneous moment in time. If we regard our salvation experience as an ongoing process which inevitably results in our ultimate glorification in Heaven at the conclusion of the ages, then we don't ever have to wonder whether we are truly saved or not. We don't have to worry about measuring up to some standard in order to "qualify" for our salvation. Virtually everyone is on that road to glory thanks to Christ's atoning sacrifice on Calvary. According to the Bible, we will ALL eventually arrive at the final destination (1 Cor. 15:22-28). It is so comforting and liberating to know that God loves us all unconditionally (John 3:16), wants all of us to be saved (1 Titus 2:4), and fully intends to accomplish all that He desires (Isaiah 24:27).

But, you might ask, doesn't the Bible make a rather clear-cut distinction between Christians and non-Christians, those who are "saved" and those who are not? Here's my answer. Although the Bible refers to Christians and non-Christians as separate "classes" or "categories" of individuals, this does not necessarily rule out the possibility of a period of transition from one category to the other. I have already made a case for the salvation experience being a process rather than an instantaneous event.

I would like to illustrate this by comparing the salvation experience with another type of experience with which we can all identify, the experience of "happiness" and its counterpart, "sadness." Although these are typically categorized as separate and distinct experiences or states of being, they nevertheless represent opposite ends of a continuum of sorts. People whom you would characterize as extremely happy would find themselves as experiencing one end of the continuum, while extremely unhappy people would find themselves at the other end. And then there are those in the middle who are neither happy nor sad, who from one day to the next experience a little of each. If one were to line all of us up based on the degree of happiness or sadness that we are experiencing in life, most of us would find ourselves somewhere in the middle, and our exact position in this line-up would change from day to day and from one moment to the next. If you were regarded as a generally happy person, then you would be experiencing happiness most, but not all, of the time. A generally sad person would be experiencing sadness most, but not all, of the time.

In the same way, the writers of the Bible classify people according to categories like godly vs. ungodly, righteous vs. unrighteous, saved vs. lost, and so on. If you find yourself straddling the middle between these categories, then you might be wondering if you are genuinely saved or not. Trying to *"serve two masters"* at the same time can be a very frustrating and unrewarding experience. If your so-called "conversion experience" was nothing more than a quick and emotional decision to obtain a fire insurance policy with not much follow-through afterwards, then you might actually be less of a Christian than the individual who can recall no salvation experience at all but is continually striving to build and improve his relationship with Christ.

Christian Universalism is regarded by some as a dangerous doctrine, because it would provide a disincentive for people to become Christians. Why go to the trouble of becoming a Christian now, if God is going to eventually save us all anyway? Christian Universalists in no way minimize or trivialize the judgments of God upon the ungodly. These judgments can be harsh indeed. It really is *"a fearful thing to fall into the hands of the living God"* (Heb. 10:31). The *"destruction"* of the soul is a terrible thing (ie. becoming "lost") (Matt. 16:26). I believe the fires of God's judgment to be symbolic of mental and spiritual anguish (with the purpose of purification). God has not set up an eternal torture chamber. Nevertheless, God's judgments can harsh indeed. Sometimes these judgments include physical death, as in the case of the people of Noah's day, and also in the case of Christians like Ananias and Sapphira (Acts 5:1-11) and some of the immoral Christians belonging to the Church at Corinth (1 Cor. 11:30). Sometimes these judgments take the form of self-imposed natural consequences of our evil behaviors.

Here's the question we should be asking ourselves. Do we want, in the here and now, to experience peace, love and joy in the ever-present company of our loving heavenly Father, and receive great rewards in the ages to come for a job well-done in this present age? Or would we rather go it alone, and find ourselves the recipients of the negative consequences of our willful disobedience.

Christian salvation is a gift from God made possible by the death and resurrection of Jesus Christ (Eph. 2:8,9). The *"working out"* of our salvation (Phil. 2:12) is another matter entirely. God has paid the price of your sins and removed the barrier of separation between you and God (Matt. 27:51), and guarantees the eventual salvation of all mankind (1 Cor. 15:22). The *"working out"* of your salvation has to do with the timing of it and the degree to which you experience it. Yes, some of us are more Christian than others. Christian salvation is not an all-or-nothing experience. We start out as mere babes in Christ (1 Cor. 3:1) and begin an ages-long journey toward God's long-term goal for us, which is our ultimate glorification in Heaven and transformation into the complete likeness of Christ (Phil. 3:14).

Becoming a Christian is not a once-in-a-lifetime experience based on the belief in and recitation of an acceptable doctrinal formula. Instead this process should be regarded as entering into and experiencing a day-to-day intimate relationship with Jesus Christ. God loves you just as you are. He's already taken care of the penalty phase of the sin in your life. Any gaps that may exist in your theological knowledge will be filled in as time goes on. Most of those gaps won't be filled in until you meet Him face-to-face in the next age, which will begin at the moment of your death. Everything that happens to you when you are walking with Jesus has a positive and loving purpose (Rom. 8:28). All who come to Him will be warmly received (John 6:37). He will never leave nor forsake you (Heb. 13:5). You will still experience plenty of trials and tribulations, but they cannot even be compared with the joys that await you in Heaven some day (Rom. 8:18 and James 1:2,3).

All of this depends on your relationship with Jesus. You cannot possibly make progress in your spiritual journey through life unless you continually *"abide in Christ."* Apart from Him you cannot achieve anything of lasting significance (John 15:5).

So, why have I written this little chapter? Because so many of you out there are hung up on being theologically correct. Perhaps you are wondering whether or not you, or those whom you love, are theologically correct enough to qualify for God's free gift of salvation. Perhaps you are struggling with an ethical or moral problem which you think might disqualify you from receiving God's love, grace and help.

Here's my advice to you. Forget everything negative you were ever taught about God, and just believe this. God's loves you unconditionally just as you are. All the necessary conditions were taken care of at Calvary by God Himself, in the person of his Son, Jesus Christ.

Let Christ into your life. Forget the past, and start over again. For the sake of your relationship with Christ, just start out again as a little child, as if there were no past to atone for. Read Matt. 19:14 and Luke 18:17. Trust Christ with every detail of your life. Let Him worry about the difficult theological questions you don't have answers to. Remember, you are just a child in His tender care. God will increase your understanding of these matters soon enough. In the meantime, just trust Him as any child would trust a loving earthly father. Trust Him through good times and bad. Remember, everything that happens will eventually benefit you in some way (Rom. 8:28). Pray without ceasing throughout the day, every day (Thes. 5:17). If you are not doing this now, try it for a while and see what happens. You will be amazed.

Chapter 31

God Loves You Unconditionally, No Buts about It!

The purpose of this chapter is to help you discover what the Bible actually teaches about the love of God, which forms the basis of His character, and leave all the "buts" out of the equation. We have all heard statements that begin like these:

It is God's desire to save everyone, but. . .

God's love is unconditional, but. . .

Jesus died for your sins, but. . .

God is a God of love, but. . .

God is a God of mercy, but. . .

God is sovereign over his creation, but. . .

Here, I will be showing you exactly what the Bible teaches about God's love and character, in what I believe to be explicit and incontrovertible terms. I will be leaving all the "buts" up to you. If you like, you can keep those "buts" and strew them all over the floor of your home and live with them. Or, you can sweep them into the closet and pretend they aren't there. Or, you can study and research each of those troublesome "buts" and examine them more carefully and thoroughly. You might want to read what others have written about them, including the other chapters of this book. See if you can discover alternate, yet equally natural and plausible, interpretations of the texts, interpretations that would harmonize with what you know to be the true character of God.

God is like the mother of a serial rapist and murderer, sentenced to death. Her son is at least partly made of her own flesh and blood, and her love for him is unconditional and undying. If she could, she would, in a heartbeat, take his place in the gas chamber. Well, that is exactly what God is like. His love for us is unconditional and "unfailing." His love is infinitely greater than that of any human being. On the cross of Calvary, God, in the person of His son Jesus Christ, literally became sin for us and took our place in the death chamber, so to speak. He made propitiation (atoned) for our sins and perfectly satisfied the demands of justice. The purpose of His death on the cross was not merely to demonstrate His love or to exert some kind of moral influence on our behavior. The Bible teaches that something supernatural happened on the cross. An actual transaction occurred which fully satisfied the demands of justice. He paid the price of our salvation while we were still sinners, long before we actually repented of our sins. It all happened before we were even born. If you believe this, then you must also believe that our sin debt has been fully paid, and our salvation from the death penalty of sin has already occurred, at least from God's timeless point of view. Here are some Scripture verses which support this

***Psalm 13:5**: "But I trust in your unfailing love; my heart rejoices in your salvation."*

***1 John 2:2**: "He is the atoning sacrifice (propitiation KJV) for our sins, and not only for ours but also for the sins of the whole world."*

***1 John 4:10**: "This is love: not that we loved God, but that he loved us and sent his Son as the atoning sacrifice (propitiation KJV) for our sins."*

***1 John 4:10**: "He himself bore our sins in his body on the cross. . . "*

***Romans 5:8**: "But God demonstrates his own love for us in this: while we were still sinners, Christ died for us."*

***Timothy 4:10:** "and for this we labor and strive, that we have put our hope in the living God, who is the Savior of ALL men, and especially of those who believe."*

***Hebrews 9:26b:** "But now he has appeared once for all at the end of the ages to do away with sin by the sacrifice of himself."*

In the Parable of the lost sheep, Jesus taught us that God is like a shepherd who is not satisfied until the last one is found (*my interpretation*). Technically it is we who repent and come back to God, but what really happens is that God first seeks us out. The correct order of events is this: God first loves us and seeks us out. Then we respond to that love and give our hearts to Him. My dad loved to tell me about how during his courting days he chased my mother "until she caught him." This is a beautiful illustration of how God works. Like my mother, God is totally in control of the situation, but He makes it look like we are the ones coming to Him. For God's love to be complete, it needs to be requited. In my view, the Calvinistic notion of God being totally self-sufficient within the triune godhead, and not needing anything at all from us, is total nonsense. The more we love, the greater the pain we feel when we are separated from the object of our love. Unrequited love is painful indeed. Do you really believe that God is so great and powerful that He feels no pain? God is the creator of our emotions. He patterned us after Himself. He created us in His own image. Because God is greater than us, He is capable of experiencing the emotions of love and sorrow to a much greater extent than we can imagine. These are not just human emotions; they are Godly emotions. Before I offer Scripture passages in support of the above, I would first like to offer a word of caution with respect to the parable of the lost sheep. In another context, Chapter 10 of John, Jesus made it clear that not all the people of his day were included in his sheep fold, especially not the Pharisees. They did not recognize his voice because at the time they did not belong to him. This does not necessarily mean that God will never add them to the fold in the future. During Jesus' earthly ministry, and also during the period immediately following his death and resurrection, the hearts of God's chosen people were hardened, and they were deliberately blinded by God to the truth of the Gospel until after the *"full number of the Gentiles has come in."* Afterwards, all Israel will be saved (See Romans 11:25). The same principle also applies to God's treatment of the Gentiles. All of us have been *"bound over to disobedience"* in order that God might eventually *"have mercy on all"* (See Romans 11: 28-32).

Luke 15:3-7: *"Then Jesus told them this parable: Suppose one of you has a hundred sheep and loses one of them. Doesn't he leave the ninety-nine in the open country and go after the lost sheep until he finds it? And when he finds it, he joyfully puts it on his shoulders and goes home. Then he calls his friends and neighbors together and says, 'Rejoice with me; I have found my lost sheep.' I tell you that in the same way there will be more rejoicing in heaven over one sinner who repents than over ninety-nine righteous persons who do not need to repent."*

John 6:44: *"No one can come to me unless the Father who sent me draws them, and I will raise them up at the last day."*

John 12:32: *"And I, when I am lifted up from the earth, will draw all people to myself."*

Jesus repeatedly likened our relationship with God to that of a parent and child. He referred to God as not only his Father, but also *"our"* Father, as in the Lord's Prayer. Sometimes God is represented by evangelicals as exclusionary and not actually the Father of all, but only of the so-called elect. There are many Scriptures that seem to support this point of view. But these exclusionary Bible passages only tell half of the story. *The "rest of the story,"* in the words of Paul Harvey, is this. From God's point of view they are still His children and He will never stop loving them. From the point of view of God's *"prodigal"* children, they are estranged from God and no longer part of His family. But in truth, God has never left them. His loving heart burns with desire for them to be reunited with Him and once again become a part of the family. The prodigal son doesn't know it, but his father has already forgiven him in advance. There are no barriers of any kind that would prevent the prodigal son from returning to the family, with full privileges, as though he had never left.

When a child responds negatively to the parent and says things like, "I hate you," the parent never stops loving the child. If the child rebels and does terrible things with his or her life, the parent keeps on loving. When a child strays, the parent continues to reach out in love. And, heaven forbid, if the child is abducted or runs away, the parent never stops looking for the child. If your child were lost or abducted, how would you respond? Well, your Heavenly Father responds in the same way. He doesn't disown you. He doesn't cease to love you. He actively seeks for you. He is always there for you, always ready to receive you back into the family. Do you really believe that God is less loving than most human parents? Do you really think that God puts some kind of time limit on his love and patience? The main difference between our Heavenly Father and a human father is that our Heavenly Father never loses touch with us. He always knows where we are and is always watching over us. He has supernatural powers and is fully capable of touching our hearts, turning us around, and leading us home, when He feels we have had enough, so to speak. Nothing can separate us from His love, not even death. God even has power over death, and there is nothing in Heaven and Earth, and even beneath the earth (demonic regions), that can prevent God from achieving His heart's desire, which is for all of us to eventually find our way home to Him.

When we leave God's family, we cease to be His child only in the sense that the parent/child relationship is broken, as in the case of the Prodigal Son. We cease to be God's children only from our human point of view. God never ceases to love us, and the door is always open when we are finally ready to return home.

Luke 15:31: *"'My son,' the father said, 'you are always with me and everything I have is yours. But we had to celebrate and be glad, because this brother of yours was dead and is alive again; he was lost and is found.'"*

Romans 9:25: *"As he says in Hosea: I will call them my people who are not my people; and I will call her my loved one who is not my loved one."*

John 3:16: *'For God so loved the world that he gave his one and only Son, that whoever believes in him shall not perish but have eternal life."*

John 1:12: *"Yet to all who did receive him, to those who believed in his name, he gave the right to become children of God."*

1 John 4:8: *"Whoever does not love does not know God, because God is love."*

1 Corinthians 13:6-7a: *"Love does not delight in evil but rejoices with the truth. It always protects, always trusts, always hopes, always perseveres. Love never fails."*

Does God hate His enemies? Does He wait until they repent before He decides to love and forgive them? If they never repent before they die, does God then punish them for all eternity? Does God only love those who are good to Him and who love him back? God commands us to love our enemies, pray for them, forgive them and return good for evil. If God himself is not willing to do the same, wouldn't that make Him the biggest hypocrite of all time?

Luke 6:27-36: *"But I tell you who hear me: Love your enemies, do good to those who hate you, bless those who curse you, pray for those who mistreat you. If someone strikes you on one cheek, turn to him the other also. If someone takes your cloak, do not stop him from taking your tunic. Give to everyone who asks you, and if anyone takes what belongs to you, do not demand it back. Do to others as you would have them do to you." If you love those who love you, what credit is that to you? Even 'sinners' love those who love them. And if you do good to those who are good to you, what credit is that to you? Even 'sinners' do that. And if you lend to those from whom you expect repayment, what credit is that to you? Even 'sinners' lend to 'sinners,' expecting to be repaid in full. But* *love your enemies, do good to them, and lend to them without expecting to get anything back. Then your reward will be great, and you will be sons of the Most High, because he is kind to the ungrateful and wicked. Be merciful, just as your Father is merciful."*

Matthew 5:43-48: *"You have heard that it was said, 'love your neighbor and hate your enemy.' But I tell you, love your enemies and pray for those who persecute you, that you may be children of your Father in heaven. He causes the sun to rise on the evil and the good, and sends rain on the righteous and the unrighteous. If you love those who love you, what reward will you get? Are not even the tax collectors doing that? And if you greet only your own people, what are you doing more than others? Do not even pagans do that? Be perfect, therefore, as your heavenly Father is perfect."*

I was raised in the fundamentalist, evangelical Christian tradition. I was completely immersed in it. I even served on Church staffs in full-time Christian ministry. I am totally familiar with all Scriptures relating to the love and Fatherhood of God. You cannot throw any "buts" in my face that I have not already read a thousand times and heard preached a thousand times from church pulpits. As you do your due diligence and study those troublesome "buts," see if there aren't ways they can be reconciled with the undeniable truth that God is all-powerful and all-loving, and everything He does is consistent with His unfailing love towards all of us.

Chapter 32

Two Sides of the Same Coin Resolving the Paradoxes

The Bible to me represents the truth of God expressed from two different perspectives. A good way to illustrate this is with the analogy of a two-sided coin. One side of the coin represents God's perspective, while the other side represents the human perspective.

Many of the words and teachings of the Bible are clearly ambiguous and difficult to understand. As a matter of fact, many Bible truths seem to be downright contradictory to one another. As a result, there is little agreement among highly educated, intelligent and sincere theologians regarding many very important Christian doctrines.

It is not always easy to separate the objective truths of God from the opinions of inspired, yet fallible, human authors. For example, in the Gospel of John it is impossible to separate the actual words of Christ from the words of the writer, John. Everything seems to run together, and there are no quotation marks in the original Greek. Another example would be that the writer of Ecclesiastes, speaking from his human perspective, made statements like *"everything is meaningless"* and that both the righteous and unrighteous share a common destiny and have no further reward after they die (See Eccl. 9).

This doesn't mean that the Bible is an unreliable source of information about God. The key to interpreting the Bible correctly is to understand that the Bible was written from both a Godly and a human perspective. While it is true that the human authors were inspired by God and were expressing truths resulting from actual interactions with God, God did not actually put the words into their mouths. Instead, He allowed the writers the freedom to express their own points of view. If you are wondering why God didn't just write the Bible Himself and hand it to us without errors of any kind, you might also ask yourself these related questions: Why doesn't He preach the Gospel directly to everyone? Why does He allow imperfect preachers to preach so many different versions of the "truth." Whatever the reasons, the fact remains that God has decided to accomplish His purposes in this world, including the writing of the Bible, through imperfect human agents.

This being true, is there some principle of Scripture interpretation that would enable us to resolve the various ambiguities, paradoxes and apparent contradictions that we find in the Bible, and arrive at the objective "truths" of the matter, so to speak?

Before answering this, I would like to point out that if God wanted us to know with certainty and clarity the absolute truth about every Christian doctrine, He most certainly would have brought that about. But He didn't. For this reason, I believe that theological correctness is not a prerequisite for Salvation. Your eternal destiny does not depend on your getting it all right before you die. If you believe nothing else about God, please believe that He is your loving Heavenly Father who loves you unconditionally and when you seek Him with all your heart He most certainly will receive you to Himself, regardless of whether you fully understand all these highly complex doctrines that even the most brilliant theologians cannot agree upon.

Now I would like to share with you a principle of Scripture interpretation that will help you resolve at least some of the ambiguities, paradoxes and apparent contradictions that are found in the Bible. When confronted with Bible contradictions it helps me to understand that in some cases we might be looking at are two sides of the same coin, so to speak, one side representing the truth from God's point of view, and the other side representing the human perspective.

Let me start with a simple example. In the Book of Genesis, after Adam had sinned he hid himself from God. In Genesis 1:9, we read *"But the Lord God called to the man, 'Where are you?'"* If we were to take a very literalistic approach when interpreting this passage, you might assume that God was looking for Adam and didn't know where he was. We know from the rest of Scripture, however, that God is omniscient, and no one can hide from God. So why does God ask, *"Where are you?"* The answer might be that Adam was unaware of God's omniscience, and God was just "playing along." Perhaps the teller of this Genesis account also did not know that God was omniscient. The writer derived his information from various oral traditions that were handed down over the centuries. Although the information might be inaccurate from God's perspective, it does accurately portray the truth from Adam's perspective and the perspective of the writer of the story. So who are we to believe, the writer of the Genesis account or the writers of the rest of the Bible who have told us that God is omniscient and no one can hide from Him? The objective truth is that God knew where Adam was hiding, but Adam didn't know that. This doesn't mean that the Bible is an unreliable source of information about God. It does mean that the Bible expresses both the human and the divine perspectives.

Here's another example. Job was perplexed and frustrated about the apparent unfairness of life. He just couldn't understand why God was treating him so unfairly. God had not yet revealed to him that there is life after death and that in the next life good will be rewarded and evil punished. We now know in hindsight that there is life after death, but this was not made plain to us until after the life, death and resurrection of Christ.

Another two-sided theological coin would be Christian salvation, which is spoken of in the Bible as both a past and future event. Some Scriptures speak of salvation as something that happened when we first received Christ into our lives. At that time we became *"new creatures"* in Christ, our sins were forgiven, we received *"aionian"* life, and were seated with Christ in the heavenly places. Yet the Bible also speaks of our salvation as a future event, something we hope and patiently wait for, something that Christ will bring with Him when He comes again. All of our sins (past, present, and future) were atoned for on Calvary, yet we remain sinners and are commanded to seek God's forgiveness on a daily basis. So which is it? Are we saved already, or not yet saved? The first side of the coin represents God's timeless point of view. God views all past and future events as though they were in the present. He views the entire course of human history as a completed event. When He looks at us, He sees not only what we are like now, but also what we will become. He views us as sinners in need of correction, and as saints, already perfected in Heaven. From our human perspective, we view and experience salvation as a process that plays out over time.

Another example of the two-sided coin involves the doctrine of salvation by grace apart from works. The Apostle Paul tells us that we have been saved by grace through faith apart from works. Our salvation is a gift and there is absolutely no room for boasting (Eph 2 8,9). James, on the other hand, tells us that faith apart from works is dead, and faith alone cannot save us. Over and over again, Jesus emphasized the importance of living a righteous life as a condition of entering the Kingdom. In Matthew 25, Jesus made it very clear that in the future Kingdom only those who produced good deeds would be permitted to enter, and many of those who thought they knew Christ would be rejected. So which is it? Are we saved by grace through faith apart from works, or do we have to earn our salvation by repenting of our sins and producing fruit (good deeds)?

Here's how I would resolve this issue. Christian salvation is given to all of us as an act of pure grace on God's part. This was made possible by the atoning sacrifice of Christ on Calvary. The sin debt was paid in full and only had to be paid once. The salvation of all mankind actually happened on the Cross of Calvary. That is the way God looks at it. That is the side of the coin that represents God's perspective.

From our human perspective, we experience God's forgiveness only after we commit a sin and repent of it. In our human experience, it seems like we qualify for salvation through our own efforts, when in actuality it is the Holy Spirit of God who produces our faith and the fruit of righteous living in us.

Chapter 33

Human Consciousness, Quantum Mechanics, and the Efficacy of Prayer

In my quest for understanding of how and why prayer works I studied not only the Scriptures but also science, quantum physics in particular, so see if there is a way to explain or validate the efficacy of prayer from a scientific point of view. In my quest for spiritual truth I began with the premise that truth is truth, no matter where you find it. There can be no conflict between true science and true religion. Jesus is the *"way, the truth, and the life,"* and if the Bible is true, then true science should also validate the truth of the Bible, and vice versa.

Not only does science validate the existence of God, but it also validates the truth of the Christian Scriptures, and the efficacy of prayer, in particular. To understand how and why prayer works, from a scientific point of view, it is necessary to understand that scientific discoveries over the past 100 years or so relating to general relativity on the macro scale and quantum mechanics on the micro scale have demonstrated through actual, indisputable, verifiable, repeatable, and almost universally accepted experimental data that the external physical world we observe actually does not exist. It exists only in the form of possibilities that may be described as quantum wave functions which do not actually collapse into realities until actually observed by conscious observers.

One experiment that demonstrates this truth is the famous double-slit experiment relating to Heisenberg's uncertainty principle, which states that you cannot determine the future state of any particle based on its current position and velocity. When you "observe" or "measure" one or the other it "collapses" into an actual reality and the particle can end up virtually anywhere in the universe. In other words, you cannot determine in advance where the particle will be the moment after you observe it.

Most likely it will end up where you expect, but in actuality it can end up anywhere in the universe based on a range of probabilities.

It has been deduced by many physicists that the universe we observe does not actually exist. No two individuals or particles exist at the same moment in time in relation to one another. Everything is "relative" according to Einstein's theory of relativity. You are separated from everything you physically observe by the amount of time it takes the light to travel from the object you are observing to the retina of your eye. Even two related subatomic particles, such as protons and neutrons in a single atom, do not occupy the same place in time relative to one another. It has been scientifically verified and universally agreed upon that the smallest possible unit of time is approximately 1×10^{-24} seconds (one Planck unit of time) and the smallest unit of distance is approximately 5.3192×10^{-44} meters (one Planck unit of distance). In between those units nothing exists. What we are viewing when we observe any object, whether in motion or not, are the discontinuous frames of space and time (similar to the frames of a movie) which occur at very small intervals of time measured in Planck units. In between those frames things only exist as waves of probability or possibility, which do not actually collapse into actual objects or events until they are observed by a conscious observer. The actual "present" that I am observing consists of an empty vacuum of nothingness, only un-collapsed quantum wave functions. The events or objects that will collapse into reality by our observations exist in the present moment in what physicists call a "super positioned state" and exist only as possibilities with an infinite number of potential outcomes spread out over all of time and space. The actual "present" moment of the universe from my unique perspective in space and time only exists as a "wave function" of possibilities. Because of the time it takes for light to reach the retina of my eyes, everything I am looking at in this current moment only exists in the past. It does not actually currently exist. Everything in the future does not yet exist. So from my perspective nothing actually exists except my own consciousness, which is not actually a part of this physical universe. I am a spiritual being, created in the image of God.

These discoveries completely changed the way scientists understand the nature of the universe. The old system of Newtonian physics that described all events as deterministic in nature based on strict laws of gravity and motion had to be abandoned in favor of the indeterministic system described by quantum mechanics. On the macro level (large things), Newtonian physics pretty well describes how the physical universe works and the results of our measurements are very predictable. But on the micro or quantum level (very small things) we are not able to make accurate predictions and are only able to describe future events as a range of probabilities, not certainties. When you combine the affects of all the micro events at the quantum level what you end up with is a world at the macro level that is totally unpredictable. True randomness actually does exist in our universe. But does this mean that God is not in control? Albert Einstein strongly resisted the indeterminism which was demonstrated by quantum mechanics, and insisted that *"God does not play dice with the universe."* He was a determinist to the end, despite overwhelming evidence to the contrary, which today is almost universally accepted by the scientific community.

To Albert Einstein the "uncertainties" demonstrated by quantum mechanics meant that God was not in control, resulting in a meaningless or purposeless existence for all of us. While I believe that God did set in motion truly random processes when He created the universe, I also believe that this did not result in a meaningless or purposeless universe. God still remains firmly in control while still allowing random processes to occur. More about this later, but first I want to discuss one more scientific discovery that helps us understand how prayer works, and that is the principle of entanglement and non-local interactions between entangled particles.

Repeated experiments have shown that when two "entangled" or related particles are separated and have no possible way of interacting with one another due to the distance between them and the limitations imposed by the maximum speed of light, changing the state of one of the particles instantaneously results in the related particle changing into the opposite state. The measurements are made so quickly that there is no possible way for one particle to communicate with the other, yet in some as yet unexplained way one particle seems to know what has happened to the other particle and assumes a state that is the opposite of the other particle. One example of this type of experiment has to do with the measurement of separated pairs of entangled bosons. The plus or minus spin of one of the particles does not occur until after the measurement is taken. Yet somehow one of the particles, which could theoretically be separated from the other particle by millions of light years, automatically knows enough about what happened to the other particle to enable it to instantly transform itself into the opposite state. Not all physicists agree that such non-local communication is possible, but to date no verifiable alternative explanation has been offered.

In this chapter, I have tried to keep things as simple as possible. Concepts involving quantum mechanics and general relativity can be extremely complex and difficult to understand, and there is no absolute agreement among physicists regarding many of the particulars. The best way to research this for yourself is to Google the various terms given above or do a YouTube search using the same terms. In this way you will find many articles and videos that explain these concepts in laymen's terminology.

The interesting thing about non-local communication between entangled pairs, is that non-local communication has also been experimentally verified to exist at the macro level. This is sometimes referred to as ESP, or extra sensory perception. It also occurs when we communicate with God through prayer and when we pray for others

We don't live in a natural world subject only to the natural laws of Newtonian physics. We actually live in a supernatural world that is in part described by quantum mechanics and general relativity. We are not natural, physical beings subject to deterministic immutable laws of cause and effect. We are actually supernatural, spiritual beings. We live in a world that is governed by probabilities and possibilities.

You might ask, if events don't actually happen until after I observe them what observer or observers are collapsing all the other wave functions of possibility that I don't observe? What about the tree in the forest that falls when no one is looking? Does it really fall? Yes, the tree really does fall. Human beings are not the only conscious entities in the universe. God is the main "conscious observer" who views everything from every possible time and place, and the other observers are the rest of humanity and other conscious entities who oversee what goes on in our lives.

The next question we need to answer relates to the apparent randomness and uncertainty of the object or event that collapses as a result of our conscious observation. Is it possible to influence the result by taking control of our thought processes? Are all human events the result of blind chance, or are human events somehow being guided by our own thoughts in combination with the thoughts and purposes of God and other conscious entities? Because the probabilities associated with quantum collapse are infinite in number, and not subject to classical time and space limitations, I would assume that an infinite variety of potential outcomes might at least theoretically be possible.

In my view, there are two irrefutable proofs that the results of quantum collapse are not totally random and that the universe that we experience and observe is not the result of blind chance. The first proof is the fact that the creation and continued existence of the universe requires a level of fine tuning that is mathematically impossible to achieve by merely random processes and must be the result of some kind of intelligent design. The second proof is the increasing order and complexity that we see in the development of life on Earth, which, according to the second law of thermodynamics should not be happening. According to this law, which is accepted by the majority of the scientific community, random processes should inevitably result in disorder, not increasing order and complexity. The only viable alternative to these proofs is the theory of multiple universes which basically states that for every quantum collapse, no matter how infinitesimal, an infinite number of alternate universes must be created to account for every possible outcome. We just happen by chance to live in the one and only universe that defied all laws of probability and developed in the way it did. This in my view stretches the limits of credulity far beyond what is required to accept the fact that the universe was created by intelligent design. It is beyond the scope of this essay to provide detailed information regarding the issues related to intelligent design, the second law of thermodynamics, and the theory of multiple universes. If you would like to learn more, simply Google these terms or search for them on YouTube.

God, in a manner of speaking, may be described as a universal conscious entity who brought the universe into being and controls its evolution and development by means of nothing more than His thoughts and active observations. Is it possible that because we are spiritual beings created in the image of God we have the ability to creatively influence the outcomes in our individual lives by means of that same process, subject perhaps to certain limitations imposed by God?

Is there truth to the Biblical teaching that with *God "all things are possible"* (Matthew 19:26) and that when we draw upon this limitless resource through prayer we are literally capable of *"doing all things"* (Philippians 4:13) and that *"nothing will be impossible"* for us (Matthew 17:20)?

Because we are spiritual beings, created by and connected in some way with God, our prayers can have a dramatic effect not only on our own lives but also on the lives of others. For this to happen two things must occur. First, what we are praying for must not be at cross purposes with God's plans for all of us. For example, if individuals are approaching an intersection from two different directions and both are "praying" for a green light, both prayers cannot be answered in the affirmative. God has an overriding blueprint which determines the general outline, purpose and culmination of all future events. He allows us great flexibility with respect to the individual routes we choose to travel, so long as the overall plan is not compromised (see 1 John 5:14-15). The result is an interesting and sometimes confusing interplay between God's sovereignty, quantum uncertainty, and mankind's freedom of choice. Secondly, we need to become "entangled" in some way with the objects of our prayers. It is the universal "consciousness" of God that "non-locally" makes the connections between the "entangled" relationships in our lives.

Ideally there would be a vertical and a horizontal component to each of our prayers. Our prayers will be more beneficial if we are praying for people we know and with whom we have become "entangled." The closer the relationship the more in sync the two lives would be, thus increasing the likelihood that the thoughts and prayers of both would correlate. We need to be both praying and doing (James 1:22). If we are praying for someone we know, we need to physically connect with them as much as possible. If we are praying for ourselves our prayers would be greatly enhanced if others were also praying for us. This I believe is why group prayer is so important. This is also why it is so important to share your requests and interact as much as possible with a local body of believers.

Chapter 34

Materialism, Dualism and Idealism

The three "isms" given above lie at the root of the controversies associated with Christian Universalism. Basically, they represent three world views that are common to scientists, theologians, and just plain ordinary people like you and I. These world views directly influence the way we process information. Our world view influences many of the underlying assumptions, or premises, that we begin with when we perform certain types of theological or scientific investigations. If the underlying premises are false, then even a flawlessly conducted investigation will yield a flawed result.

I believe that faulty underlying premises are the root cause of many paradoxes or contradictions that scientists and theologians are forced to live with after their investigations have been concluded. That is why equally brilliant individuals can arrive at totally different conclusions after examining exactly the same information. For example, if an evolutionary biologist has a materialist philosophy and begins his investigations with the assumption, or premise, that God does not exist, he would most certainly conclude that the evolutionary process is guided by random chance and nothing else. He would have to live with unexplained gaps in the fossil record, and results which are in conflict with the universally accepted second law of thermodynamics. If a Biblical literalist examines the same evidence, he might conclude that the geological strata were laid down by a single cataclysmic event, the Genesis flood, just a few thousand years ago. He would have to live with apparent contradictory evidence that these strata were laid down over millions of years. Or he might conclude that the universe and the earth were created with the illusion of age built in.

During the course of my scientific and theological research and inquiry I have come to appreciate the brilliance and impeccable logic of those who disagree with me. Nevertheless, I still don't agree with their conclusions. It would be pointless to engage in debate with them, because the underlying premises which form the basis of their logic are not the same as mine.

This brings me to a discussion of the three "isms" mentioned in the title of this essay. These three different world views form the basis of our logic when we read the Bible and formulate doctrine. The materialists believe that everything is material in nature. To them, even our thoughts are nothing more than electrical and chemical processes which occur in our physical brains. If you begin with this premise when examining the Bible, your conclusions are going to be quite different from those of a theist and/or dualist. A dualist is a person who believes that the material and the supernatural worlds are separate and distinct. Most Christians are dualists. They believe that because God is separate from the physical world, He must intervene "supernaturally" to influence the course of human events.

The idealist, on the other hand, has a totally different world view than either the materialist or the dualist. The idealist believes that the physical and the spiritual worlds are one and the same, and there is no difference between the natural and the supernatural. The idealist believes that both the spiritual and material dimensions of reality are comprised of and created by the "thoughts" of God and to a lesser extent those of other conscious beings created by God. Some quantum physicists also view reality in this way. They believe that the present universe that we observe currently exists only in the form of un-collapsed quantum wave functions. These wave functions do not actually collapse into reality until observed by God and/or other conscious observers. This has been demonstrated by repeatable and universally accepted experimental data. To date, no viable alternative has been offered. Not all physicists are idealists. As a matter of fact, the overwhelming majority are died-in-the wool materialists, despite the experimental evidence to the contrary. As a result, materialist physicists are forced to live with many as yet unresolved contradictions and paradoxes associated with quantum physics.

In like manner, religious dualists must live with many unresolved contradictions and paradoxes associated with their belief systems. Most Christians, and also many non-Christians, are dualists. They view almost all theological issues in black and white terms and approach all religious inquiry with an either/or mentality. This forms the basis of their world view and is one of the underlying premises on which their logic is based. Here are some examples of these "black and white" dualisms: God vs. Satan; good vs. evil; physical vs spiritual; Heaven vs. Hell; saved vs. lost; God of love vs. God of wrath; faith vs. logic; grace vs works; the Bible is literally true or not true at all; and so on.

When studying the Bible and searching for spiritual truth, our logic is flawed if we begin with the premise that there can only be two possible results. If neither result is the correct one, then at the conclusion of our investigation we will inevitably be left with unanswered paradoxes and contradictions. The actual "truth" of the matter might lie somewhere in between two extremes, or it might be a solution that incorporates them both, or it might be something altogether different that disproves both of the alternatives you originally had in mind.

Dualism lies at the heart of religious fundamentalism. The opposite of fundamentalism, however, is not liberalism. Most liberals also think in dualistic terms, though perhaps somewhat less so than fundamentalists. Christian fundamentalists and liberals have more in common with one another than they do with the materialists.

Idealists, on the other hand, believe that the so-called material world is not actually material at all and is not really separate and distinct from God Himself and the spiritual world. According to them, everything created by God is a part of God. Many adherents of Eastern religions also view the world in this way. Idealism is far less common in Western thought. If everything that exists is technically a part of God, created by God, and controlled by the thoughts of God, and if God is by nature loving and good, then everything that happens or exists must be consistent with God's character and would have a loving purpose. In other words, things or events that we would normally think of as at "cross purposes" with God's intentions (Satan, evil, suffering, hell, and the like) must instead fit into God purposes and be consistent with His loving nature.

As you approach the study of the Bible, don't be afraid to think outside of the box, so to speak. Do not dismiss out of hand all approaches to truth that might conflict with the prevailing dualistic Christian world view.

Studying the Bible with an open mind is a very scary proposition, especially for the Christian fundamentalist, because for this person a lot is at stake. Entertaining the possibility that he or she might be wrong about one of these very rigid fundamentalist doctrines could be viewed as an admission of doubt. Faith, in the view of many fundamentalists, is an absolute requirement for salvation. Without it, there is no chance of escaping endless, infinite punishment in Hell. Any open minded investigation which has the potential of eroding a person's faith is very scary. They are stuck in the black and white box of dualism. For them,

God is either your best friend or your worst enemy. There is no in between. To them, God is extremely “schizophrenic,” so to speak. He is an “either-or” God. Either He forgives and overlooks your sins or He never forgives you at all, and instead punishes you forever in Hell. You are either saved or you are not saved. Most fundamentalists will tell you they believe in God’s unconditional love for all mankind. At the same time, their description of God’s actual behavior is not even remotely consistent with that kind of love.

So, here’s the problem. Because dualists begin their study of the Scriptures with the underlying assumption (premise) that people are either saved or not saved and are going to Heaven or Hell when they die, they interpret all the Scriptures they read in such a way as to be consistent with this dualism. As a result they have to live with huge unresolved paradoxes and contradictions, and a very schizophrenic God.

A few years ago, I embarked on a very scary journey of discovery. I decided to engage in a serious attempt to study the Bible with an open mind and see if it was possible to interpret the Scriptures in such a way as to retain the essence and truth of the Gospel, and at the same time remove the paradoxes and contradictions. I hope you can appreciate how scary this was for me. In order to be intellectually honest, I also had to entertain the possibility that the materialists might be right and the Bible is not true at all. My main criteria for interpreting the Scriptures was to accept the most natural interpretation and avoid as much as possible work-a-rounds and the twisting of meanings and semantic tricks in order to arrive at conclusions which were consistent with the result I was seeking. If the materialists were right, and the Bible was just a hopelessly flawed human document, then so be it.

The result of my investigation over a period of several years was a validation of most of the core beliefs of evangelical Christianity, but with some important differences. Most of the dualisms have been replaced by their idealistic counterparts. The one major doctrine that emerged, and made possible a resolution of the dualisms, paradoxes and contradictions, was the doctrine of “universal reconciliation.” This doctrine is also called “Christian universalism” because most of the core Christian beliefs and doctrines are retained and strongly affirmed. The one major teaching that went by the wayside is the doctrine of “eternal conscious torment in Hell” (ECT) for all unbelievers.

Chapter 35

NDE's, Reincarnation, and Christian Theology

It is beyond the scope of this book to provide evidence for the validity of near death experiences (NDE's) and past-life and between-lives hypnotic regressions. Many books have been written about the subject, which I would encourage you to read for yourself. Literally millions of people have reported NDE experiences, and tens of thousands have experienced past-life hypnotic regressions in a clinical setting. If you are not comfortable reading about this topic, you may just skip this chapter of my book. Nothing in this chapter conflicts with any of the theological views expressed in the rest of this book. What we learn from NDE's and past-life regressions is in complete harmony with the Scriptures as I understand them. I believe that NDE's and past-life regressions are the most reliable forms of communications from Heaven and the afterlife, mainly because they are "eye witness accounts." Other forms of communication from the "other side" mostly take the form of second-hand accounts that are "channeled" by a third party such as a medium or clairvoyant. In my view, the second and third-hand accounts are less reliable because they are more subject to fraud and deception.

I am sure we are all puzzled by the differences in the NDE experience from one individual to the next. There are also many similarities. I believe the experience is real, and not based on thoughts that occur in the physical brain, because most of the subjects are "brain dead" during the NDE experience. I do believe that our human consciousness exists separately from our physical brain, and all sensory experiences of our lives are stored not only in the brain but in our spiritual consciousness as well. I believe that what is going on during the NDE is a kind of shaping of our own individual realities. Apparently, in the Heavenly realms we are to a great degree able to create our own realities. This also occurs during our earthly plane of existence, but to a much lesser degree. Quantum theory ties in very nicely with this. *"As a man thinks, so is he."* After death, some people can remain trapped for a while by their negative thoughts which are holdovers from their earthly existence, while others are liberated. So in the NDE's we do see a variety of both Heavenly and sometimes "Hellish" experiences and settings. Those experiences, though varied, are still real. After death, each of us experiences a different reality because we come from different places in our thinking and all have different issues to work out.

What we see in the NDE experience is a picture of what happens immediately after death. We don't ever see is what comes later, because people who experience NDE's always return to their physical bodies. For information about what happens afterwards we must rely on past-life and between-lives hypnotic regressions. Psychiatrists discovered the art of past-life regression quite by accident. While regressing their patients backwards in time during hypnosis to discover childhood events that might be impacting a patient's current well-being, occasionally one of those patients would accidentally regress to a previous life. Sometimes an individual would regress to a place between lives in Heaven or the spirit world. Over the years, many therapists have made past-life regression their main practice. Some therapists have regressed literally thousands of patients to their past-life and between-lives states. Usually these sessions are tape recorded and well documented. Information coming from these sessions has been verified over and over again as accurate and which could not be known by the subjects from any other information sources. It is interesting to me that what happens between lives in Heaven is remarkably consistent from one patient to another, much more so than with the NDE experience. Amazingly, thousands of patients from all backgrounds and religions, even atheists, report pretty much the same things. Their descriptions of the afterlife are very similar. Apparently, once we get past the initial stages of entering the Heavenly realms and make a cleaner separation from our life on earth we all tend to end up in similar circumstances.

Based on most near death experiences (NDE's), it appears that God's judgments in the afterlife, or Heaven, initially take the form of a life review. During the life review we observe every detail of the life we have just lived from our own perspective and also from the perspective of those whose lives we have touched. We are able to see and feel how our actions affected others. We feel their joy if we did something good to them, and we also feel their pain and anger if we caused them physical or emotional harm. Here's where the cross of Calvary comes in. Almost all NDE accounts of the life review describe the experience as totally non-judgmental in nature. And almost all report an overwhelming experience of unconditional love and acceptance by God. During the life review the individual feels as though he or she is judging or evaluating him or herself. God is not the judge. Instead, God is the one who is viewed as dispensing unconditional love. The message of Calvary is that Christ made atonement for everyone's sins. Most who encounter God in the NDE experience are pleasantly surprised at God's non-judgmental attitude towards them and how much God loves them, despite their sins and shortcomings.

I do not believe that we enter the Heavenly realms with fully reformed characters. Based on my study of the Scriptures, I believe that more learning and character development will take place after we die, either in the Heavenly realms or in future incarnations on Earth. In between our earthly incarnations much learning takes place, including the life review and a needs assessment. In addition, some very interesting group learning sessions take place as well as very high tech forms of "book learning." Lots of time is also allotted for various forms of recreation and enjoyment. After much time goes by, we then decide with the help of our friends and guides in Heaven when and where to reincarnate. The particular time, place and body that we choose for our next life on earth depends on what lessons we want to learn. Spiritual growth occurs much more rapidly during an earthly incarnation than in Heaven for obvious reasons. In heaven there is no pain or sorrow or problems of any sort. Learning and growth takes place much more rapidly in the difficult and challenging environment here on Earth where we are exposed to real life and death situations. It is on earth where the "rubber meets the road," so to speak. The lessons we learn in the "crucible" of our earthly life can be viewed as a purification, refinement, and self-improvement process. No one achieves perfection in one lifetime. As I have said many times in this book, I believe that growing into the likeness of Christ is an "ages-long" process.

Much of the eschatology (doctrine of the last things) of the Bible suggests that rewards and punishments will occur during physical ages to come on planet Earth. Some, called Preterists, believe that the Kingdom Age actually began two thousand years ago, and that Christ is growing and perfecting His Kingdom right now on Earth. I personally am sympathetic with the Preterist view. I also believe that the descriptions of God's Kingdom ages in the Book of Revelation are mostly symbolic and allegorical in nature. Reincarnationists would say that rewards and chastisements of God are carried out during our current and future lives here on Earth.

Some of you might be wondering, when do we meet Jesus in Heaven? This is a difficult question for me to answer because most people who experience NDE's make no mention of Jesus. Some Christians identify a "being of light" as Jesus, while some non-Christians identify this being as a religious figure from their own religious tradition. Most don't recognize this being by name or as any particular religious figure. After progressing further into the heavenly realms, this "being of light" is often recognized as a "spirit guide" who was assigned as one's teacher during the time spent in between lives. A spirit guide, and other entities as well, act as "guardian angels" during our incarnations here on earth.

The name Jesus was given to Christ during his earthly existence, but He would not necessarily be called by that name in the afterlife. The "Jesus of history" and the "Christ of faith" are indeed one and the same, but the name Jesus belongs for the most part to the earthly life of the Christ, who in a larger sense is the divine *"Logos,"* the co-creator of the universe. When the Bible speaks about every knee bowing at the *"name"* of Jesus, those worshippers were not technically bowing to a name, but instead to the person who bore that name during His earthly sojourn. It is not the name Jesus that we worship. Instead, we worship Christ Himself.

The descriptions of God the Father in most NDE's and between-lives regressions are very impersonal. God is mostly referred to as the "source," or "creator," or the "energy" from which everything is made and holds together. The Creator is always described as incredibly loving. Love is the chief attribute by which God is described. God is further described as the greater whole of which we are all a part. There is a strong sense of connectedness in Heaven. We are all connected with God and with each other. I believe that Christ is the only begotten Son of God, the first-born of all creation, and the entity through whom everything else was created. But in Heaven this "person" of the Godhead is not called Jesus. I would guess that most of what Christ does in Heaven is done behind the scenes, similar to the way He works on Earth. There are many levels of exaltation or *"dwelling places"* in Heaven. Not all of these levels are accessible to most of us. It takes untold ages to progress to the highest levels where Christ may perhaps be known in a different way. In the meantime, we all remain indwelt by the Spirit of Christ by whom we are all connected with each other. In Heaven, as on Earth, we would still be regarded as Christ's body, His hands and feet as it were, through whom He accomplishes His master plan of transforming all of His created beings into His own likeness. Of course, Christ is not really a "he" or a "she." In Heaven, these anthropomorphisms no longer apply.

Appendix

Additional Thoughts Since Writing this Book

Why do people reject Christianity?

According to Christian apologist Don Johnson, the top six reasons people reject Christianity are:

1. *Christians behaving badly*
2. *Disappointment with God*
3. *Weak or absent father*
4. *Social pressure*
5. *Cost of discipleship*
6. *Immorality (especially sexual immorality)*

Source: http://donjohnsonministries.org/sexual-immorality-and-five-other-reasons-people-reject-christianity/

While those reasons might be relatively common among the unthinking and uninformed, I personally believe that the most common reason, worldwide, would be cultural bias against Christianity, for which people in non-Christian cultures can hardly be blamed.

Another very important reason, not mentioned above, especially among those with a rational mindset, is the Christian portrayal of God as both loving and, at the same time, immensely unfair and cruel. Popular Christian theology is full of absurdities and blatant contradictions regarding the true nature of God. You can find this anti-Christian mindset reflected in the following testimonial which I extracted from a website, called ExChristian.net:

"Christianity would have us believe in an angry, jealous, judgmental, all powerful, loving god that: demands worship, keeps a running tally on everything you do, contradicts itself, and will punish you to the end of

time simply for exercising your right to question its nonsense! But although this god-man in the sky will damn you to torment for all of eternity, simply for questioning, or not believing or worshipping a certain way, he loves you! What an asshole this Christian god is eh?

There are so many reasons why I reject the Christian faith, and all religions, but simply, I reject Christianity because it is completely illogical, nonsensical, hypocritical, superstitious myth, and has no place for an enlightened humanity. Merely studying the history of the Christian church, with its grotesque torture, its vast intolerance and hypocrisy, and even today, with the rampant Catholic sexual abuse of young children, It's amazing to me that so many still blindly accept this crap, and give their lives away to it. Christianity, and religion in general, is a retirement home for the mind. It is a morass of nonsense, promulgated through fear. It is a spiritual prison.

My religious philosophy is simple: live to do the most good, and the least evil. I need no bibles, priests, prophets, saints, cardinals, and especially no non-existent crucified saviors to rescue me by demanding conformity. If humanity is to evolve than it is time to let the source of our greatest fears and superstitions fall into the dust where it belongs...Religion."

Source: http://testimonials.exchristian.net/2003/10/why-i-reject-christianity.php

Within the pages of Scripture, God does reveal to us His true nature. However, for a correct understanding of the true character of God, as described in the Bible, we must do three things. . .

1. Discard the notion of Scriptural "inerrancy," as it is commonly taught.
2. Eliminate mistranslations of important Bible terms, such as "eternal," "destruction," "death," "life," "Hell," and so on.
3. Exercise sound logic, common sense, and reason when "interpreting" the Bible and applying its teachings in the context of our current day and age.

The Bible does teach that God is love. He loves everyone equally and He has already redeemed all mankind. Eventually, all the gaps in our knowledge about God will be completely "filled in." All of us are in the process of being drawn into a loving relationship with God. Yes, some of us are farther along in this process than others, and some of us think we are farther along than we really are, but eventually Jesus will be leading all of us home. One day, every knee will bow to Jesus, and every tongue will confess Him as Lord. (Philippians 2:10-12)

Ours is a message of reconciliation.

Most of us like to think of ourselves as being relatively tolerant, broadminded individuals, preferring to give the benefit of the doubt whenever possible, to those who differ with us. No one wants to be thought of as a "know it all," or a "narrow minded bigot." Our society in recent years has become increasingly diverse and pluralistic, and traditionally held religious and moral beliefs are no longer widely held in the popular culture. Those who resist the growing secularization of governmental, educational, and even religious, institutions are labeled as intolerant, religious extremists, who wish to impose their narrow minded beliefs on society.

The truth is, however, that there is no virtue in being "broad minded." What is there to admire in a person who has no convictions or firmly held beliefs? As Christians, we should be "sticking out like sore thumbs." We should be living our lives in radically different ways from mainstream society.

At the same time, however, we should be viewed as both loving and non-judgmental towards those who have not yet "found their way" back to God. Jesus reserved most of His harsh words for the self-righteous religious elite, and seemed most welcoming and forgiving towards "sinners" and outcasts of society. Without condoning their sin, He taught them that God loved them and so did He. Our ministry should be one of reconciliation, not judgment, "for God was in Christ, reconciling the world to himself, no longer counting people's sins against them. And he gave us this wonderful message of reconciliation." (2 Cor. 5:19

Inch by inch, anything's a cinch.

According to the Chinese proverb, "a journey of a thousand miles begins with a single step." Another proverb goes like this, "inch by inch, anything's a cinch." Christian salvation, I believe, is an ages-long process that begins by entering into a relationship with Christ and does not end until the conclusion of the ages. In the words of the Apostle Paul, in Philippians 3:13-14, "I do not consider myself yet to have taken hold of it. But one thing I do: forgetting what is behind and straining toward what is ahead, I press on toward the goal to win the prize for which God has called me heavenward in Christ Jesus."

When we enter into relationship with Christ we become new creatures. (2 Cor. 5:17) Old things pass away and all things become new. This is not an instantaneous process. It is a life-long journey that I believe continues after death. Progress, not perfection, is the best indicator that we have been genuinely "converted" to Christ. We all struggle with sinful habits in our lives, and like all addictions, they are very hard to break. Some are impossible to overcome without God's help. Here's a suggestion for those of you who are struggling with a major problem or goal in your life. Try and break down the solution into very small bite-sized pieces, or steps. Decide what your first step will be, and make a commitment to do it each day, religiously, no matter what. Continue to do this until it becomes a daily habit and becomes a part of your lifestyle. Daily habits can be difficult to form, often with many missteps along the way, but once formed, they are just as difficult to break. Once you have formed your little "first-step" habit, then take another very small step, and form another habit that will advance your progress towards overcoming a major sin problem or achieving any positive life goal.

You can catch more flies with honey than with vinegar.

The best way to persuade your dog to let go of the filthy bone that he/she just dug up in your back yard, would be to offer him/her a nice, juicy steak, instead. Have you noticed that the largest, and fastest growing, churches in our country today almost never mention Hell in their worship, or in their sermons, or in their Bible studies? Nearly 100% of the focus in these churches is on principles of Christian living and on how much God loves us in Jesus Christ. Why is that? If the main purpose of the Gospel of Christ is to rescue people from everlasting torment in Hell, why is this aspect of the Gospel message almost never spoken of? Well, I can tell you why. If those dynamic, inspiring, full of the Holy Ghost preachers were to give this a place of prominence in their sermons and Bible studies, their churches would quickly be emptied.

A frequently expressed criticism of Christian Universalism is that it would remove the incentive for missions and outreach. I believe that the contrary is true. Many Universalists have the same passion for missions and outreach as believers in ECT (Eternal Conscious Torment), actually more so in my case, because I know that the Gospel of Christ is good news for all. The main religion of Japan, Shintoism, is based on a worship of, and reverence for, one's ancestors. Missionaries to Japan, in the early days, were forced, due to their incorrect theology, to proclaim, along with the message of salvation in Christ, that there was no hope for their ancestors, who they believed were eternally lost in Hell. Is it any wonder that Japan, despite our best efforts, remains largely unreached by Christianity?

There is no such thing as "blind faith."

Recognizing and admitting contradictions in our current belief system is how we grow morally, ethically, and spiritually. If you feel that your beliefs do not have to be "logical" in order to be true, why do you believe that? What arguments would you present to prove that logic is not necessary? All belief systems have at their root basic logical assumptions, even religious beliefs. "Blind faith" is not really blind at all. It is a decision one makes, with eyes wide open, to accept someone else's belief system, rather than one's own, without fully understanding the logic behind it or the underlying premises on which it is based. Why would anyone want to become a Christian if there are no good "reasons" to do so? Sadly, most people cling to illogical and harmful belief systems mainly due emotional dependence and fear. Reason, common sense, and logic should lie at the foundation of your religious belief system. My faith in the Gospel of Christ is stronger today that it was years ago, mainly because it is no longer illogical and self-contradictory. According to the Bible, perfect love casts out fear, and God is love. If you can believe that, then you don't need to be afraid to ask the tough questions. Don't be afraid of the answers you might find. All truth is God's truth. Jesus is the way, the TRUTH, and the life. If God is love, He will continue to love you, no matter what.

The "Lie Question"

When I was in College, nearly 50 years ago, my psychology professor had the whole class take a personality assessment test. Several of the questions in this were called "lie questions," the purpose of which was to determine whether the test subject was answering truthfully all of the questions on the test. They were all "forced choice" questions, meaning that only a "yes," or "no" answer was permitted. You couldn't answer "maybe," or "most of the time," or "most probably," and so on.

Here is one of the lie questions: "If you were passing by a movie theatre showing a movie you really wanted to see, and you were able to walk into the movie unseen, without buying a ticket, would you do so?" The presumption was that most people would walk in, without paying, under those circumstances. Well, I answered "no" to the question. I did not answer truthfully. I gave what I believed was the "best" or "right" answer, but it was not the truthful one. Well, if I had answered untruthfully to enough of those cleverly disguised "lie questions," then the results of the test would have been nullified and thrown out. The presumption was that if I answered the "lie questions" untruthfully, I was probably answering many of the other questions untruthfully, as well.

If I were to take the same test again today, I would be able to "truthfully" answer "no" to the same question. There are two reasons for this. First, the cost of admission, at this point in my life, is trivial. Second, and most important, regardless of the cost of admission, purchasing a ticket is the right thing to do, and I am able to fully empathize with the owner and employees of the theatre. They deserve to earn a fair return/wage on their investment of time and money into that business. I was a business owner myself for many years, and I now know how hard it is to succeed in any business. I have also been cheated and swindled out of some pretty large sums of money in my earlier years. On many occasions I was cheated by men who presented themselves to me as ardent Christians. About twelve years ago, despite the best of intentions, and a lot of very hard work, I went through an utterly humiliating bankruptcy, which was the result of many bad financial decisions. I know what it's like to be on the receiving end of business failure and financial loss.

Since then, I have made a remarkable financial recovery, due, in no small part, to the lessons I learned from those previous failures and losses. My relationship with God is also much stronger as a result of those struggles.

Would the moral and ethical decisions you make in life be different if you knew no one was watching, not even God? If you knew for absolute sure that Heaven, Hell, and God did not exist, would you still be the same loving, kind and generous person that you are currently (cough, choke)? I know this is counterintuitive, but might there be some benefit to having the freedom to make decisions in life without feeling like God is watching over you, rewarding you for every good thing you do and punishing you for every wrong choice you make? I believe that God loves us unconditionally, and will "save" us all, regardless of how good or bad we are. It is all based on grace, which I would define as "underserved" love. There is absolutely no room for boasting.

This does not mean that we do not pay a price for our misdeeds. God does give us the freedom to suffer, as well as enjoy, the earthly consequences of our actions. The reason He gives us this freedom is that we may learn from those experiences and become better able to empathize with those who are less fortunate than ourselves. The life we live in the flesh is like a "crucible" or "furnace" by which we are refined and purified. All of God's judgments have the purpose of cleansing us from sinful attitudes and behavior

I am here to tell you that God does not want you to be good because He is standing over you with rewards in one hand and a club in the other. He wants you to be good because you have become a genuinely good person on the inside.

Who's really in charge here?

No one splits hairs more than I, when it comes to Bible interpretation and theology. At the same time, we need to distinguish between what is "essential" or "foundational" and what is not. I am referring to basic truths of Scripture on which most can agree. At the same time, I believe that "diversity" of thought and opinion is a good thing. It keeps us humble, knowing that we ourselves do not have all the right answers. If we can become like children and just focus on God's love and love him back, and try to live our lives accordingly, we can find great happiness and joy in our lives and our worship of God, and are freed from fear of what might happen to us if we get some of the "finer nuances" of theology wrong.

When I was in college, a Christian friend, who was also a skeptic, asked me this question. If those who reject Christ spend eternity in Hell, what happens if a native in Africa gets a "lousy missionary," and rejects Christ because the message was presented in the wrong way? Well, at that time, I had no answer for him. Today, I would answer in this way. No one will be going to Hell, or Heaven because of anything I do or say. No one should have to live with that burden. Some word or action on my part might be the immediate, or "surface" cause of someone accepting or rejecting Christ, but the underlying cause is God, the Holy Spirit. It all boils down to our belief in the Sovereignty of God. Who is really in charge? In whose hands does the destiny of our souls rest, God's or ours? This is another way of approaching the old Calvinism vs. Arminianism debate. The Calvinists are right about the sovereignty of God, and the Arminians are right about God's good intentions for all mankind.

Principles of good scripture interpretation

Quoting a scripture, that has more than one reasonable interpretation, in order to support one's particular point of view, proves nothing at all. And it makes no sense to suggest that the opposing point of view is not supported by Scripture. Being inspired by the Holy Spirit does not guarantee error-free interpretation of the Bible, otherwise we would not be hearing a variety of opposing points of view being preached from the pulpits across America, and everywhere else, by so-called "inspired" preachers who got their "inspired" message directly from the same source (ie. the Bible through the Holy Spirit). It flies in the face of logic. Most of the dogmas of the Christian evangelicals are derived not directly from an impartial study of the Scriptures, but instead from traditions that have been passed down over the centuries. The main reason for this is the threat of "excommunication" or "eternal punishment in Hell" for deviating, even in the slightest way, from established dogma.

This all sounds very complicated, the truth of the matter is simpler than one might expect. Jesus said that unless we become like children we won't enter the Kingdom. All that the children of Jesus' day knew, theologically speaking, was that Jesus loved them, and they loved Him back. Each aspect of most “statements of faith” may be given a variety of detailed and highly specific "interpretations," any one of which may be used as a means of excluding most of the human race from the salvation that God has provided for all on Calvary. We especially see this in the first few ecumenical councils of the church in the 4th and 5th Centuries AD. Prior those councils, there were many, many different descriptions relating to who Jesus was/is, exactly. Was he fully divine or fully human, or both, or something in between. There were many different views on this, all derived from Scripture. It was decided at these councils that you would be condemned to Hell for all eternity unless you subscribed to only one highly detailed and specific point of view.

Good Scripture interpretation does not have to be complicated. It's not rocket science. Here's a good rule of Scripture interpretation. The least important doctrines are the ones that are the most highly disputed. The most important ones are the ones on which most people agree, both Christians and non-Christians. You can boil it all down to the children's song, "Jesus loves me, this I know." Many people, who would never set foot in a Christian church, have a more correct view of the scope of God's love than many "card-carrying" church members. When discussing, and arguing over Christian theology, what parts of the conversation would you want your children to hear.

Separating the sheep from the goats

When the nations were gathered before Christ in Matt. 25, and the sheep were separated from the goats, Jesus didn't ask, "OK, which of you prayed the sinner's prayer before you died?" When the teacher of the law asked Jesus what he must do to inherit eternal (aionian) life (Luke 10), Jesus didn't answer, "simply pray the sinner's prayer." The religion of Jesus is a "way" of life, not a "get-out-of-jail-free card." That is why the early Christians were called "followers of the way." All have been "saved by grace." That happened at Calvary. Now Christ asks us to live accordingly

The love of God

It's odd that Christians can sing this song by Frederick M. Lehman with great emotion, and the same time believe that God gives up on most of humanity and sends them to unending torture in a place called Hell. It distresses me greatly that many of the very people who sing this song have declared me a heretic for believing its words with all my heart.

"The love of God is greater far
Than tongue or pen can ever tell.
It goes beyond the highest star
And reaches to the lowest hell.
The guilty pair, bowed down with care,
God gave His Son to win:
His erring child He reconciled
And pardoned from his sin.

•*O love of God, how rich and pure!*
How measureless and strong!
It shall forevermore endure—
The saints' and angels' song.

•*When hoary time shall pass away,*
And earthly thrones and kingdoms fall;
When men who here refuse to pray,
On rocks and hills and mountains call;
God's love, so sure, shall still endure,
All measureless and strong;
Redeeming grace to Adam's race—
The saints' and angels' song.

•*Could we with ink the ocean fill,*
And were the skies of parchment made;
Were every stalk on earth a quill,
And every man a scribe by trade;
To write the love of God above
Would drain the ocean dry;
Nor could the scroll contain the whole,
Though stretched from sky to sky.

Wisdom should not be equated with certitude.

"The whole problem with the world is that fools and fanatics are always so certain of themselves and wiser people so full of doubts." Bertrand Russell

When I was young I felt cursed by my intellect, because I was unable to "prove" to myself the truth of Christianity. Though I desperately wanted to be "saved," I never felt that I qualified, because I was told over and over again that in order to be saved, one had to "believe." How on earth was one to know what "level" of belief was required, since belief can only be measured in degrees, and is rarely "absolute." The more I tried to believe that the Bible was "inerrant," the more questions I found. The more I tried to understand Christian theology, the more new questions that arose in my mind. After a lifetime of searching (about 50 years since my spiritually troubled youth), I do believe I have found most of the important answers. However, I still have many more questions than answers. Could it be that honest atheists might be "closer" to God than intellectually dishonest or unthinking evangelicals? Does "theological correctness" have anything at all to do with our "standing" with God.

The best reward for doing good

"So when you give to the needy, do not announce it with trumpets, as the hypocrites do in the synagogues and on the streets, to be honored by others. Truly I tell you, they have received their reward in full." Matt. 6:2

The best reward for doing good is becoming a better person. We can "see" God and future rewards only by faith, not by sight. By definition, an "act of faith" is done in the presence of doubt. Otherwise we would not call it "faith," but "certainty." Of the three examples below, who do you feel is making the most progress towards the goal of becoming like Christ?

1. The church member who tithes to the church, knowing that God will "open up the windows of heaven" (as in Malachi) and bless him financially in greater measure than what was given.

2. The seeker who gives his life to Christ in order to escape the torments of Hell and go to Heaven after death.

3. The agnostic who joins the Peace Corps because he/she genuinely wants to help people.

I do believe that one of the reasons that God "hides Himself" from us, and does not provide us with absolute "certainty" on all doctrinal matters, is so that we might more easily become good simply for goodness sake. He wants us to be good, not for immediate or future rewards, but because we have actually become good people.

I know this is controversial, but I believe that even Christ had to live with a degree of uncertainty while on Earth, hence the agonizing outpouring of grief in His prayer at Gethsemane.

Is God the author of sin and evil?

We are all prone to sin and helpless to avoid it. That's the way we're made. We are born with basically selfish desires. Babies are very self-centered and selfish by nature. They need to be taught to be unselfish and put the needs of others before their own. Evolutionists would say that our innate selfishness is a "survival" mechanism. So, in that sense you could say there is an obvious need for God to make us that way. Unfortunately, this basic "survival" mechanism also leads to sin, when we "harm" others for our own benefit. Obviously, God wants us all to rise above our basic "carnal" desires and learn to love God and others unselfishly. So, while our natural built-in selfishness serves a good purpose, from a "survival" of the species standpoint, God created us for more than just survival. So this built-in selfishness also serves the higher purpose of creating the circumstances that result in our need for His love and forgiveness.

There would be no merit in doing good if we were not also capable of doing bad. One benefit of this is that in our fallenness, we most appreciate God's love and mercy. To fully appreciate God's love and forgiveness, we must first find ourselves in need of it. I just don't see where God's perfect nature is diminished in any way when He creates us with a built-in need for His love and forgiveness. As a matter of fact, I think it's an act of pure genius on His part. We cannot find true happiness and fulfillment except in union with our Savior God. God created us with a "built-in" need for a loving relationship with Him.

What about Hitler?

Believe it or not, God loves Hitler just as much as He does anyone else. Have you ever heard the phrase, "There, but for the grace of God, go I?" If you had the same genetics and life experiences as Hitler, you might well have made many of same bad decisions as he. Christ died for all, and He saves all. The worse our "sin" condition, the more glory we give to God for our salvation. Most people resist the doctrine of universal reconciliation because they believe that people like Hitler "deserve" to go to Hell for all eternity. Conversely, they must also believe that they, on the other hand, "deserve" to go to heaven. Well, you can't have it both ways. If we are saved by grace, apart from works, so must Hitler become saved in the same manner. Christ made atonement for the sins of everyone on Calvary, including Hitler. It might take a bit longer for Hitler to "work out his salvation," but God will get the job done. It is God who saves us, and not we ourselves. God has all "eternity" (age upon age) to get the job done. One day, at the end of the ages, death will finally be abolished, and Christ will have drawn every last individual to Himself, as He promised He would, and we will all be presented "faultless before the throne of God," and God will be "all in all." See Ephesians 2:8,9, John 12:32, Philippians 2:10-11, Ephesians 1:9-10, and especially 1 Corinthians 15:22-28.

The first word of the Gospel

The first word of the Gospel is "repent." Most places where Jesus and His disciples went, the first words out of their mouths were "repent for the Kingdom of Heaven is at hand." The Gospel of Christ should not be equated with the false message, "turn or burn forever." Instead, it should be worded, "turn or face the righteous judgments of God," the purpose of which are to eventually bring everyone to repentance and entrance into the Kingdom. The Gospel of Christ is "good news" for everyone (Christ died for all), though some (actually all of us) will be required to experience a measure of God's "tough love" before entering the Kingdom. When I speak of entering the Kingdom, I speak a bit metaphorically (as did Jesus, I believe). We are not talking about a physical kingdom or a "place" that is separate from everywhere else. Entering the Kingdom should be equated with a process of submitting oneself to the rule of Christ in one's heart and deepening one's relationship with God. We are currently living in the Kingdom Age.

Pantheism and the immanence of God

In my view, there is a very fine line between pantheism and the traditional Christian view of God as both immanent and transcendent. I believe this is why we have such difficulty understanding exactly who Jesus was/is. We read in John 1 that the Word (Jesus) was "with" God which implies a separate existence and a distinctly separate personality. The verse doesn't actually say He, at the same time, "was" God. The literal translation is this: "What God was, the Word was." In other words, Jesus was made out of the same "stuff" as God, but was/is not actually "God Himself."

I would speculate, at the same time, however, that God is all there is. He is omni-present. The universe, right down to the smallest sub-atomic wave of energy, is infused by God. All creation is a part of God in the sense that we came from God and are not technically separated from God. He is omnipresent.

Jesus said that He was one with the Father and that we have the same potential. Although we are at the same time distinct and different from God, one day we will all become like Christ, and God will be *"all in all."* When Jesus became incarnate, according to Philippians, he *"emptied"* himself , in a manner of speaking, and divested himself of many of his God-like qualities. These qualities and attributes were all restored to him when he ascended back to heaven. It is quite likely that Jesus, especially as a child, was not fully aware of his divine nature and his status as the only begotten son of God. Although, he was, by nature made up of God parts (begotten of God), in his subjective consciousness he was not fully aware of this connection. The Bible says he *"grew in wisdom and stature and in favor with God and man."*

Just as Christ was made of "God parts," so we are made of "Christ parts" because the world and everything in it were created by and through Christ. So, we are part of Christ, and Christ is part of God. Christian salvation, in my view, is an ages-long process of discovering and experiencing our true nature as children of God in Christ. We are made from God's and Christ's DNA, so to speak.

The sovereignty of God

Romans 9:16-18 *"It does not, therefore, depend on human desire or effort, but on God's mercy. For Scripture says to Pharaoh: "I raised you up for this very purpose, that I might display my power in you and that my name might be proclaimed in all the earth." Therefore God has mercy on whom he wants to have mercy, and he hardens whom he wants to harden. One of you will say to me: "Then why does God still blame us? For who is able to resist his will?"*

Romans 11:30-32 *"30 Just as you who were at one time disobedient to God have now received mercy as a result of their disobedience, so they too have now become disobedient in order that they too may now receive mercy as a result of God's mercy to you. For God has bound everyone over to disobedience so that he may have mercy on them all."*

God is the "first cause" of everything. Everything that happens happens because God's wills it. This is even true with respect to our *"disobedience."* Everything happens for a purpose. No one is able to resist God's will. The purpose of evil is that God's power and love might be manifest. God has *"bound everyone over to disobedience so that He may have mercy on them all."*

If you carefully read Romans 9-11 (the favorite Bible passage of Calvinists), from beginning to end, you can easily see how God's *"election"* fits into the overall picture. He has created some vessels for honor, and some for dishonor. He uses the nation of Israel, Jacob and Esau, and Pharoah as examples. He *"elected"* (ie. *"chose"*) the nation of Israel as His vessel of honor to be a *light to the nations*. Then God turned the tables and hardened their hearts, and Jews became vessels of dishonor, which was the occasion of bringing salvation to the Gentiles. Eventually, in the fullness of time, God will turn the tables again and *"all Israel will be saved."*

God, *"who desires all people to be saved and to come to the knowledge of the truth,"* (1 Tim. 2:4) will most certainly accomplish this, *"for who is able to resist His will?"*

The judgments in Matt. 24 and 25

I believe that the Olivet Discourse (Matt. 24) refers to the destruction of Jerusalem in AD 70, but not necessarily the parables. There was an "earthly" judgment that fell upon the nation of Israel in AD 70. Beyond that, there is a judgment we all face after death. The separation of the sheep from the goats in Matthew 25 is symbolic of the kind of judgment we all face in this life and after death. It is not, however, a separation of Christians from non-Christians. Both Christians (those who acknowledged Christ as Lord) and non-Christians (those who comforted and aided the "least" of Christ's brethren, without realizing they were at the same time serving Christ) were treated impartially during this judgment. Those who were "sent away" to "aionian chastisement" included both Christians and non-Christians. This parable should not be taken literally. My take on it is that each of us will be rewarded for the good that we do and judged for our misdeeds. Our attitudes will also be judged. In other words, a good deed, which was done for wrong motive, will actually be judged negatively. I believe the judgment will take many forms, including self-judgment, the reaping of various rewards and punishments, and the requirement of making restitution and seeking forgiveness from those we have harmed.

The real reason most Christians resist universalism

Most Christians resist the doctrine of universal reconciliation because they don't feel that everyone "deserves" to go to heaven and/or be forgiven. They believe there are two kinds of people, "good" people and "bad" people, and only two eternal destinies, Heaven or Hell. That would put Jesus in Hell forever, because He said that He was not good, only the Father in Heaven. The reality is that people are not innately good or bad. All are the same in the eyes of God. He is not a respecter of persons. He loves all equally. Bad thoughts lead to bad actions. Jesus taught that it all begins in the heart. What differentiates us is our level of ignorance of who we really are (in Christ) and how much God really loves us, and how much more wonderful our lives could be if we would yield ourselves to His leading. If we could put ourselves in the place of an enemy, or someone we despise, and be able to understand why they think and feel as they do, we wouldn't be so quick to rush to judgment. While suffering horribly on the cross of Calvary, Jesus asked God to forgive His tormentors, *"because they don't know what they are doing."* I believe God answered that prayer in the affirmative.

Faith and reason

Ever since childhood, I was unable to believe the scriptures with absolute conviction because so much of what I read did not square with reason, especially many of the stories in Genesis. Now that I have come to understand the truths of Scripture in a different way, I can cling to them with great conviction. My faith in God is so much stronger as a result. The Bible is an amazing document, inspired by God, yet written by fallible human beings. When you add a bit of common sense and reason to the equation, the important truths become self-evident. Earlier in my life, I felt that my intellectual approach to matters was a spiritual disadvantage, because it prevented me from believing the Bible at face value. Now, I believe that my intellect is a wonderful gift from God that has enabled me to understand and believe many truths about God, mainly His unconditional love for all of mankind, which many so-called "Bible-believing" Christians are unable to accept.

The key to successful Christian living

We need to know that God loves us and accepts us as we are. We all have "sins" that we are not yet willing to let go of. Destructive behaviors are like "addictions" that are extremely difficult to overcome. And it seems that no matter how hard we try to be better, there is always more that we could do. We deal not only with "sins" of "commission" but also with sins of "omission." I had the hardest time earlier in my life learning to believe that God wanted to bless me despite my unwillingness and/or inability to live up to what I have now come to realize are impossible standards. I do believe the Apostle Paul was onto something as he repeatedly emphasized the fact that our standing with God is based on grace rather than good works. Technically, in the words of Paul, *"all things are lawful."* God doesn't hold our sins against us. Successful Christian living flows from our relationship with God. It's not the other way around. Although I hate much of Augustine's theology, he hit the nail on the head when someone asked him how to make correct moral decisions. He answered, "Love God and do as you please." First God loves us and saves us. Then He helps us deal with our sin. It's not the other way around. He loves to give good gifts to His children. When we look up at Him and pour out our soul to Him and ask for His blessings and help, it melts His heart. Yes, God has emotions. He will always give us, in those moments, exactly what we need.

Where good theology begins

Take delight in the Lord, and He will give you the desires of your heart. I believe it pleases God for us to have a loving relationship with Him. It pleases God to give good things to His children and answer our cries for help, when life becomes too much for us to handle. If we are going to establish and maintain a healthy and loving relationship with God, it must be based on grace, not works. That is not to say that good works are not important, but we be begin with grace. We begin by establishing that loving relationship. We begin by recognizing that God is more loving and kind than any human father.

Why you can never win an argument with an ardent fundamentalist.

The most devout and brilliant theologians in the world, even Christian fundamentalists, do agree on many of those so-called fundamental truths. Nevertheless, many Christian fundamentalists insist that the beggar on the streets of Calcutta, because does not correctly understand and believe in those fundamentals before he dies, will be tortured in Hell for all eternity. There is no use in explaining to these fundamentalists that this is not logical. Instead of presenting logical argument to defend their position, they will simply tell you that logic is the enemy of faith, and that faith always trumps logic on important theological issues. This is why you will never win the argument.

Why atheists hate Christianity

The fundamentalist view of a vengeful and cruel deity provides rich fodder for militant atheists. I once heard a panelist on the TV show hosted by Madeline Murray O'Hair, say this: "The Christian God hides from view and makes it very difficult for people to believe in Him, and then condemns to everlasting torture in Hell all those who don't." That statement really shook me up and bothered me for the rest of my life, until I finally changed my theology and my view of God. If Christians are ever to fully "evangelize" the world, they are going to have to start preaching the "good news" of the true Gospel, that God is the Father of all and loves us all unconditionally. Can you imagine how differently non-Christians and atheists would view Christianity if we were to do this?

My view of Bible inspiration

I don't believe God is good because the Bible says God is good. I believe the Bible when it says God is good.

Why does God permit sin and suffering?

One law of physics states that for every action there is an equal and opposite reaction. You can call it Karma or you can call it the law of sowing and reaping. Our life in the flesh is a learning experience. Some things can't be learned by the acquisition of second-hand knowledge. For example, we know that if we touch a hot shove we will be burned and it will be painful, but we have not really learned this until we actually touch the stove and are burnt by it. It's one thing to know about love. It is quite another to actually experience it. We cannot truly experience love until we find ourselves in need of it. True Agape, self-sacrificing, love can only be experienced in the midst of some kind of suffering or need. Just existing in a purely spiritual state in perfect communion with God in the heavenlies cannot teach us these lessons. So God, in His infinite wisdom, has placed us in this crucible of our earthly existence, so that we can learn first-hand, through actual human interactions, just how much pain sinful actions and attitudes cause to ourselves and others. We also learn and experience first-hand God's love and forgiveness, and the joy that results from loving and helping others. These feelings of love and joy are intensified when we finally emerge on the other side and are able to contrast where we have arrived with where we have been. Someone once asked the marathon runner why he endures so much pain to finish the 26-mile course. His response, "because it feels so good when I stop." Romans 11:32: *"For God has bound everyone over to disobedience so that he may have mercy on them all."*

The moral dilemma of compartmentalization

We are not normally disturbed by the misfortunes of others unless we actually make physical contact with them. While leaving choir rehearsal one night, I walked past a man who was sitting in the doorway of the church in much distress. He was a mess and would not make eye contact with anyone as we walked past him on our way out. A minute or two after I drove away, my conscience got the best of me and I circled back and eventually found him outside on the other side of the church crying uncontrollably. He said his wife just kicked him out for the last time and he had walked about 15 miles from there to where he now was. He was filthy and unkempt and apparently all of his worldly possessions fit in a very small knapsack. Both he and his wife, who were on public assistance, were addicted to drugs, fought all the time, and he was prone to violence. To make matters worse, she has a small child. I couldn't persuade him to let me take him back home or anywhere for help. Eventually he walked away and didn't want me to follow. I did anyway, gave him some money, and left him there in the freezing cold. I felt so helpless.

Of course, I was emotionally devastated by this. At the same time, I was reminded that the world is full of such people, and almost 100% of the time, I do not actually care at all, and feel no strong emotions about the plight of the homeless, as I did this evening. It reminds me of the Gaither chorus, singing and praising the Lord, with huge smiles on their faces, and at the same time believing that most of the rest of the world is going to suffer eternal torment in Hell. We do tend to compartmentalize our lives and our feelings, and tend to concern ourselves only with those people with whom we come into close physical proximity.

I'm not saying this is right or wrong. It only illustrates why people are able to believe in eternal torment in Hell for most of humanity, without being bothered by it.

Just so you know, the way I decided to handle my moral dilemma with respect to what happened last night was to become a regular contributor to the Jesus Center, in a town nearby, whose mission it is to minister to people like the one I was personally unable to help that night.

What is the true message of Calvary?

It is assumed by most Christians that the atonement that took place on Calvary somehow changed the way God deals with our sin. According to Newton's laws of motion, for every action, there is an equal and opposite reaction. The same can be said of our moral and ethical choices. According to the Scriptures, sin has negative consequences, and righteous attitudes and deeds have positive consequences. Sometimes this is referred to the "law of sowing and reaping," which Jesus clearly taught. It is assumed by Christian evangelicals that, on Calvary, Jesus paid the price of our sins, resulting in an exemption from the law of sowing and reaping for believers. The idea is that Jesus was "punished" for our sins, in our place, thereby removing the negative consequences of our sin. To qualify for this special exemption, one must repent of one's sins and acknowledge Christ as Savior and Lord. At the same time, most Christian evangelicals believe that, even as born again Christians, God still lovingly chastises and corrects us, and allows us to suffer the negative consequences of our sins, at least during our temporal lives here on earth.

If Christ's death and resurrection on Calvary did not remove all negative consequences of sin, exactly what was accomplished? According to the Apostle Paul, the "wages of sin is death." Jesus death on Calvary did not remove all consequences of sin, which have the purpose of correction and remediation. Instead, what was removed at Calvary was the single consequence of spiritual death, or what I would refer to as a loss of our connection with God. Of course, God is omnipresent. He is never far from any of us, not even the worst of sinners. Spiritual death may best be defined as a subjective feeling of isolation from God, not real, but only imagined.

What God accomplished on Calvary is to demonstate to the world that He loves us unconditionally, in spite of our sins, and that nothing can separate us from His love, not even physical death. Not all have received and internalized the message of Calvary, and as a result, not all are spiritually alive. Not yet, anyway. The Bible clearly teaches that eventually all will be made alive in Christ. Eventually, if not in this life, then most certainly in the next, all will come to the subjective realization that God loves them and has never left them.

Why I am a Universalist

1. Universalism is fully supported by the Scriptures.

2. Regardless of whether works or faith, or a combination of both, are required for salvation, they do not exist as absolutes, and can only be measured as points on a continuum. So, it is impossible to categorize individuals as "saved" or "not saved" and spending eternity in only one of two possible states, ie. saved or lost,

3. Regardless of whether you believe in determinism or free will, it appears that our decisions are strongly, if not completely, influenced by "external" forces. Nothing is self-caused. Therefore, it makes absolutely no sense that anyone should be punished eternally for the choices they make.

4. The only way that God's justice can be compatible with His loving and all-powerful nature, is for His justice to be tempered with mercy and restoration.

5. No decent human being would punish anyone infinitely for temporal crimes, and God must be greater, better and more loving than any human.

Scriptural inerrancy vs. progressive revelation

For the most part, our view of God today is quite different from that of the ancient Hebrews. Their view of God was a mixture of truth and error. It would be logical to conclude that the history on which their notions about God are based are also a mixture of truth and error, ie. pious fiction. The religious and cultural identity of the Hebrews and, by extension, modern day Christians, is deeply rooted in those ancient legends. Consequently, proponents of Biblical inerrancy must deal with many contradictory and paradoxical religious doctrines. In order to resolve these contradictions, one must break free of the literalism and try to identify the progression of thought that we see in Bible history.

Valuable lessons are often learned through a process of trial and error, and this is evident in the lessons learned by the Nation of Israel and the Christian Church throughout history. Even the teachings of Christ and the Apostles that we find in the New Testament have no doubt been somewhat distorted by a degree of historical revision.

It is unsettling for most of us to realize that the particular religious doctrines that form the basis of our purpose in life, including our final destiny after death, are based on an imperfect document. It is helpful for me to understand that our view of perfection may not be the same as God's. A vessel does not have to be perfectly shaped, and free from surface cracks, to be perfectly suited for holding water. It apparently suits God to accomplish His goals for mankind through imperfect human intermediaries. He does almost nothing directly. We have been given the privilege of being used by God to accomplish His purposes, despite our weakness and imperfections.

Why we sometimes react strongly against "incorrect" theology

Many Christians, even universalists, react very negatively to certain doctrines or beliefs related to predestination vs. free will, Scripture inerrancy, the Trinity, soul sleep after death, homosexuality, and so on. As universalists, these issues should not be as bothersome, because we all believe that in the end things will work out well for everyone.

I think the reasons why emotions are so strong in some of these areas is that they all relate in some way to the authority and inspiration of Scripture. An attack on one of these controversial doctrines might be regarded as an attack on Scripture. Some universalists are universalists only because of what the Scriptures teach. Others are universalists because of extra-biblical sources of information, such as intuition, common sense, NDE's, and so on, which they feel contradict many teachings of Scripture. Still others, like myself, believe that both the Scriptures and extra-biblical sources may be relied upon, and are not contradictory when correctly analyzed and interpreted.

Some of us get pretty emotional when the foundation of our belief system is directly, or indirectly, challenged. I take great comfort in realizing that God obviously has chosen not to reveal these truths in clear and unambiguous terms. He could have easily accomplished this, if He had so desired. So, in my view, it is perfectly OK to be theologically incorrect. Even atheists would probably agree with us on many of the fundamentals, including basic concepts of morality, generosity, kindness, love, and justice. God has built these values into all of us, although in the case of some, they might be buried deep within the subconscious mind and not outwardly known or expressed. God's Holy Spirit is a Spirit of truth. In the end, the whole and complete truth will be known to all. Christian salvation is a process that occurs gradually over time.

Fear-based religion discourages independence of thought.

The average pew sitter has appallingly little knowledge of the Bible, and spends almost no time at all seeking answers to the tough theological questions. Most are not even capable of asking good questions. They would rather have their pastor and teachers do their thinking for them. The problem is most pastors and teachers accept, without much critical thought at all, what their pastors and teachers taught them, and so on. So, we've got the blind leading the blind, so to speak. That is not always such a terrible thing, because there is a lot of good theology mixed in with the bad, and because of this, most Christians, are still able to make good life decisions. Somehow, God is able to get the important truths across to us, despite our confusion over many theological issues. We instinctively know right from wrong, that it is better to love than hate, and so on. Most instinctively know that God exists and rewards those who seek to do His will. Most are not very adept at logic and reason, but that's OK. The heart has reasons that reason cannot know. God will fill in the gaps in our knowledge soon enough.

God's self-adjusting universe

In a manner of speaking, does not evil punish itself? Has God not set moral laws in motion, by which we sow what we reap? Could it be that the chastisement and correction by God might happen, not directly by his hand, but would instead result from the laws He has set in motion? Conversely, would not goodness and love create their own rewards in our hearts? God has created a universe which is to a great extent self-adjusting.

The price of our sins

We do pay a price for our sins. The law of sowing and reaping still applies to "born again" Christians. Christ's sacrifice on Calvary did not remove the need for God to "chasten those whom He loves." I see the message of Calvary not as means of removing the penalties associated with our sins, but as removing the single consequence of a perceived "separation" or "isolation" from God that result from feelings of guilt that are associated with our sin. I would define the "death" penalty for sin, not as eternal Hell, but as a kind of "spiritual death" or feeling of abandonment and isolation from God, which is only our subjective perception, not an actual reality from God's point of view. It is possible that Christ actually "experienced" this on Calvary on behalf of whole of humanity. Or, perhaps, this was more of a demonstration of God's love, instead. Regardless of how you view the atonement, Christ did not suffer vindictive retribution from God for the sins of mankind. God never has, and never will, punish us in this way. Instead, He allows us to suffer the natural consequences of our sin, one of which is "spiritual death." These consequences are removed for those who turn to Calvary and turn to God for forgiveness and receive the wonderful "gift" of eternal (age abiding) life, which I would define as "fellowship with God" in this life and the next.

The problem with pragmatism

The problem with Christian evangelicalism is that while it works very well for some, it doesn't work at all for others. This has to do with the foundation on which one's faith in God is built. Many evangelical Christians are very passionate about their faith and derive huge benefit from it. They are able to passionately love God and devote their lives to Him. God's work in their lives, and in the lives of people they know, provides validation for their belief system. Pragmatically speaking, many of them believe it primarily because it works.

Christian evangelicalism did not work for me, on the other hand, because I could not convince myself that it was objectively true. For me, the fact that Christianity worked well for many of its adherents did not validate the truth of their belief system. It has been said that ignorance is bliss. It is easy for me to understand how genuine bliss can result from a faulty belief system. If a con artist convinces you that he is going to make you very rich, you will indeed become very happy about that. On the other hand, if you know the Con artist is lying to you, the result will be doubt and skepticism, not happiness.

I personally could not benefit from a faith in God until after I was able to verify the validity of my belief system as objectively true. In order for that to happen, my beliefs had to square with objective reality, including the external realities of science, history and universal human experience. It also had to be internally consistent with itself and free from logical contradictions.

As a result of my investigations, I discarded the doctrine of Scriptural inerrancy and embraced the doctrine of Christian universalism. In addition, some of the biblical terminology needed to be more carefully and accurately defined, or should I say redefined. Pragmatically speaking, my faith works very well for me, mainly because it based on reason and logic. I still call it faith because nothing can be absolutely proved. The objective facts, however, have made it easier for me to take that "leap" of faith.

The key to correct Scripture interpretation

When interpreting Scripture, it is very important to begin with basic assumptions and premises that are self-evident, universally accepted, and consistent with common sense and logic.

I personally would begin with the existence of a Creator God who is the first cause of everything that exists. Additionally, God, by definition, must exist outside of the created space-time universe. In order to exist outside the boundaries of the physical universe, the creator must be a spiritual and not a physical being. I would also have to believe that God is good, not evil. I believe this because it is universally believed by virtually all mankind, except for a few whom most would consider mentally unbalanced. The truth of God's goodness is attested in the sacred scriptures of virtually every world religion. Because the creator is obviously greater than any created being, He must possess the highest and noblest qualities of human character to a greater degree than any human being. It is universally agreed upon by almost everyone that these qualities of character include love, kindness, justice, mercy and forgiveness. God is therefore more loving, kind and just than any human being.

Our belief in the truth and validity of the Christian Scriptures must be based on the above self-evident truths, and not on any internal claims made by the Scriptures themselves. The doctrine of Scriptural inerrancy is not self-evident. The Scriptures are a compilation of man-made stories and opinions about God. They were not written by the direct hand of God. The truths contained in the Bible come to us through the filter of imperfect human understanding. Because the Bible is an imperfect document, great care must be taken when evaluating and interpreting the truths contained in it. For example, we shouldn't believe God is good because the Bible says so. Instead, we should believe the Bible when it describes God as being good. If one of the Bible characters or narratives portrays God as unloving, unfair, or unjust, then we must reject that teaching or dig a little deeper to see if that is what the writer is really saying.

It has been argued by Christian fundamentalists that if the entire Bible is not completely true, accurate and inerrant in every respect, then none of it can be trusted. The claim is made that if the Bible contains a mixture of truth and error there would be no way to authoritatively determine which parts to believe and which parts to reject. The problem with this line of reasoning is that by all objective scientific, historical and logical standards of evaluation, the Bible is full of errors and contradictions. Separating truth from error in the Scriptures, however, is not as difficult as you might expect. Those teachings which are consistent with what we know to be the true character of God, as described above, may be accepted. Those teachings which are inconsistent with the true character of God must either be rejected or reinterpreted in ways that would resolve the discrepancies.

The Christian Bible may absolutely be relied upon as a source of information about the nature of God and how we may relate to him, but it must be studied and interpreted with respect to the historical, linguistic and cultural context in which it was written. Unfortunately, due in no small part to mistranslations in the text and a misguided belief in literal inerrancy, modern Christian evangelical theology is full of blatant contradictions relating to the nature and character of God. When properly understood and interpreted, however, the Bible contains the highest expressions of truth about God ever written, culminating in the life and teachings of Jesus Christ.

Mathematical proof that we have always existed

Many times in the past, during my morning runs, I have contemplated the nature of my existence and the sheer improbability of my being alive and consciously self-aware at this exact point in time. I cannot imagine or comprehend the possibility of the annihilation and subsequent non-existence of my consciousness. Intuitively, I know that the true nature of my existence is spiritual, not physical. No matter how hard I try, I am not able to believe that the non-existence of my soul is even possible.

We all know that the space-time universe which we are now experiencing is finite, not infinite, in size and duration. It had a beginning in time, and linear time as we know it has only existed since the big bang. Outside of the known universe there must exist an infinite, timeless realm of a Creator God, whose existence has no beginning or end. God is an infinite being. He is also a spiritual being, and all of His created offspring (that would be us) are spiritual beings as well. Technically, because we are spiritual beings, our "real selves" actually reside outside of this finite physical universe, in a timeless realm called Heaven by some.

I believe it can be mathematically proven that we have always existed. All we have to do is try and calculate the odds against our being physically alive and self-aware during the 100 years or so of our current earthly existence.

The odds of my being alive during my current 100-year lifespan are less than 100 in 14 billion (the approximate age of the universe). That would be expressed as the fraction 1/140 million. Those are pretty slim odds, about the same odds as winning the state lottery. Of course, you would have to multiply those odds by the odds of a particular sperm and egg coming together to create me, at a particular moment in time during the 14 billion year history of the universe. Those odds may be expressed as the fraction 1/one cajillion cajillion. I'm sure you catch my drift.

In addition, you would have to multiply those odds against the probability of a planet existing in the universe that is even capable of supporting life. According to astrophysicist Dr. Hugh Ross, those odds are less than one in a hundred thousand trillion, trillion, trillion, trillion, trillion. Those odds were calculated by multiplying the individual probabilities of over 75 criteria that must be satisfied for a planet existing that can support life. To be honest, it is beyond my mathematical ability to multiply that fraction by the fraction given in the previous paragraph of 1/one cajillion cajillion.

I'm sure that with a little thought you could come up with many more conditions that must be met in order for me to exist at this particular point in time. Multiplied by one another, the odds against my being alive and consciously self-aware today are very nearly infinitely great.

If it is true, however, as many quantum theoretical physicists attest, that my consciousness actually resides in a timeless realm outside of the observable universe, then it may be deduced that I have always existed. The odds of my being consciously self-aware in this point in time are zero, unless my consciousness has always been in existence independently from my physical body.

Is man basically good or evil?

Well, that depends on which "man" you are talking about, the spiritual man or the carnal (fleshly) man, the inner man or the outer man, our immortal soul (ie. spirit) or our fleshly physical body (including our physical brain). We were all created in the image of God, and at the innermost core of our being we are made of the same stuff as God, who is spirit. Our spirits, or souls, are basically good, because God is good and we are made of "God parts."

The Apostle Paul explains it this way in Romans 7 and 8. He says that he was once "alive" apart from the law, but when the commandment came (ie. the knowledge of good and evil), sin sprang to life and he "died."

Romans 7:9: *"Once I was alive apart from the law; but when the commandment came, sin sprang to life and I died."*

What Paul is saying here is that we all start out as spiritual beings and are spiritually alive and free from sin. (There is no such thing as "original sin.") When Paul talks about "life" and "death" here, he is obviously not talking about physical life and death. When Paul "died" as a result of his sin, he did not die physically. Spiritual life and death refer to our relationship with God, which is severed when we fall into sin. When we die spiritually, we lose touch with our connection with God in our innermost selves, and allow ourselves to be controlled instead by our physical, fleshly natures.

Paul further explains that when he fell into sin it was not his true inner self that was doing this. Paul identifies his "sinful nature" as the one who is really committing those sins. Each of us has two natures, our spiritual nature and our physical or fleshly nature. The saying of Jesus is very true that *"the spirit is willing but the flesh is weak."* (Matt. 26:41)

Romans 7:17-18: *"As it is, it is no longer I myself who do it but is is sin living in me. I know that nothing good lives in me, that is, in my sinful nature. For I have the desire to do what is good, but I cannot carry it out."*

Paul then explains that in his "inner being" he delights in God's law, but another part of him, his fleshly nature has imprisoned him. In his *"mind"* (ie. his human spirit or Godly nature) he is *"alive,"* but in his "sinful nature" he is a slave to sin.

Romans 7:22: *"For in my inner being I delight in God's law; but I see another law at work in the members of my body, waging war against the law of my mind and making me a prisoner of the law of sin at work within my members."*

When the Spirit of Christ indwells us, we are in a sense "reconnected" with our true spiritual nature and are given the power to overcome our fleshly, sinful nature and "live" according to the Spirit of Christ who has enlivened our human spirit and imparted to us "super human" powers.

Romans 8:1-4: *"Therefore, there is now no condemnation for those who are in Christ Jesus because through Christ Jesus the law of the Spirit of life set me free from the law of sin and death."*

We see from this that, according to Paul, Christian salvation has nothing to do with physical life and death. It has nothing to do with physically "living" forever. The *"aionian"* life (literally: *"age abiding"* life) that Christ gives us is something that we experience in the here and now. It's not something that anyone experiences "completely" at any instantaneous moment of time, however. It may best be regarded as a process of transformation that will not be complete until after we die and finally shed these fleshly bodies for good.

A lesson in practical Christianity

What you think and visualize in your mind tends to form its own reality. When we allow the indwelling Spirit of Christ to *"transform us by the renewing of our minds,"* then we literally become new creatures. Old things pass away and all things become new. Christ forgave sins, healed the sick, and even raised the dead, and He said we would be able to do even greater things than He. The key to unlocking this potential within us is to change the way we think. Mental and spiritual healing come first, then comes the emotional and physical healing. Just as there are physical laws that govern our physical universe, there are spiritual and moral laws that govern our relationship with God and others.

The greater reality is this. There is actually no difference between physical and spiritual laws. The physical universe in which we reside is actually not material at all, but instead is spiritual in nature and substance, and it is governed by the universal consciousness (Spirit) of

God in combination with our own consciousness (human spirit). God does not reside apart from His created universe. He dwells within it (and within us), holds it all together, and is in direct control of every aspect of it. When we allow the Spirit of God to exercise control over our human spirit, nothing will be impossible to us. It doesn't matter what our desires might be, whether physical or spiritual in nature. If we can learn to control our thinking, we truly can achieve the desires of our heart.

We do this through prayer and meditation. As a practical exercise, I would encourage you to meditate on the following Scripture passages several times a day, and pour out your heart to God. Ask Him for whatever you want for (1) yourself, (2) those whom you love, and finally for (3) those whom you ought to love.

Proverbs 23:7a: *"For as he thinketh in his heart, so is he. . ."*

Romans 12:2: *"Do not conform to the pattern of this world, but be transformed by the renewing of your mind. Then you will be able to test and approve what God's will is--his good, pleasing and perfect will."*

Philippians 4:8: *"Finally, brothers and sisters, whatever is true, whatever is noble, whatever is right, whatever is pure, whatever is lovely, whatever is admirable--if anything is excellent or praiseworthy--think about such things."*

Proverbs 3:5-6: *"Trust in the LORD with all your heart and do not lean on your own understanding. In all your ways acknowledge Him, and He will make your paths straight."*

Psalm 37:3-4: *"Trust in the LORD and do good. Dwell in the land and cultivate faithfulness. Delight yourself in the LORD; and He will give you the desires of your heart."*

Psalm 1:1-3: *"Blessed is the one who does not walk in step with the wicked or stand in the way that sinners take or sit in the company of mockers, but whose delight is in the law of the Lord, and who meditates on his law day and night. That person is like a tree planted by streams of water, which yields its fruit in season and whose leaf does not wither. Whatever they do prospers."*

Matthew 6:33: *"But seek first his kingdom and his righteousness, and all these things will be given to you as well."*

We need to give in order to receive

The great motivational speaker, Zig Ziglar, often repeated this formula for success: "If you help enough people get what they want in life, they will help you get what you want." This formula obviously applies to the acquisition of material wealth, but it applies to the acquisition of Heavenly treasures as well. Lasting happiness, peace and contentment, both in this life and the next, result from placing the needs of others ahead of our own.

It is not sinful to seek love, happiness and financial security for ourselves. We are never told in the Scriptures that it is wrong to seek "the good life" for ourselves and our families. It is sinful, however, to covet what does not belong to us and to pursue personal gain without regard for the needs of others. As a practical matter, it so happens that the best way to acquire both material and spiritual wealth is by helping others to find it.

The best way to receive love is to give it out. The best way to receive forgiveness is to be in the habit of forgiving others. The best way to find happiness is to do things that make others happy. The best way to get that job promotion is to unselfishly do more than the job requires. The best way to learn is to become a teacher. The best way to find your way in life is to help others find their way. The best way get the other guy to agree with you is to first find ways to agree with him. And so on.

If you have needs and desires that are not being met, and who of us doesn't, then here is a practical exercise that will help you get what you want and need:

1. Make a list of your needs and desires, and prioritize them. To the right of each item list one unselfish thing you can do for someone else that might help you achieve your goal.

2. Pray about it daily.

3. Meditate on the following verse of Scripture and visualize in your mind what it would be like to have the object(s) of your desire.

"Psalm 37:3-4: *"Trust in the LORD and do good. Dwell in the land and cultivate faithfulness. Delight yourself in the LORD; and He will give you the desires of your heart."*

Little things can make a big difference

I once had an acquaintance in college who was different in one small respect from anyone else I knew back then or have ever known since. You might ask, what was so very special about this person? Well, he wasn't particularly religious, and he posted playboy pictures on the wall of his dorm room, which I thought was quite immoral. Here's why I never forgot him. Every once in a while he would do something nice for one of us, without being asked. He would make someone's bed, or clean up someone's space in their dorm room, or present one of us with a small, thoughtful gift. I almost never think about anyone else I knew during my four years of living in that college dormitory, but I have never forgotten him.

Hudson Taylor, a great man of God and founder of the China Inland Mission, once said, *"A little thing is a little thing, but faithfulness in little things is a great thing."* In the words of Rick Warren, *"small tasks often show a big heart."* Jesus said, in Luke 16:10, that *"whoever can be trusted with very little can also be trusted with very much."*

When you find yourself heartsick, depressed or discouraged, take time to do a small favor for someone else who could use a lift. See if it doesn't lift and enlarge your own heart as well.

When life hands you a lemon

"And we know that in all things God works for the good of those who love him, who have been called according to his purpose." Romans 8:28

All of us have been handed a few lemons in our lives. We should regard these not as abnormalities, but instead as normalities. If you've got a few lemons in your life, well, welcome to the human race. It should not be your goal to get rid of the lemons, but instead you need to learn how to use them for your benefit and turn them into lemonade, as the saying goes.

In James 1:2-4, we are told to *"consider it pure joy, my brothers and sisters, whenever you face trials of many kinds, because you know that the testing of your faith produces perseverance. Let perseverance finish its work so that you may be mature and complete, not lacking anything."*

You have probably read these scriptures and been given this advice more than once, but do you really believe them in your heart? Take time right now to list on a piece of paper the most distressing lemons in your life. Now let's be honest. You wouldn't be putting them on the list if they were making you happy or joyful, right? So, you need to admit that you do not really believe with your heart the Scriptures quoted above. Are you still with me? Your faith will grow with each success. Put your faith to work and give it a chance to grow.

We can benefit from those lemons in two ways. First, we can learn to be joyful in spite of them. Secondly, we can turn them into lemonade. We need to learn both lessons.

IN THE SHORT TERM, we need to learn how to be content in all circumstances and rejoice even in the midst of suffering. What better example of this than the Apostle Paul who was able to rejoice even as he wrote the book of Philippians from a filthy prison cell. Here are two tips on how to accomplish this.

1. When you get the blues and are facing an unhappy circumstance, go to God in prayer and pour out thanksgiving to Him for all the terrible things that happened to you in the past and tell Him how grateful you are that He brought be through them all. When viewing your current distressful situation from the perspective of what God has done for you in the past, you will be able to transfer those feelings of gratitude to your current situation.

2. It also helps to think about people you know, or know about, who are in much more dire circumstances. By comparison, your problems will seem much smaller. You could even take matters a step further and take some sort of action to help alleviate the suffering of one of those unfortunate individuals. You could donate to a special charity, or put a little extra into the offering place at Church, or offer your help to someone who is in greater need than you. The Apostle Paul was so passionate about his ministry and so focused on the wonderful things that were happening to the people he was helping that he was able to rejoice even in prison. The happiness he was bringing into the lives of others turned the negative of his imprisonment into an occasion for joy.

OVER THE LONGER TERM, you need to figure out how to use your negative experience to create something new and good in your life, something you can really be happy about. Here is a list of practical tips that will help you to do just that.

1. Don't blame God. God didn't hand you this lemon, life did. God is the one who is going to help you.

2. Don't complain, take action instead. Negative thoughts create negative results. Positive thoughts create positive results. Try not to harbor and savor negative thoughts, and do not allow them to turn into spoken words.

3. If the situation is temporary, continually visualize in your mind how good it will feel when it is over.

4. If the situation is permanent, or of indeterminate length, pray about it continually. You are not necessarily going to beg for a "miracle," but instead ask for the strength to bear it and the wisdom to learn from it. It needs to be OK with you if God does not miraculously remove the lemon.

5. Ask yourself this. Is there something else in life you would like to have that would make your present difficulty easier to bear? Is there something new and good that you have the resources to accomplish in your life that will make your present difficulty pale in comparison. For example, if you have recently lost your job, what steps could you take to get an even better one? If your marriage is failing, what steps can you take to help your spouse love you even more than when you were first married? If you are seriously ill, how can you use your time in the hospital or at home to enhance your relationship with God or shine a little light into the lives of those around you?

6. Ask yourself this. How can God use this current situation to help you become a better person? What weaknesses in your character has this situation revealed, and what steps can you take to improve yourself. The trials and tribulations of life are like sandpaper that God can use to smooth out your rough edges. They are like the pruning shears that God uses to lop off old tired branches in order to make room for new ones. They are like the

chisel the diamond cutter uses to make the dull, rough stone sparkle.

7. Be patient and wait on the Lord. Time is the greatest healer in your life. If your troubles clear up too soon, you won't have time to learn from them, grow from them, or replace them with better things. Meditate daily on Isaiah 40:31, *"but they that wait upon the Lord shall renew their strength; they shall mount up with wings as eagles, they shall run and not be weary, and they shall walk and not faint."*

I'd rather have a bottle in front of me than a frontal lobotomy

Years ago, a friend of our family, who struggled with alcoholism, jokingly made the above statement. The idea of partitioning the human brain, as with a lobotomy, came to my mind this morning as I contemplated the irrationality of fundamentalist Christian theology. How is one able to believe that God is both loving and at the same time unimaginably cruel and hateful at the same time? How can any rational person take pleasure in a loving relationship with God, knowing that the same God they worship will be torturing most of humanity in a place called Hell for all eternity? How will anyone be able to enjoy the pleasures of Heaven one day, and at the same time remain aware of what is going on in Hell. The most common answer that I get from believers in ECT (Eternal Conscious Torment) is that God will "lobotomize" (my word, not theirs) them when they get to heaven and remove the memory of their loved ones in Hell. This is sort of like the ostrich that sticks its head in the sand, pretending that the outside world is not really there.

Yesterday, I spent a few minutes on the phone with the head of a very large and fast growing charismatic Christian movement. Their website was full of positive affirmations about God's love and power to change lives. Because there was no statement of faith on that website, I thought they might be open to the doctrine of universal reconciliation. When I asked their leader if he believed that God would be sending most of humanity to everlasting punishment in a place called hell, he dodged the question and would not answer me directly. I asked the question several different ways. In each case, I did not get a direct answer. He did emphatically state, however, that he never mentions Hell or anything negative in any of his messages. This man has successfully "lobotomized" his followers into pretending that the elephant of "Eternal Conscious Torment" in a place called Hell is not really in the room.

Sadly, there is no room for "people like me" in the evangelical Christian church today, mainly because I take seriously the Bible teaching that God is love. Any theology that portrays God as unloving, unforgiving, and unable or unwilling to save all of His "lost sheep" is not Biblical, in my view.

Please be patient, God is not finished with me yet.

The first word of the Gospel is "repent." The opening sentence to the gospel message of Jesus, John the Baptist, and Jesus' disciples was, "Repent, for the Kingdom of Heaven is at hand." Christian Salvation, in my view, is not an instantaneous event. It is an ages-long process. All were redeemed on Calvary. They just don't all know it yet and for this reason they are not experiencing a relationship with Christ that is available to all because of Calvary. Repentance is a change of mind or attitude toward God, when God opens our eyes and removes the blindness and enables us to enter into a living relationship with Jesus Christ. It may be equated with a change in the direction of our lives. We need to keep in mind that repentance occurs in degrees. We don't usually start out by repenting of every known sin and completely turning from every ongoing sin. We start out as *"babes in Christ,"* in the words of the Apostle Paul. We don't become perfect right away. Becoming perfect is an ages-long process of the Holy Spirit working in our lives. No one is "completely" saved in that sense. The goal of our salvation experience it to become like Christ in every respect and become perfected in heaven one day. Repentance should not be equated with praying a sinner's prayer and then thinking that we are now done with it. We should not regard our salvation experience as something that occurs only at one single moment in time. I like the acronym that was popularized many years ago by Bill Gothard: PBPGINFWMY - "Please Be Patient, God Is Not Finished With Me Yet."

The goal of Christian missions

Matthew 28:19,20 – *"Therefore go and make disciples of all nations, baptizing them in the name of the Father and of the Son and of the Holy Spirit, and teaching them to obey everything I have commanded you."*

Romans 10:15b – "How beautiful are the feet of those who bring good news!"

Which makes the most sense to you?

Plan A: The goal of Christian missions is to save people from the wrath of an angry God and help them avoid everlasting torture in a place called Hell. The message goes something like this. "Hi folks, I would like to introduce you to the Gospel of Jesus Christ. If I can persuade you to sincerely pray this simple, one or two sentence prayer, you will go to Heaven when you die. If you don't, then when you die you will be tortured for all eternity in Hell, along with all the rest of your ancestors and loved ones, who weren't lucky enough to hear and respond to this wonderful good news of the Gospel."

Plan B: The goal of Christian missions is to make disciples of all nations, introduce them to the Savior of the world, Jesus Christ, and teach them to obey His commandments. The message goes something like this: "Hi folks. God loves you and so do I. God demonstrated His love for you by dying on the Cross of Calvary in the person of His Son, Jesus. The penalty for sin is death, and it was paid in full for all of you on that cross. The price only had to be paid once, so all of you are off the hook. God offers to each of you the opportunity of experiencing a personal relationship with Him and His Son, Jesus Christ. When you enter into relationship with God, He will give you many wonderful gifts including, but not limited to, love, joy, peace, patience, kindness, goodness, faithfulness, gentleness and self-control in this life and also in the next life after you die."

God is love

I recently posted the following comment on a Calvinist/Arminian discussion forum:

"God is love, and if you don't believe it He will burn you in Hell for all eternity."

No one in that discussion forum challenged the truth of my absurd post. Instead, they offered many scriptures in support of it. Can you imagine? This was a site where both Calvinists and Arminians post, each accusing the other of blasphemy for their respective theologies, while both sides subscribe to the biggest blasphemy of all, accusing God of being unloving and unforgiving.

"Dear friends, let us love one another, for love comes from God. Everyone who loves has been born of God and knows God." 1 John 4:7

"And so we know and rely on the love God has for us. God is love. Whoever lives in love lives in God, and God in them." 1 John 4:16

Happiness comes from within

The happiest people I ever knew were the people I met in the early 70's while stationed in Thailand during the Vietnam War. Most of the Thai people were dirt poor and lived in small, cramped apartments in a hot, humid climate with no air conditioning. When you walked down the damp, dingy streets, you were greeted with huge smiles everywhere you went. The rice paddies and tropical fauna held no attraction at all for me, but the Thai people thought they lived in the most beautiful place on Earth.

I, myself, could hardly wait to get out of Thailand and get back to the 'States. During my 2-year stay, I continually daydreamed about living back in the 'States again, especially in some beautiful, forested area with a temperate climate and many rivers and lakes. To me, Thailand was an ugly, dirty place, and I had a difficult time understanding why the Thai people were so happy all the time.

After returning to the 'States, I quickly moved to a place near the rivers and lakes and forests similar to what I had envisioned while in Thailand. For a while, life was great. Eventually, after settling into marriage and a career, life got a little bumpier and I found myself overwhelmed much of the time by financial pressures, and the various trials and tribulations that we all face in life, no matter where we live. During the times of greatest stress, I wished that I had opted for a simpler, less expensive lifestyle. I often thought of those happy Thai people who were poor in material goods, but rich in so many other ways.

Just as beauty is in the eye of the beholder, so it is with happiness. It may be found in almost any circumstance. If the external circumstances of your life are making you unhappy, look within for the help you need.

"Do not be anxious about anything, but in every situation, by prayer and petition, with thanksgiving, present your requests to God. And the peace

of God, which transcends all understanding, will guard your hearts and your minds in Christ Jesus." Philippians 4:6-7

Just as important as believing in God is believing in yourself.

"Truly I tell you, if you have faith as small as a mustard seed, you can say to this mountain, 'Move from here to there,' and it will move. Nothing will be impossible for you." Matthew 17:20

"I can do all this through him who gives me strength." Philippians 4:13

According to the Scriptures, we are all spiritual beings, with almost limitless potential. This is also supported by recent discoveries of quantum physics. We are non-physical, conscious beings who by the power by our observations alone bring into being the physical realities of the universe in which we temporarily reside. When energized by the Spirit of God, the human spirit, which is technically part of God, is theoretically capable of almost anything. The key to unlocking the nearly limitless potential of the human mind is "faith," or "belief."

Our limitations are mostly self-imposed and result from our inability to believe in ourselves. The famous motivational speaker, Zig Ziglar, called it *stinkin' thinkin'*. It's one thing to believe in God. It is quite another to believe in ourselves. Few people would doubt the power of God to accomplish anything He sets His mind to. A problem arises when we view ourselves as unworthy, incapable and separated from God. For a variety of reasons, we are unable to convince ourselves that God loves us unconditionally and wants us to thrive and prosper. The words of Christ (in John 10:10) that He came to give us life abundant, have fallen on deaf ears. We conjure up all sorts of alternate interpretations of what Jesus said, rather than accept the plain and obvious meaning. Some of us refuse to believe those words because we feel that due to our sinful condition we don't deserve the blessings of God. Others refuse to believe because of Scriptures that speak of "suffering" as a natural and expected result of following Christ. We forget that the disciples, in the face of suffering and hardship, were able to perform great miracles. Suffering and hardship in the name of Christ is supposed to bring us *"pure joy"* (James 1:2-4), and *"the fruit of the Spirit is Love, Joy and Peace"* (Galatians 5:22).

It is one thing to suffer persecution for our faith in Christ. It is quite another to suffer continual failure and defeat in the normal course of our secular lives. This was never God's intention for us. It is not normal or expected that Christians be unhappy. We all have the resources within us to be successful in life. Our relationship with God is based on grace, not works. Every possible sin of commission or omission on our part was already atoned for on Calvary. If you are unhappy for any reason with the hand that life has dealt you, a good first step in the right direction would be to change your thinking and start believing that God wants you to be successful despite any feelings you might have of unworthiness or inadequacy. What greater resource could you possibly need than the power of the Holy Spirit within you?

Sin is our enemy, not God

It has been asserted by many evangelical Christians that no one is "good enough" to be saved. Some would go so far as to insist that even if a person were guilty of only one sin, and perfect in every other respect, God would be just in condemning that person to everlasting torment in Hell. The idea is that God demands perfection from us.

The actual truth of the matter is just the opposite. God is love. He is more loving and forgiving than any human being. Because of this, there is absolutely no need to qualify for salvation. We are not saved by works, because works are not necessary. They are not necessary because God loves us just as we are. We are slaves of sin, true. But sin is our enemy, not God. Jesus did not come to save us from God. He came to save us from sin, from our own self-destructive behaviors. God is the *"Savior of all men, especially those that believe"* (1 Timothy 4:10). God is the one who saves, not the one who condemns. According to John 3:17, *"God did not send his Son into the world to condemn the world, but to save the world through him."*

"For by grace you have been saved through faith. And this is not your own doing; it is the gift of God, not a result of works, so that no one may boast." Ephesians 2:8-9

La La Land or Law Law Land

It seems that most people are uncomfortable with shades of gray, especially with respect to Christian theology. Most of us like to wrap up our religious, moral and ethical concepts into neat little "dualistic" packages. We view people as either saved or lost, basically good or basically bad, saved by grace or saved by works, spiritual or carnal, and going to only one of two places when we die, Heaven or Hell.

Some of us live in spiritual La La Land, and view Christian salvation as something that is a gift of God, given by grace, with no judgment of their sins after that. They view their conversion experience as obtaining a ticket into Heaven where they will not be held accountable for their sins.

Others live in spiritual Law Law Land, and view Christian salvation in the same dualistic terms, but instead of being saved by grace apart from works, they view it as something that one achieves by obeying God's laws. Hopefully, on judgment day after they die, the scales of God's justice will weigh in their favor.

Whether in politics, religion or everyday life, the truth of the matter generally lies somewhere in the middle. We are saved by grace, apart from obedience to the Law, but we are still held accountable by God for every sinful thought or action, even every careless spoken or unspoken word. Being saved by grace, does not exempt us from the "Law of Sowing and Reaping." God doesn't stop loving us when we fall into sin. However, because He loves us He allows us to suffer the negative consequences of our sinful actions in order that we might grow and learn from those experiences. What loving and caring human father would not do the same for his children?

"...the Lord disciplines the one he loves, and he chastens everyone he accepts as his son." Hebrews 12:6

Our sins Are "covered" but Not "ignored"

There is a difference between "forgiving" someone, and "ignoring" the sin in their lives. Sin causes harm to the sinner and those whose lives are touched by the sinner. There is a difference between "correction" and "retribution." 1 John 1:9 has more to do with God's correction than retribution. God loves all of us unconditionally, but for our sakes, not His, He wants to hear those words, "I'm sorry," when we stray from the path which He has chosen for our highest good.

"If we confess our sins, he is faithful and just and will forgive us our sins and purify us from all unrighteousness." 1 Jn. 1:9

How to get the dirty bone out of your dog's mouth

"Do not get drunk on wine, which leads to debauchery. Instead, be filled with the Spirit." Ephesians 5:18

We all have sin addictions, some great and some small. This is part of being human. We always fall short of God's best for us. The best way to overcome sinful habits and addictions is to focus on the positive, not the negative. I you want your dog to let go of that dirty old bone he just dug up in the back yard, you won't succeed by trying to yank it from him. If, instead, you offer him a nice juicy steak, he will drop the old bone in a heartbeat.

If you can get in the habit of rededicating your life to God's service anew each morning in prayer, and remain in a "state of prayer" throughout the day, just one day at a time, you will find yourself replacing bad attitudes and habits with good ones. Start out each day with a fresh infilling of the Holy Spirit, and as the day progresses "top it off" over and over again as the level drops. Don't worry about the specifics of how to overcome an addiction or bad habit. Don't worry about how to rid yourself of bad thoughts. Just focus on filling yourself to overflowing each day with the love of God. Understand that God loves you just as much when you fail as He does when you succeed.

It's not easy to curse your neighbor and praise God at the same time. They are mutually exclusive activities. I can assure you that the latter activity is much more pleasurable than the former. Love is so much more gratifying than hate. Freedom is so much more pleasurable than addiction. God is much better company than fair weather friends who tempt you to sin. Keeping busy with the Lord's business is so much more gratifying than sitting around doing God knows what else and hoping for nothing bad to happen because of it.

Finally, don't worry about results. Results will come eventually, sometimes all at once, sometimes a little at a time. Your God is a God of miracles, so don't worry about the "mechanics" or the "how-to's" either. And look within for the help you need. Yes, God is out there everywhere, but He is also in you and will give you whatever strength you need to overcome any negative habit.

You must be born again.

Recent events in the Middle East have caused many of us to rise up in righteous indignation against those who commit heinous atrocities against innocent people. We view evil people as deserving of Hell. It is easy to understand how God can save us, because we are not nearly as evil as they are. It is a lot more difficult for us to envision God saving militant Islamic Jihadists, especially those who commit murder and rape for the sheer pleasure of it.

It helps me, personally, to understand that sin is a form of blindness. Islamic Jihadists are no different than the Apostle Paul who believed he was serving God by persecuting Christians. Moderate Moslems today are very much like the Jews of Jesus' day, who practiced a very legalistic form of religion. Non-religious people who commit acts of atrocity out of pure self-interest are also blinded. They think that their crimes serve their self-interest, and they are unable to empathize with the feelings of those whom they are hurting. Lack of empathy is a form of blindness. When we judge these people as not worthy of salvation, we fail to realize that they are inherently good in their innermost being, in their spirits, but in their carnal existence in the flesh they suffer from a disease of blindness that may be instantly cured by God when the timing is right. Paul makes this case in Romans 7 & 8.

For those of you who have read up on the Near Death Experience (NDE), you know that during the life review, the subject relives every moment of his/her life, and experiences it from two perspectives, their personal perspective and also from the perspective of those whose lives they touched. For the first time ever, some are able to completely empathize with the feelings of others. During this exercise, God removes the blinders and restores their spiritual sight. When we shed our mortal bodies and put on immortality, we leave the fleshly, sinful body behind. For most, this happens very soon after death. Others cling to more tightly to their earthly existence and experience a "Hell" of their own making after death, but eventually the love of God reaches them and they are rescued from the illusion of Hell, and God opens their eyes to the truth.

"And even if our gospel is veiled, it is veiled only to those who are perishing. In their case the god of this world has blinded the minds of the unbelievers, to keep them from seeing the light of the gospel of the glory of Christ, who is the image of God." 2 Cor. 4:3-4

"For the mind that is set on the flesh is hostile to God, for it does not submit to God's law; indeed, it cannot. Those who are in the flesh cannot please God." Rom. 8:7-8

"For we know that the law is spiritual, but I am of the flesh, sold under sin. For I do not understand my own actions. For I do not do what I want, but I do the very thing I hate. Now if I do what I do not want, I

agree with the law, that it is good. 17 So now it is no longer I who do it, but sin that dwells within me. For I know that nothing good dwells in me, that is, in my flesh. For I have the desire to do what is right, but not the ability to carry it out. For I do not do the good I want, but the evil I do not want is what I keep on doing. Now if I do what I do not want, it is no longer I who do it, but sin that dwells within me." Romans 7:14-20

"Jesus answered him, 'Truly, truly, I say to you, unless one is born again he cannot see the kingdom of God.' Nicodemus said to him, 'How can a man be born when he is old? Can he enter a second time into his mother's womb and be born?' Jesus answered, 'Truly, truly, I say to you, unless one is born of water and the Spirit, he cannot enter the kingdom of God. That which is born of the flesh is flesh, and that which is born of the Spirit is spirit. Do not marvel that I said to you, 'You must be born again.' The wind blows where it wishes, and you hear its sound, but you do not know where it comes from or where it goes. So it is with everyone who is born of the Spirit." John 3:3-8

"No, in all these things we are more than conquerors through him who loved us. For I am convinced that neither death nor life, neither angels nor demons, neither the present nor the future, nor any powers, neither height nor depth, nor anything else in all creation, will be able to separate us from the love of God that is in Christ Jesus our Lord." Romans 8:37-39

Ten pillars on which the doctrine of Universal Reconciliation is based

1. Making good use of common sense and logic

2. Understanding the nature and character of God

3. Understanding the purpose of God's judgments

4. Understanding the nature and scope of the Atonement

5. Understanding Christian Salvation as a process, rather than as a single event

6. Examining Scriptures which explicitly teach universalism

7. Examining Scriptures which imply universalism

8. Correctly translating and interpreting scriptures which seem to negate universalism

9. Correctly translating and defining important words like "eternal," "condemn," "death," "life," "destruction," and "salvation"

10. Interpreting individual scripture passages in accordance with their immediate context and the entire body of Scripture

Note: It is not at all necessary to discard the doctrine of Scriptural inerrancy in order to support the doctrine of Universal Reconciliation.

Positional vs. experiential truth

Romans 8:18-25: *"I consider that our present sufferings are not worth comparing with the glory that will be revealed in us. For the creation waits in eager expectation for the children of God to be revealed. For the creation was subjected to frustration, not by its own choice, but by the will of the one who subjected it, in hope that the creation itself will be liberated from its bondage to decay and brought into the freedom and glory of the children of God.*

We know that the whole creation has been groaning as in the pains of childbirth right up to the present time. Not only so, but we ourselves, who have the firstfruits of the Spirit, groan inwardly as we wait eagerly for our adoption to sonship, the redemption of our bodies. For in this hope we were saved. But hope that is seen is no hope at all. Who hopes for what they already have? But if we hope for what we do not yet have, we wait for it patiently."

In the past, I felt that the above passage of Scripture should not be taken literally. I presumed that *"all creation"* would include both animate and inanimate objects. How can an inanimate object *"wait with eager expectation"* or *"groan?"* After much study and contemplation, not only of the Scriptures, but also of physics, I have come to realize that the above passage of Scripture may be accepted as literal truth. Consider the following passages of Scripture which deal with both the omni-presence and creative activity of God, in the person of Jesus Christ. In the Bible, God the Father and Jesus the Christ are used interchangeably, two distinct personalities but one in essence. The third person on the Trinity, the Holy Spirit, is also used to describe both God the Father and Jesus Christ interchangeably.

"You, however, are not in the realm of the flesh but are in the realm of the Spirit, if indeed the Spirit of God lives in you. And if anyone does not have the Spirit of Christ, they do not belong to Christ." Romans 8:9

"For in him (Christ) *all things were created: things in heaven and on earth, visible and invisible, whether thrones or powers or rulers or authorities; all things have been created through him and for him."* Colossians 1:16

"'For in him (God the Father) we live and move and have our being.' As some of your own poets have said, 'We are his offspring.'" Acts 17:28

God's creation is "separate" from God Himself only in the sense that Jesus Christ is Separate from God the Father. Jesus is God's offspring, His only begotten Son. Well, guess what? We are also God's offspring, according to Acts 17:28 (see above). We are actually divine, in the same sense that Jesus Christ is divine, except that we are "begotten" of Christ and are made up of "Christ parts," Because Christ is in turn made up of "God parts," we would by extension also have divine natures. We do have separate and distinct personalities, but we are made of the same "stuff" (spirit) as the triune Godhead. I also believe that all creation, including both animate and inanimate objects and entities, are part of God. Another way of terming this would be to say that we are all "manifestations" of God. Nothing is separate from God Himself. God is omnipresent. There is nowhere that God is not. We are all intimately connected with God, and with each other for that matter.

So why does the Bible describe humanity as "lost," or "separated from God," or "under condemnation," or "enemies of God?" The reason is that most of us are not consciously aware of our divine natures. We are not aware of God's presence in our lives. We have no conscious relationship with God. We live in the "Hells" of our own making. I don't believe that Hell is a place, but where ever we find ourselves, we are separated from God only in our conscious awareness, or should I say, lack thereof. There is no place we can go, or be sent, where we can escape the presence of God.

I like to distinguish between our "true spiritual selves" and our "fleshly self-awarenes" (See Romans 7) by using the terms "positional" and "experiential" truth. Positionally, we have divine, spiritual natures, and were redeemed by the blood of Christ on Calvary, and have been raised up with Christ and reside with Him in the heavenly realms. (See Eph. 2:6). Most non-Christians are not at all aware of this. Christians have experienced these positional truths only partially, and have experienced only the "first fruits" of the Spirit.

POSITIONAL:	**EXPERIENTIAL:**
Alive	Dead
Spiritual	Fleshly/Carnal
Redeemed	Under condemnation
At home	Lost
Cleansed from sin	In need of forgiveness and cleansing
Saved	Unsaved
Children of God	Children of Satan
United with God/Christ	Separated from God/Christ

Both Christians and non-Christians are in a process of transition from one mental state to the other. The process of Christian salvation is not instantaneous. It is an ages-long growth process. No one is completely "saved" or "lost." The Spirit of God is at work in our lives before, during, and after our profession of faith in Christ. All are at some stage in a process which culminates at the end of the ages. In the end, everyone will be presented faultless before the throne of God, and every knee will bow to Christ and acknowledge Him as Lord, and God will become *"all in all"* in everyone's conscious awareness. (See 1 Cor. 15:22-28)

All creation is a manifestation of God Himself and literally made of "God parts," even inanimate objects. According to the discoveries of quantum physics, general relativity, and the law of conservation of energy, the universe is spiritual, not physical in nature. When you break down physical matter into its fundamental components you arrive at nothing more than "unrealized" quantum potential. Others would describe it as "potential" energy, which can neither be created nor destroyed. This is the fundamental spiritual building block for all reality. Again, all reality is spiritual in nature. The entire universe is a manifestation of God Himself. At the very deepest level of reality, the universe is actually conscious and alive, because God is conscious and alive. And the entire universe (including every person in it) literally *"groans with birth pains"* and *"waits in eager expectation for the children of God to be revealed."*

My biggest question

Over the past eight years, I have progressed in my thinking to where I have become a committed Christian universalist. The biggest question that remains for me is this. If Christianity is true, why doesn't God reveal this to everyone in clear and unmistakable terms? Why do most Christians cling to many irrational beliefs about the true nature of God? Why does God allow most of them to believe in eternal conscious torment for most of humanity in Hell? Why does the mass of humanity today remain unconvinced about the truth of the Christian Gospel? If believing the Gospel is necessary for salvation, why is this truth so difficult for most people to accept?

The best answer I can come up with is this. God is both loving and just and fully intends to save all mankind. He is also omnipotent and fully capable of saving each of us whenever He so desires. Because of this, I must also assume that from God's perspective, it is not important that all find Christ in their current lifetime on Earth. So why the urgency that we see in the Scriptures to get the word out before people die? Here's my best answer. Entering into relationship with Jesus Christ is a very import step in the salvation process, and it is a very helpful one. Part of the "package" that comes with one's profession of faith in Christ is a change of attitude toward sin and an increased ability to live a righteous, Godly life. For those who are already committed to a generous and loving lifestyle, the only missing ingredient is the correct theology about the person and work of Christ. I would imagine that this deficiency can be quickly and easily rectified immediately after death. I like the illustration Jesus gave, in Matt. 25, of the separation of the sheep from the goats, where some are admitted into the Kingdom even though they never consciously served Christ by name.

But, you might ask, what about those who have no desire to know Christ or live righteous lives? Why doesn't God intervene to help them change their thinking? Here's my best guess. Losing our way in life and falling into sin must have some positive benefit or God wouldn't allow it to happen. Remember, He is both loving and omnipotent. One must experience the negative aspects of life to fully appreciate the positive. I would assume that our negative experiences in this life benefit us in the long run. In the words of Paul, in Romans 5:20, *"But where sin increased, grace increased all the more."* The fact remains that God does not "save" all of us at once. There are two ways to *"grow in grace."* One is to change your life in relationship with Christ by the power of the Holy Spirit. The other is to be refined and purified in the crucible of negative life experiences (ie. God's judgments and/or the Hells of our own making). We need both. So, we must leave it up to God which method of growth best suits our current situation.

I no longer fret over whether the people I meet are technically "saved" or not. I know that all of us are loved and accepted by God just as we are, and that all of us are somewhere in the process of being or becoming "saved." I never hesitate to share the Gospel with people I meet. The difference for me now is that the Gospel I preach is "good news" for all, not just some.

Make today the best day of your life.

Matt. 6:34 "Therefore do not worry about tomorrow, for tomorrow will worry about itself. Each day has enough trouble of its own."

Phil. 4:11-13 "I am not saying this because I am in need, for I have learned to be content whatever the circumstances. I know what it is to be in need, and I know what it is to have plenty. I have learned the secret of being content in any and every situation, whether well fed or hungry, whether living in plenty or in want. I can do all this through him who gives me strength."

Ask yourself these questions. How much of your present happiness and peace of mind depends on something happening tomorrow or sometime in the future? What do you hope will happen in the future that will make your life happier or more satisfying than it is today? What is missing from your life today that you hope you can add to your life tomorrow? What goals, dreams and aspirations do you have for the future? What tasks do you plan on accomplishing in the future that will make you feel better about yourself?

Now ask yourself this. What can I do today that can make me feel better about myself and cause me to be happier today? How much of what I plan on accomplishing in the future can I experience and/or get started on today? What changes can I make in today's schedule that will make me happier right now? What changes can I make in my life today that will make me feel better about myself right now? How much better can my life be today if I make better use of my time, beginning right now?

Finally, ask yourself this. How would the pattern of my life change if I were to ask these questions of myself each morning, pray about them, and then jot down on a piece of paper one or two action items for the day?

Persuasive deeds are more effective than persuasive words

"Be ye doers of the word and not hearers only…" James 1:22

"Do not repay evil with evil or insult with insult. On the contrary, repay evil with blessing, because to this you were called so that you may inherit a blessing." 1 Peter 3:9

The best way to change someone is with actions, not words. We've all heard about how hard it is to live with nagging wives, verbally abusive husbands, dictatorial bosses, complaining employees, and excessively judgmental individuals. Words are not as powerful as we would like them to be. Most often, our attempts at "constructive criticism" backfire and make matters even worse. It seems that, despite our best efforts, our powers of verbal "persuasion" tend to fall on deaf ears. We find ourselves saying things like, "some people just can't or won't change," or "I'll never be able to change him/her," or "I'll just have learn to live with his/her imperfections and faults." And so on.

When attempting any important task, more can be accomplished from a position of strength than weakness. If you view yourself as a "helpless" victim, the results will match your expectations. On the other hand when you approach a task with strength and confidence, you will most likely succeed. According to 1 Peter 3:9, the secret to overcoming evil is to attack it with blessing. In other words, return good for evil. According to James 1:22, actions are more important than words. Talk is cheap.

When two individuals experience conflict, in most cases at least a portion of the guilt lies with each party. Each generally regards the other as the most guilty. You might regard yourself as only 10% or 20% at fault. Not surprisingly, the other party probably views him or herself as only 10% or 20% at fault. This impasse cannot be bridged with words alone. In order mend and restore the relationship, you need to focus on the 10% to 20% of the fault that lies with you and overcompensate for your own deficiencies.

The advice I giving here is not for victims of severe spousal abuse or other forms of criminal behavior. If you are being victimized in this way, you need to get out of the relationship altogether, and the sooner you do it the better. Instead, my advice is for those of you who are experiencing conflict in an otherwise valuable personal or professional relationship.

If you are unhappy in a relationship that you want to maintain and make better, then here is a suggestion that might work for you. Try to improve the relationship with persuasive deeds, rather than with persuasive words. If you must use words, the most helpful are words of apology for the portion of the guilt that lies with you, with absolutely no mention of the guilt that lies with the other. You goal is to use actions alone to restore or improve the relationship, and make it better than it ever was. If the conflict is with your spouse, your goal is to rekindle the intensity of love that you first had for one another. If the conflict is in a professional relationship, then you want to earn maximum respect from your boss, employee, or coworker and make yourself as valuable an asset as possible to the company that you manage or work for.

Believers will enter the Kingdom ahead of unbelievers

"Jesus said to them, "Truly I tell you, the tax collectors and the prostitutes are entering the kingdom of God ahead of you. For John came to you to show you the way of righteousness, and you did not believe him, but the tax collectors and the prostitutes did. And even after you saw this, you did not repent and believe him." Matthew 21:31-32

Since becoming a universalist, I notice little things in the Scriptures that support universalism, things that I never noticed before. In the above passage, which I read in church today, Jesus pointed out that the tax collectors and prostitutes would enter the Kingdom ahead of the chief priests and elders of Israel. The reason is that the tax collectors and prostitutes believed the Gospel message and the chief priests and elders of Israel did not. Notice that Jesus did not say unbelievers would never enter the kingdom, only that believers would enter first. Interesting, huh?

God's ways are higher than ours.

Believers in Eternal Conscious Torment (ECT) often quote from Isaiah 55 to justify God's apparently cruel and inhumane actions. They ask, "Who are we to judge God? God's ways are above our ways. His thoughts are above ours. We should not be invoking human reason when evaluating God's actions." Well, they are right about not evaluating God's actions according to human reason. Most reasonable human beings believe that people should be severely punished for their evil actions. Most reasonable human beings believe that punishments should fit the crimes. But God is not reasonable. His ways are not our ways. God returns good for evil. He forgives His enemies. While we were yet sinners, Christ died for us. He saved all of us by grace on the Cross of Calvary, and does not require us to earn our salvation. When He does find it necessary to chastise and correct us, it is always done in love and with the loving purpose of correcting our evil ways. We serve a mighty and loving God who is not at all reasonable when it comes to handing out mercy and pardon to undeserving humanity.

Isaiah 55:

"Come, all you who are thirsty,
come to the waters;
and you who have no money,
come, buy and eat!
Come, buy wine and milk
without money and without cost.
2 Why spend money on what is not bread,
and your labor on what does not satisfy?
Listen, listen to me, and eat what is good,
and you will delight in the richest of fare.
3 Give ear and come to me;
listen, that you may live.
I will make an everlasting covenant with you,
my faithful love promised to David.
4 See, I have made him a witness to the peoples,
a ruler and commander of the peoples.
5 Surely you will summon nations you know not,
and nations you do not know will come running to you,
because of the LORD your God,
the Holy One of Israel,
for he has endowed you with splendor."

6 Seek the LORD while he may be found;
call on him while he is near.
7 Let the wicked forsake their ways
and the unrighteous their thoughts.
Let them turn to the LORD, and he will have mercy on them,
and to our God, for he will freely pardon.

8 "For my thoughts are not your thoughts,
neither are your ways my ways,"
declares the LORD.
9 "As the heavens are higher than the earth,
so are my ways higher than your ways
and my thoughts than your thoughts.
10 As the rain and the snow
come down from heaven,
and do not return to it
without watering the earth
and making it bud and flourish,
so that it yields seed for the sower and bread for the eater,

[11] *so is my word that goes out from my mouth:*
It will not return to me empty,
but will accomplish what I desire
and achieve the purpose for which I sent it.
[12] *You will go out in joy*
and be led forth in peace;
the mountains and hills
will burst into song before you,
and all the trees of the field
will clap their hands.
[13] *Instead of the thornbush will grow the juniper,*
and instead of briers the myrtle will grow.
This will be for the LORD's renown,
for an everlasting sign,
that will endure forever."

God is saving the best for last

"And, for that matter, the only God we can maintain belief in is the one who is careful to be utterly concealed, all the time, whose action is, by definition, indistinguishable from what might possibly happen anyway. Because this is how God functions, if God is." Peter Bradford Martin

Why does God conceal Himself? Why does He interact with us in ways that are nearly indistinguishable from mere chance? Why are truths about God revealed only through the filter of imperfect human understanding and intuition? I don't know why. I only know this is the case. I intuitively believe that God is by definition both loving and omnipotent. I am most likely right about this, because this belief is shared by most of the human race. This truth is central to every major world religion. It would follow, then, that God must be perfectly OK with our imperfect and conflicting religious belief systems.

This is not to say that Christianity is not true, only that God must be perfectly OK with our imperfect understanding of it. It is perfectly OK with God that not all find Christ in this lifetime. It is OK with God that we don't all agree on the "fundamental" truths of the Bible. If the truths relating to the Christian Gospel are also "fundamental" in God's eyes, then I must assume that God will make them clearly and unmistakably known to all of us sooner or later.

I do believe that if we seek God with all our heart, He will reveal to us what we need to know to live a successful life, when we need to know it. God is saving the best for last, the frosting on the cake as it were, until after we die.

A word about extra-biblical truths of God

There seems to be a genuine paranoia among many Christian evangelicals about investigating extra-Biblical sources of spiritual truth. These information sources include the discoveries of science, psychology, sociology, history, archaeology, metaphysics, and the scriptures of non-Christian religions. If the Bible contains accurate information about God, why on earth would you expect this to be contradicted by extra-Biblical sources of truth? Many evangelical churches sometimes attempt to control their flocks in a very "cultish" manner by exercising a form of "mind control." Church members are encouraged to submit to the spiritual "authority" of their leaders and avoid exposure to sources of truth outside of the Scriptures. They are especially warned to avoid those sources which seem to contradict their particular interpretation of the Scriptures.

In my view, they have got it just backwards. We shouldn't rely exclusively on the Scriptures to "authenticate" or "evaluate" the truths found outside of the Scriptures. Instead, we should be exploring those extra-Biblical sources of information in order to authenticate the truths found in the Bible. If you don't agree with this, ask yourself why you believe that the Bible is true in the first place. No religious text may be accepted as truth solely on the basis of its internal claims. In a court of law, the defendant is not declared innocent solely on the basis of his or her own testimony. That would be ludicrous. A proper defense can only be made by carefully examining many forms of evidence which are external to the statements of the defendant. This evidence would be historical and scientific in nature, but would also include the experiences and testimony of impartial observers.

Most of you are aware by now that I do not believe that the Christian Scriptures are historically, scientifically or theologically inerrant. At one point in my life, it was difficult for me to affirm the truths in Scripture while at the same time discarding the doctrine of inerrancy. This is no longer a problem for me for two reasons.

First, my investigation of extra-Biblical sources of information has provided strong evidence for the truths contained in the Scriptures.

Second, and equally important, this investigation has helped me to more correctly interpret and apply the truths of Scripture.

Truth is truth, no matter where you find it. All truth is God's truth. Many extra-Biblical truths are in my view reasonable, logical, and incontrovertible. Over the next few days, I will be providing you with many specific examples of how these extra-Biblical truths have influenced my theology and my interpretation of the Scriptures.

Extra-Biblical Truth Case Study No. 1: The Stories in Genesis

When I was a young man, struggling with my faith, I desperately wanted to believe the Gospel of Christ and find assurance of my salvation. A huge obstacle for me was the difficulty I had accepting the literal truth of many Old Testament passages of Scripture, especially the creation account in Genesis and the events relating to human origins, the fall of man in the Garden of Eden, the flood story, the story of the Tower of Babel and the confusion of languages, and so on. I was completely unable to believe that they are literally true. As I read the narratives, they seemed rather absurd in many ways. Although I believed that God is completely able to circumvent and violate the laws of science, I couldn't believe that there would be any logical reason for Him to do so. Why would God choose to accomplish supernaturally what He could just as easily do through the natural processes which He had already set in motion? A bigger question for me was this. Why would God create the world is seven literal 24-hour days and then create a false geological, linguistic, cosmological, and archaeological history that would make it appear that the process occurred over billions of years? Why would God attempt to fool us in this way and in so doing make it nearly impossible for reputable scientists and rational thinkers to believe the Bible?

To make matters even worse, these stories lacked plausibility. Why would God need to rest on the seventh day? Why would God need to scoop up a handful of clay, or a rib from the side of Eve, to create the first male and female? Why would God, who is supposedly omniscient, be walking around in the garden calling out to Adam in order to find out where he was hiding? And a talking snake? Give me a break. If God wanted to destroy all mankind and start over, why would there be any need at all for the worldwide flood and the ark? Why not just snuff out all the bad guys instantaneously? This would eliminate the need to put millions of species of animals onto an ark that was not nearly big enough to accommodate them. Why would a man-made tower that reaches at most a few hundred feet into the air be such a threat to God? The confusion of languages at Babel seems not only unlikely but makes no sense at all. A confusion of languages would not at all be necessary in order to encourage mankind to spread out and explore their world. I could go on and on. These ancient stories bear all the earmarks of legend and myth, and they are contradicted by the findings of science, especially geology, cosmology, and paleontology.

If the stories in Genesis are not historically true and accurate, in what sense may they be relied upon for discovering truths about God and for guidance in making important life decisions? According to 2 Timothy 3:16, *"All Scripture is God-breathed and is useful for teaching, rebuking, correcting and training in righteousness..."* This passage says nothing about the Hebrew Bible (ie. the Old Testament) being historically accurate or literally true. In the Bible we find many different genres of literature, including historical narratives, legends, myths, poetry, songs, sermons and homilies, symbolism, imagery, parables, similies, and proverbs, none of which need to be scientifically or historically accurate in order to convey spiritual and moral truths. The Bible was derived from many oral and written sources, none of which originated with the intent of being incorporated into an infallible, inerrant Bible which would be identified by many as the authoritative word or words of God Himself. Their original intent and purpose was to communicate information that would motivate people to conduct their lives in a manner pleasing to God and beneficial to mankind.

So, with this in mind, what can we learn from extra-Biblical sources that will help us better understand, interpret and benefit from the stories and legends in the Book of Genesis? First of all, we learn from science, geology, linguistics, cosmology, and paleontology that the stories are not literally and historically true. Because of this, I personally would be reluctant to base any critical theological teaching on a literalistic interpretation of these stories. In order to believe Christian doctrines relating to observance of the Sabbath, capital punishment, the existence of Satan, original sin, human depravity, and so on, I personally would need to find support for those doctrines elsewhere in Scripture.

What we learn from archaeology is that these stories are a huge improvement over the creation myths and legends of the surrounding Babylonian and Sumerian cultures, from which they are partially derived. We see evidence of an evolution in thought. God is still described in largely anthropomorphic terms, but is now viewed as the creator of the universe, and He is a righteous God who enforces a moral code that will develop into something quite sophisticated over time.

Extra-Biblical Truth Case Study No. 2: God-Approved Genocide

Second only to the doctrine of eternal conscious torment (ECT) in Hell, God-approved genocide in the Bible has been the most troubling to me. If one believes in the inerrancy of the Bible, then one must also accept that genocide is an approved method of achieving God's purposes. Examples include the Genesis flood, the killing of all the first-born of Egypt prior to the Exodus, the subsequent conquest of Canaan, and God's continuing support of Israel in various wars against her enemies. The idea that God destroys His enemies in the form of mass genocide has, by extension, also found its way into the New Testament, especially in the Book of Revelation.

It's one matter to defend yourself against enemies who are seeking to kill you or your loved ones. It is quite another matter to employ the use of violence to advance a religious or territorial objective, especially when other options are equally available to you. Most Christian conservatives, who are strongly opposed to fundamentalist Islamic jihad on moral and ethical grounds, are perfectly comfortable with exactly the same methods being used by the nation of Israel in the Old Testament, and by God Himself in the Book of Revelation.

In the Bible, God is depicted as loving, yet at times very harsh in His judgments. God-approved Genocide has been rationalized as having a loving and redemptive purpose. The question then arises, does the end justify the means? When tempted to return evil for evil and employ violence to resolve problems or achieve righteous goals, are we able to do this in the spirit of what Christ taught us about loving our enemies and returning good for evil? Is there a conflict between what Christ taught and what was previously taught in the Old Testament? Was God really approving, even commanding, the use of genocide, or was man incorrectly ascribing this to God?

In order to successfully resolve this issue, we need to discard the doctrine of Scriptural inerrancy, and employ a different basis for the interpretation of Scripture. Separating truth from error in the Scriptures is not as difficult as you might expect. Those teachings which are consistent with what we know to be the true character of God, as described by Christ himself, may be accepted. Those teachings which are inconsistent with the true character of God must either be rejected or reinterpreted in ways that would resolve the discrepancies.

For the answer I seek, the primary extra-Biblical information source I would draw on is the use of common sense, logic, and the lessons of history. The answer that satisfies me most has to do with the concept of progressive revelation. I view the Bible as a man-made, yet God-inspired, record of an evolution of thought, a learning process. Through a process of trial and error we learn and grow in our personal lives. Even Jesus, Himself, started out with a blank slate and grew in wisdom and stature with both God and man. The same is true for humanity as a whole. Just as various plant and animal species develop and adapt through a process of God-directed macro and micro evolution, so it is with societies. God directs from behind the scenes. He works in and through us, not outside of us. Supernatural intervention is the exception, not the norm. He has chosen to accomplish His goals for mankind through us, not for us. He doesn't just hand us wisdom and all the answers to life in completed form, on a silver platter, as it were. Instead, He helps us to learn and grow in a better way, through actual human interactions. Spiritual, moral and ethical lessons are best learned first-hand, not second-hand, in the crucible of both positive and negative life experiences. In the Bible we find a record of this painful process on the societal level, and especially in the experience of one particular society which God has chosen to be an example for all the others, the nation of Israel. The Bible records their successes and their failures. It records their wisdom and also their misconceptions and misunderstandings.

This process reaches an apex of sorts in the life and teachings of Jesus Christ. All that has gone before should be evaluated on the basis of what Christ taught. Since the time of Christ, society has continued to evolve and change, and progress has not been easy or smooth. Many of Christ's followers have not been able to fully assimilate much of what He taught, because they remain stuck in the past and have not been able to discard many of the mistaken religious beliefs and ethical mores of the ancient Hebrews.

Extra-Biblical Truth Case Study No. 3: Soul Sleep

There are two main schools of thought regarding what happens to us immediately after death.

Some believe that the soul and body are so closely connected that when the body dies, so does the soul. When Christ comes again to earth, those who are dead in Christ (or "asleep," in the words of Paul) will be made alive again and their physical bodies will be resurrected and made immortal. Proponents of this view believe that non-Christians will also be resurrected, but at a much later date, at which time they will be either annihilated in the Lake of Fire or punished there for all eternity. Universalists, who subscribe to this view of the body-soul connection, believe that the Lake of Fire is symbolic of a purification and refinement process, after which all will eventually be saved and granted admission into the Kingdom of Heaven.

The second major school of thought is that the body and soul are separate and distinct, and the soul lives on in spiritual realms after the body dies. Non-universalists, who subscribe to this view, believe that punishments in Hell begin immediately after death. Some Universalists who believe this also believe that the purpose of those punishments is to bring sinners to repentance. Other Universalists believe that the "hellish" experiences after death are only temporary mental constructs and are not imposed by God.

A pretty good case from Scripture can be made for each of the above views. I myself, subscribe to the latter view, and can make a strong case for it solely from Scripture. However, various extra-biblical sources of information also support my view.

According to virtually all NDE's (Near Death Experiences), the soul immediately leaves the body upon death and enters the spirit world (ie. heaven or heavens). If you believe that soul dies when the body dies, then you cannot at the same time believe that NDE's are valid out-of-body or after-death experiences. In my view, the evidence for the validity of NDE's is much stronger than the arguments against it. If you have not read up on this, I would encourage you read a few good books on the subject or research it on the internet. The testimony of those who have experienced NDE's also supports Universalism. Almost all of them testify that they are welcomed into the spirit world (ie. heaven) with open arms and experience nothing but an overwhelming feeling of being loved unconditionally. This is true of both Christians and non-Christians, even atheists. Of the very small minority who have "hellish" experiences, virtually all of them are eventually rescued as they call out for help.

Additional support for the immortality of the soul can be found in the findings of quantum physics. These findings support the view that the physical body is not actually physical at all, but is made up of non-physical probability wave functions. Human consciousness is not an artifact of the physical body, but exactly the opposite. It exists independently from the physical body and actually creates all physical realities, including the physical body, solely through the power of observation. Some very excellent books have been written on this subject, in terms that the layman can understand. Many excellent YouTube videos have also been produced on the subject.

Extra-Biblical Truth Case Study No. 4: Paul's Sermon on Mars Hill and Progressive Revelation

Acts 17:22-31 *"So Paul stood in the midst of the Areopagus and said, 'Men of Athens, I observe that you are very religious in all respects. For while I was passing through and examining the objects of your worship, I also found an altar with this inscription, 'TO AN UNKNOWN GOD.' Therefore what you worship in ignorance, this I proclaim to you. The God who made the world and all things in it, since He is Lord of heaven and earth, does not dwell in temples made with hands; nor is He served by human hands, as though He needed anything, since He Himself gives to all people life and breath and all things; He made from one man every nation of mankind to live on all the face of the earth, having determined their appointed times and the boundaries of their habitation, they would seek God, if perhaps they might grope for Him and find Him, though He is not far from each one of us; in Him we live and move and exist, as even some of your own poets have said, 'For we also are His children.' Being then the children of God, we ought not to think that the Divine Nature is like gold or silver or stone, an image formed by the art and thought of man. Therefore having overlooked the times of ignorance, God is now declaring to men that all people everywhere should repent, because He has fixed a day in which He will judge the world in righteousness through a Man whom He has appointed, having furnished proof to all men by raising Him from the dead.'"*

From this passage it appears that Paul believed that all mankind originated with one man, although the word "man" is not in the original

Greek. He was presumably speaking about Adam. Paul was a product of his age and was probably a Biblical literalist. At the time he preached the above sermon in Athens, he also probably believed in a future judgment of all mankind on a single, fixed day in the future. I believe all human beings on Earth are descended from a single man and woman, but I don't believe this because of the Genesis myth. Instead, I believe it because it has been discovered scientifically through mitochondrial DNA analysis. It has also been established by science that other human beings existed prior to the "mitochondrial Eve," from whom all present day humans are descended. It has been estimated that our current lineage branched off from the rest of humanity between 100,000 and 200,000 years ago. So, it appears that Paul didn't know everything there was to know about human origins.

Paul's sermon also raises another difficulty. His teaching that God will judge all mankind in a single *"appointed day"* in the future is contradicted by the NDE (Near Death Experience) during which, at least for many of us, a "life review" or "self-judgment" occurs almost immediately after death, and it appears that we for the most part judge ourselves and are not judged by God at all. This reminds me of the saying in John 3:17 that *"God did not send his Son into the world to condemn the world, but to save the world through him."* Paul also seems to contradict his teaching of a universal judgment in the future when He says in 1 Cor. 5:8 that *"to be absent from the body is to be at home with the Lord."* Early on in his ministry, I'm sure that Paul believed in the imminent return of Jesus to Earth to judge all mankind and set up an earthly kingdom. As time went by, this hope faded and was replaced by another concept, that of a spiritual kingdom, not of this Earth. The seeds of this belief may also be found in the Paul's above sermon on Mars Hill, where he states that God is not a physical being who dwells in physical places. Instead, God exists everywhere including inside all of us. *"In Him we live and move and exist"* and *"we also are all His children."* This obviously refers to non-Christians, as well as Christians, as Paul was speaking to non-Christian Athenians.

Eventually, the focus of the early Christian community shifted from an emphasis on a physical Kingdom to that of a spiritual Kingdom which exists everywhere. This transition did not occur at the same time for all the writers of the New Testament. The idea that Jesus' kingdom is *"not of this world"* was introduced later on, and may only be found in the Gospel of John, the last of the Gospels to be written (See John 18:36). Even Jesus, Himself, in my view, probably did not come to this realization until late in His ministry, perhaps not until after His resurrection. According to Paul's sermon above, God's revelations to mankind are progressive in nature. In the past, mankind has been kept pretty much in the dark about many spiritual matters and it was determined by God that "*they would seek God, if perhaps they might grope for Him and find Him, though He is not far from each one of us*." Because of this, God *"overlooks our ignorance."* God apparently judges us only on the basis of what He has revealed to us.

In the following passage in 2 Corinthians, Paul suggests that the *"judgment seat of Christ"* occurs for each of us immediately upon death, rather than as a single mass judgment day in the distant future.

2 Cor. 5:1-10 "For we know that if the earthly tent we live in is destroyed, we have a building from God, an eternal house in heaven, not built by human hands. [2] *Meanwhile we groan, longing to be clothed instead with our heavenly dwelling,* [3] *because when we are clothed, we will not be found naked.* [4] *For while we are in this tent, we groan and are burdened, because we do not wish to be unclothed but to be clothed instead with our heavenly dwelling, so that what is mortal may be swallowed up by life.* [5] *Now the one who has fashioned us for this very purpose is God, who has given us the Spirit as a deposit, guaranteeing what is to come.* [6] *Therefore we are always confident and know that as long as we are at home in the body we are away from the Lord.* [7] *For we live by faith, not by sight.* [8] *We are confident, I say, and would prefer to be away from the body and at home with the Lord.* [9] *So we make it our goal to please him, whether we are at home in the body or away from it.* [10] *For we must all appear before the judgment seat of Christ, so that each of us may receive what is due us for the things done while in the body, whether good or bad."*

So, what do we learn from all of this?

My first take-a-way is that the progressive nature of God's revelation to us did not stop with the life of Christ, but continued afterwards. I believe this process continues today, and I would expect that with further advances in science, parapsychology and various forms of critical analysis of the Scriptures themselves we can gain additional insights that will help us better understand the true nature of God and the purpose for our existence here on Earth.

My second take-a-way is that the Christian Scriptures, though not inerrant, are still useful for *"teaching, rebuking, correcting and training in righteousness."* They do not provide us with definitive and incontrovertible answers to the exact nature of the afterlife and what happens after death. A great deal of mystery still remains. According to Paul's sermon above, up until the time of Christ, God was OK with our not having all the answers. Our understanding has grown since then, but we still have a long ways to go. I'm sure God is OK with that. Is there value in not knowing all the answers, or having to dig for them, at the very least? I would assume so.

Extra-Biblical Truth Case Study No. 5: The Holy Spirit

You might never have thought of it this way, but the Holy Spirit of God is actually an extra-Biblical source of information. According to John 16:13, the Holy Spirit *"will guide you into all truth."* In John 14:26, Jesus said, *"the Advocate, the Holy Spirit, whom the Father will send in my name, will teach you all things and will remind you of everything I have said to you."*

The question I have for you is this. If the Scriptures are self-explanatory and easy to interpret, why do we need the Holy Spirit? The truth is that the Scriptures are in many places self-contradictory and contain a mixture of truth and error. I'm not at all sure that Christ ever intended His teachings to be written down by fallible men and then passed on to others as the actual words of God Himself. If we are going to make sense of the Scriptures and benefit from them, we need to seek guidance from the original source on which the Scriptures themselves are based. The Scriptures are at best second and third-hand accounts of the working of the Holy Spirit in the lives of fallible men. I realize that this sounds like a rather negative and cynical view of Scripture. But we must remember that we don't worship a book. We worship a living God who is more than able to directly interact with us truthfully and intimately. He will not lead us astray if we seek Him with an open heart and good intentions.

Rather than trusting in the guidance of the Holy Spirit when interpreting Scripture, most Christians have ceded this God-given right to their religious authorities. Instead of trusting in their own intellect and intuition under the guidance of the Holy Spirit, they have decided to let their pastors and teachers do all their thinking for them. The problem is that most of those pastors and teachers have done the same thing. So we basically have the blind leading the blind, resulting in many contradictory Christian belief systems and denominations, with many factions accusing others of blasphemy and heresy.

So, the question is this. Would the situation be better if every individual Christian decided to take back their God-given right to access spiritual knowledge directly from the original source, the Holy Spirit? At first glance, one might conclude that this would result in even more disunity and an even greater variety of competing beliefs. I believe exactly the opposite would happen, and here's why.

Let me begin by using a secular example. Totalitarian ideologies are only able to deceive their subjects in the absence the free flow of information. To avoid this, they implement massive propaganda campaigns, and don't allow their subjects access to a free press, or travel outside their borders. The idea is that the masses are too ignorant to make good decisions. They aren't capable of thinking for themselves. They will all be better off if they allow their leaders to do their thinking for them. Due in no small part to the free flow of information across national borders, totalitarianism has gradually been giving way to democracy in many parts of the world. The most successful nations in the world today are the democracies. They are imperfect, but not nearly as bad as the totalitarian systems.

The same is true with respect to the Christian religion. Various denominational leaders strive to maintain a rigid orthodoxy in their respective groupings. They do this primarily by restricting the free flow of information and threatening dissidents within their ranks with excommunication and damnation in Hell. As long as these leaders are successful in maintaining their ecclesiastical authority and their status as gatekeepers of spiritual truth, the Christian church will remain divided and will become increasingly isolated from the popular culture. They will continue to lose ground to advances in spiritual growth and evolution that are currently taking place in the popular culture.

Here's what I believe. As more and more people begin to question their religious authorities and seek to guidance of the Holy Spirit instead, two things will begin to happen.

First, it will become apparent that no one knows all the truth. People will have to humbly admit that there is more that they don't know than what they do know. They will be less dogmatic in their thinking and far less judgmental of those who disagree with them.

Secondly, common threads of truth will begin to emerge as people begin to realize that the most important truths are those which the Holy Spirit reveals to all of them, truths relating to the loving, forgiving and just nature of God and the importance of developing and expressing in our lives qualities of character like love, kindness, justice, mercy and forgiveness.

Christian scholars and leaders will still play an important role, but they will exercise their roles with more tolerance and humility. The Christian church will become more inclusive and far more effective in leading back to Christ those who have lost their way.

Universalism and the Scriptural inerrancy debate

It is troubling to some Christian Universalists that not all of us view the Scriptures as literally true and/or inerrant. Virtually all Universalists believe that regardless of one's views on the Scriptural inerrancy all will be redeemed sooner or later. The worst case scenario would be for someone to reject the Scriptures altogether, stop believing in God, fall into a grievously sinful lifestyle, and then suffer temporal (ie. age-during) corrective judgments of God.

In this book, I make a very strong case for Universalism based on a pretty strict interpretation of the Scriptures, largely consistent with the doctrine of inerrancy. I also make a pretty good case based on science, reason and logic. It doesn't really matter whether you view the Bible as inerrant, partially inerrant, or whether you reject the Scriptures altogether, there is plenty of evidence out there to prove the existence of a loving and benevolent Creator God who has nothing but good intentions for all of humanity.

Theological correctness is not required for Christian Salvation. For example, does it really matter what theory of the Atonement we subscribe to? There are a variety of views on this, in addition to the penal substitution theory, some of which are derived from a literalistic interpretation of Scripture passages, and some not. The important question is this. Does what we believe in any way change what actually happened? Does it really matter what mechanism God uses to redeem all mankind? Is not the end result what really matters? God is loving and just. He does not overlook sin, but at the same time He doesn't punish anyone with endless retribution in a place called Hell. All of God's judgments are consistent with His loving and forgiving nature.

I would encourage each of you to pause, breathe deeply, and then let out a sigh of relief, knowing that your eternal destiny in firmly in the hands of a loving Creator God, *"who is the Savior of all men, especially of those who believe."* 1 Timothy 4:10

The importance of visualization

Over the past few years my concept of God has changed. The popular view of God as a male father figure who exists separately from us is not at all accurate. It is an imperfect way of visualizing a spiritual being who is neither male nor female and has no physical body. Everything that exists is infused by God, including us. We actually share God's divine, spiritual nature. There is no nook or cranny in this or any other universe where God does not exist. The physical world in which we live is also spiritual in nature. There is nothing physical about it. The basic building blocks of the space-time universe in which we live are nothing more than vibrating strings of potential energy which continually blink into and out of existence. The physical bodies we inhabit are also spiritual in nature. We are spiritual beings created in the spiritual image of God. As part of God's creation, we are one of many vehicles through which God expresses Himself.

This being the case, how does one visualize and relate to a non-local, omni-present, invisible, God, who is so much bigger than any image that we can conjure up? Is there any value in visualizing God as a human father figure who lives in a place called Heaven, as depicted in the prayer that Jesus taught his disciples? Is there any value in viewing God as a "person" who is separate from us and who does not indwell us until invited in, as in Revelation 3:20, where Jesus, who is the incarnation of God, stands at our heart's door asking to be let in? Is there value in visualizing God in the form of the historical Jesus, who told us, in John 14:7, that seeing Him was the same as seeing the Father? Is there any value in visualizing Jesus as a rather handsome and kindly appearing bearded man in a white robe? Is there value in visualizing and experiencing God's presence through liturgical objects, including the bread and wine of the Eucharist?

I will try to answer that question with an analogy from secular life. Napoleon Hill once wrote an extremely influential book, called *"Think and Grow Rich."* The idea is that if you are able to create and continually focus your attention on a visual image of something you desire to accomplish or achieve in life, you have the power within you to achieve it. It is amazing what can be accomplished through the power of visualization. It has been scientifically verified, for example, that basketball players can improve their shooting accuracy without even picking up a basketball, merely through a process of mentally shooting baskets. The Bible does say, in Proverbs 23:7, that *"as a man thinks, so is he."* Throughout the Scriptures, especially, in the teachings of Christ, the power of faith is continually emphasized. The process of visualizing a desire or goal and continually meditating on it, through spoken and unspoken prayer, is very effective. I personally believe that the Spirit of God dwells within us, and at the deepest level of our consciousness we are inseparable from God Himself. This being the case, it is not surprising to me that visualization can be a creative process with almost unlimited potential.

Why does God reveal Himself to us imperfectly through images that only convey partial truths? My answer is that there are no words or images that can fully and accurately describe the indescribable. As Paul said, in 1 Cor. 13:12, *"for now we see only a reflection as in a mirror; then we shall see face to face. Now I know in part; then I shall know fully, even as I am fully known."*

This world is not my home, I'm just passing through

Sometimes I get emotionally overwhelmed when I contemplate the evil in this world. It helps me to understand that this so-called physical world is not real, nor is it our real home. Although there is no actual physical substance to this world, our experience of it is very real indeed. Those of us who take seriously our "baptism" into Christ, understand that our real home is in Heaven with Christ, and with all those who have preceded us in death. When our physical bodies die, it is not our real selves that die, but our sinful, fleshly bodies. All those who are saved by Christ now, or ever will be saved in the future, have already been *"crucified with Christ"* before the foundation of the world (see Eph. 2:4-6; Rev. 13:8; and 1 Pet. 1:20). We were all *"seated with Christ in the heavenly places"* before we were born into this world. When we die and shed these mortal bodies, we will wake up from this "dream" of our earthly existence and find ourselves at home with Christ.

If we all end up in Heaven with Christ after we die, what point is there in living a Godly life during our Earthly existence? Well, the Christian Gospel message is this. Those of us who receive the Spirit of Christ into our lives now can experience spiritual life and fellowship with Christ in this age, as well as the age to come. Eternal life in Christ is not something that we experience only after we die. It has nothing to do with living forever. It is all about experiencing life before we die, during this current evil age, in our fleshly bodies. The Greek world *"aionias,"* which is mistranslated as *"eternal"* in the New Testament, actually means *"age-during"* or *"belonging to the current age"* in which we now live. It refers to "spiritual life" in the here and now.

Why would a loving God subject us to the evil in this world, evil so great that we are revolted by it every time we turn on the news? For many, existence in this world is full of sorrow, hardship and misery. It helps me to remember that this Earthly existence is only a temporary condition, and that all of us are not only loved by God, but we are actually at home with Christ in the *"heavenly places"* as we speak. We just have not all been made aware of this, and thus are not able to experience it in the here and now. That is what the Gospel of Christ is all about. It is the Good News that Christ died for all and paid the price of our redemption. When we receive the Spirit of Christ into our hearts and minds, we can experience in the here and now much of the life to come. God gives us the strength and ability to overcome our fleshly nature and find release from many destructive habits. He gives us a new perspective on life and enables us to see our Earthly existence from the perspective of a pilgrim just passing through on our way to a much better place. When we make sacrifices for the benefit of others, we are able to see this as a "win win" situation. As we help others, we also *"lay up treasures for ourselves in Heaven."* Instead of shaking our fist at God for putting us in this world of sin and sorrow, we can love and praise Him for what He has done for all of us. When contrasted with the joys of Heaven, the difficulties of our present circumstances seem very small indeed.

Romans 6:1-14

"What shall we say, then? Shall we go on sinning so that grace may increase? By no means! We are those who have died to sin; how can we live in it any longer? Or don't you know that all of us who were baptized into Christ Jesus were baptized into his death? We were therefore buried with him through baptism into death in order that, just as Christ was

raised from the dead through the glory of the Father, we too may live a new life.

For if we have been united with him in a death like his, we will certainly also be united with him in a resurrection like his. For we know that our old self was crucified with him so that the body ruled by sin might be done away with that we should no longer be slaves to sin— because anyone who has died has been set free from sin.

Now if we died with Christ, we believe that we will also live with him. For we know that since Christ was raised from the dead, he cannot die again; death no longer has mastery over him. The death he died, he died to sin once for all; but the life he lives, he lives to God.

In the same way, count yourselves dead to sin but alive to God in Christ Jesus. Therefore do not let sin reign in your mortal body so that you obey its evil desires. Do not offer any part of yourself to sin as an instrument of wickedness, but rather offer yourselves to God as those who have been brought from death to life; and offer every part of yourself to him as an instrument of righteousness. For sin shall no longer be your master, because you are not under the law, but under grace."

Situational ethics and the Law of Love

Situational ethics has long been maligned by religious conservatives, for obvious reasons. It is troubling that in our modern society we are experiencing a breakdown in traditional morality, with the devastating consequence of the breakdown of the family. During the turbulent social upheaval that occurred in the 1960's, one of the catch phrases was "if it feels good, do it." During the period of the Judges in Israel, the nation ignored the commands of God and the people "did what was right in their own eyes." When we lose our connection with God, there is a strong tendency to lose our moral compass and engage in all sorts of sinful and destructive behavior.

In Jesus' day, the religious authorities went too far in the opposite direction and established a very complex and detailed moral code of behavior. Often, the letter of the law violated the spirit and intent of the original precepts on which it was based. There were so many do's and don'ts that the people lost touch with the reasons why those laws were created in the first place. In the Sermon on the Mount, Jesus addressed this problem by redefining several of those commands in such a way as to conform to their spirit and intent. Jesus crossed many social, religious and ethical boundaries, in both word and deed, when He reinterpreted the commands of Scripture to conform to the one law that supersedes and overrides them all, the law of love. Every law that God has given to us is based on His love for us, and He wants us to be like Him. Jesus summed up the Law with the two commands, that we love God with all our heart and our neighbor as ourselves. According to 1 John 4:7 *"Beloved, let us love one another, for love is from God, and whoever loves has been born of God and knows God."* Christ has set us free from the demands of the Law, according to the Apostle Paul. Because our standing with God is based on grace, not works, Paul said, *"I have the right to do anything. . .but not everything is constructive."*

The law of love does not give us license to do as we please or make up our own rules, regardless their negative impact on others. It does however, give us the option of departing from some of the commands of Scripture that were culturally based and no longer apply today.

So how does one separate the wheat from the chaff, so to speak, and throw out those rules which are opposed to the law of love which is strongly taught throughout the New Testament? One of the best ways to do this is to love your neighbor as yourself. Put yourself in the place of the people who are the most affected by your actions and make your decision based on what is best for them and draws them closer to God. In the link below, a Southern Baptist minister did just that, with respect to many homosexuals who came to him for help. Over a period of years, he finally decided to make this a major focus of research and study, and was finally able to changes his views and courageously explain them to his congregation, knowing full well that it might cost him his career.

Jesus was welcoming and kind to the outcasts of society and criticized the religious elite of His day for their self-righteous attitudes. How do those religious authorities differ from those of our day who refuse admission to, or expel from, their churches the very people who most need to be loved, accepted and helped by the people of God?

Please take time to listen to the entire sermon on this link:

https://www.youtube.com/watch?v=WqYvkVqVLFo&feature=share

The Pearl of Great Price

"Again, the kingdom of heaven is like a merchant looking for fine pearls. When he found one of great price, he went away and sold everything he had and bought it." Matthew 13:45-46

The wonderful gift of *"aionian"* or *"age-abiding"* life (usually mistranslated as *"eternal"*) escapes many so-called "born-again" Christians. When we view our reward as something external to us, something that we receive after death in a faraway place called Heaven, we miss out on the joys of Heaven within that are available to us right now.

An interesting analogy would be Jesus' parable about the *"pearl of great price."* When we read this parable, many of us might view it as some sort of treasure hunt. Somewhere, in the depths of the ocean, lies an oyster, with a beautiful pearl inside. In order to find it, we would need to rent a boat, perhaps hire a guide, and diligently scour the ocean bottom in search of it. The search for this pearl could be very long and arduous, and very few would be able to find it.

My theological studies over the past few years have led me to the understanding that each of us has a hidden identity as a child of God. In the deepest recesses of our consciousness, we are all intimately connected with God. The oyster that contains the pearl of great value is not to be found somewhere at the bottom of the ocean. Instead, we are the oyster, and the pearl actually lies within us. To find it, we need to look within.

Christian salvation is not an instantaneous event, based solely on a one-time confession of faith whereby we ask an external God to come to us and dwell within us. In my view, salvation should be visualized as a process of discovering our true identity as children of God, already redeemed by Christ. It is the process of discovering and experiencing the Kingdom of God (ie. the rule of Christ) that already exists within us. God loves us unconditionally before we become saved in our conscious awareness. It is not God who changes when we experience salvation. Instead, it is we who change. We don't have to be anxious about whether or not we qualify by our faith or works for salvation. We don't have to worry about the timing of it, or how long it might last. All of us are loved and accepted by God, just as we are, right now. All that remains for us to do is recognize it and experience it.

The law of Sowing and Reaping

What we reap for our misdeeds is not retribution from God. Instead, we reap the opportunity of being "on the receiving end" of what we dish out, so that we may learn and grow by it. What we reap from the good that we sow is the love and gratitude of those whom we love and help and the knowledge that we are making progress in becoming all that God wants us to be.

True repentance from sin involves more than simply asking for forgiveness in order to avoid punishment from God. Acknowledging the lordship of Christ in our lives does not exempt us from the law of sowing and reaping. It's one thing to be sorry and repent of our sins because we don't want to suffer punishment from God. It's quite another to be sorry because we are able to genuinely empathize with those we have harmed. There is a huge difference between *"Godly sorrow"* and *"worldly sorrow."* According to 2 Corinthians 7:10, *"Godly sorrow brings repentance that leads to salvation and leaves no regret, but worldly sorrow brings death."*

When Paul talks about *"salvation"* and *"death,"* he is not talking about going to Heaven or Hell after you die. He is referring to your present experience in the age in which you currently live. *"Salvation,"* also referred to as *"life,"* has to do with our relationship with God. If we are connected with God, we are *"alive"* spiritually. If we have lost that connection, then we are *"dead"* spiritually. In our day-to-day walk we most often find ourselves experiencing a little of each. Christian salvation is something that we grow into.

Praying the sinner's prayer, or asking forgiveness for a particular sin or shortcoming, only marks the beginning of a process. Of course God forgives. Then He helps us to empathize with and love those whom we have wronged. In some cases, the best way to learn to do this is to spend a while in their shoes. The law of sowing and reaping has nothing at all to do with forgiveness, nor does it allow us to escape personal responsibility for our negative thoughts and actions. The purpose of this law is to mold us into the image of Christ and prepare us for life in God's Kingdom. And don't forget, the law of sowing and reaping also includes rewards for making the right decisions and doing good.

The God within

Philippians 4:13 *"I can do all things through Christ who strengthens me."*

When I was a young man, I would look up into the sky at night and contemplate the immensity of the universe. This made me feel very small and insignificant, and I would wonder how or why a God, who is even bigger than the universe, would take time to focus on me. How could God be in a million places at once and pay attention to millions, perhaps billions, of simultaneous prayers all over the planet? For this reason my prayers lacked power and effectiveness.

Over the past few years, my view of God has significantly changed. I now believe, based on my study of the Scriptures, quantum mechanics, and NDE's, combined with common sense and logic, that God is not some immense being who lives outside of the universe and merely looks in on it from time to time, taking time out of His busy schedule to listen to millions of prayers. I now realize that the universe and everything in it is actually a part of God. It is an extension of God's consciousness. In the deepest recesses of our consciousness we are not only intimately connected with God, we are actually made up of God parts, ie. spirit, and are part of God himself. We are actually God's "body." Paul refers to us as the "body of Christ," which to me is the same as saying the "body of God the Father," because Christ is in God the Father and God the Father is in Christ, and we are in Christ and Christ is in us. In His prayer in John 17:20-22, Jesus prayed that we would all experience that oneness: *"I do not ask on behalf of these alone, but for those also who believe in Me through their word; that they may all be one; even as You, Father, are in Me and I in You, that they also may be in Us, so that the world may believe that You sent Me. "The glory which You have given Me I have given to them, that they may be one, just as We are one;..."*

I believe that deep within we are literally "one with God." Christian salvation is the means by which we become aware of this and experience it in our daily walk. We are the body of Christ through whom God experiences His creation. When we pray to God the Father, we are not just talking to a spiritual entity who exists separately from us. Yes, God is "out there." He is everywhere. He is also within us. He is us. To some this might seem blasphemous, but it is Scriptural. When we talk to ourselves, we are talking to God. He not only hears us, He is us. The Apostle Paul believed that he could "do all things." We don't have to depend on God to do everything for us. He has given us the power and authority to do things for ourselves. We have at our disposal the power of God Himself, within us, to accomplish almost anything we set our mind to. The only limitation is our lack of faith.

Understanding this has greatly helped me with my prayer life. I talk to myself a lot more than I did before. I pray now with more conviction. I know that if I am paying attention, so is the God the Father.

The question of Scriptural inerrancy is moot

It has occurred to me that it really doesn't matter whether the Scriptures are "inerrant" or not. The result is the same. Theologians disagree on most important doctrines, regardless of their views on inerrancy.

There are literally thousands of different Christian denominations and sects, most of which subscribe to the doctrine of Scriptural inerrancy. They differ in significant ways on the requirements for salvation. The list of requirements include: 1. Belief in the substitutionary atonement, 2. Belief in the deity of Christ, 3. Water Baptism, 4. Repentance from Sin, 5. Receiving Jesus as personal Savior, 6. Belief in the bodily resurrection of Christ, 7. Producing a sufficient amount of good works, and 8. Continuing to believe and not "falling away." In addition to those supposedly "essential" doctrines, there are a host of less important doctrines on which they also disagree, relating to morality, Heaven and Hell, modes of baptism, eschatology, soul sleep, spiritual gifts, speaking in tongues, healing, miracles, tithing, homosexuality, abortion, politics, materialism, and many, many more.

Those who believe that the Scriptures are inspired by God, but not inerrant, also differ on the same doctrines, some holding more or less orthodox views and some not.

Does it seem odd to you that God, who is infinitely smarter than all of us, would be incapable of communicating to us in clear and unambiguous terms? Does it trouble you that the Bible does not convey truths in such a way as to avoid distortions due to errors in translation and interpretation? If I believed in a place called Hell, where "unbelievers" and "incorrect believers" are tortured for all eternity after they die, I would be deeply troubled by God's unwillingness to communicate the saving Gospel message in a format that is easily understood by all.

I believe that the Bible, when correctly understood and interpreted, teaches that God is the Savior of all men regardless of what they believe.

Yes, there are benefits to believing in Christ, but all are saved, or will be saved, regardless. I believe this is what is expressed in 1 Timothy 4:10, that God *"is the Savior of all men, and especially of those who believe."*

To me, it is ironic that the correct interpretation of the Scriptures is that it is not necessary to interpret them correctly.

The parable of the persistent widow

Luke 18:1-8 *"Then Jesus told his disciples a parable to show them that they should always pray and not give up. He said: "In a certain town there was a judge who neither feared God nor cared what people thought. And there was a widow in that town who kept coming to him with the plea, 'Grant me justice against my adversary.'*

"For some time he refused. But finally he said to himself, 'Even though I don't fear God or care what people think, yet because this widow keeps bothering me, I will see that she gets justice, so that she won't eventually come and attack me!'"

And the Lord said, "Listen to what the unjust judge says. And will not God bring about justice for his chosen ones, who cry out to him day and night? Will he keep putting them off? I tell you, he will see that they get justice, and quickly. However, when the Son of Man comes, will he find faith on the earth?"

God is not a reluctant judge who needs to be pestered continually before He answers our prayers. The point Jesus was making is that even an imperfect earthly judge will reward your persistence and eventually give in. God is more loving and just than any earthly judge and is more than willing to answer our prayers, especially when we persist.

There are two reasons why persistence is needed.

First, we need to wait on God's timing. God knows our situation better than we do. He knows when the time will be exactly right.

Secondly, when we pray we are drawing upon the power that God has already granted us within our human spirit to accomplish miracles. God works through us, not for us. He builds us up and empowers us to accomplish seemingly impossible tasks on our own. As Paul said in Phil. 4:13, *"I can do all things through Christ who strengthens me."* The more we visualize and focus on our goals and desires, the more concrete they become in our consciousness, and the more likely they are to manifest in the physical world in which we live. Practice makes perfect. The more we pray, the more powerful our prayers become. When we see positive results, we are encouraged to pray even more, and our faith grows stronger.

Ninety percent of what my wife, Arlene, and I pray for each morning is exactly, word for word, the same as the day before. I can tell you from personal experience that God answers prayer.

Universalism and Mysticism

Many universalists believe that we all have a "higher self," which is that portion of our soul or spirit that remains in heaven when we incarnate on earth. The portion we take with us into our mortal bodies is not only intimately connected with our "higher self" but also with God. The human soul or spirit is actually a part of God and an expression of God. We were created from God's own DNA, so to speak. We are all God's offspring. Our "real or true" selves may be discovered by looking within, where our human spirit resides and connects with our "higher self" and with God. Biblical support for this concept may be found in Ephesians 2:6, where Paul states that all Christians, and by extension all who are destined to become Christians, have already been "seated" with Christ in the heavenly places. In his speech on Mars Hill in Acts 17, Paul tells us that we are all the offspring of God. In Romans 7, Paul talks about our two natures, our inner self or "mind" and our physical self or "flesh." Through our physical bodies, we, and by extension God Him/Her/Itself, experience life and the created world through the senses of a physical body. This concept may also be found in 1 Corinthians 12, where Paul describes us as individual parts of the "body of Christ," through whom Christ accomplishes his purposes here on Earth.

The goal of both Christian and non-Christian mystics is to bypass the physical senses and directly connect with God and our "higher selves." This has been achieved by various means through prayer, meditation, out-of-body experiences, hypnotic regression, near-death experiences, and the like. Sometimes this experience is referred to as "enlightenment," whereby we actually experience what it is like in heaven. To the mystic, the fleshly body hinders us from connecting with our inner self. In Romans 7, Paul likened this to a war of sorts, with our physical nature warring against our spiritual nature. To win this war we need God's help and the help of the indwelling Spirit of God. See Romans, Chapter 8.

The goal of mysticism, however, should not be to escape from the trials and tribulations of this world, but to view them from a heavenly, rather than an earthly perspective. The achievement of various "mountain top experiences," or "enlightenment," in both Christian and non-Christian settings, does not represent the goal or purpose of our earthly existence. God did not send us to Earth to escape from the Earth and earn a place in heaven after we die. We already had that before we came. Our purpose here on Earth is to learn and grow into the likeness and character of Christ. He is our example. When we return to heaven, after death, we take with us the lessons learned. The reward we receive for a life well-lived is not Heaven itself, but the treasures we have laid up for ourselves in Heaven while on Earth.

I believe that "enlightenment" or "mountain top ecstatic experiences" can in many ways detract from our life mission and purpose. It is God's plan for us to live by faith, not sight. There is value in not knowing all there is to know about Heaven and our pre-existence there. There is value in the experience of doubt, fear, and a healthy dose of sufferings and disappointments. There is value in making mistakes and learning from them in this "crucible" of our earthly life. There is value in not knowing for sure if God is even there to rescue us from our negative experiences. God hides from us on purpose and with good intentions. Yes, God may be found if we look deep enough within ourselves, and it is wonderful to discover faith in God and experience God's presence in our lives. But the greatest rewards are to be found primarily during our journey, and not after arriving at the final destination. The reward you receive when you finally arrive back at home in Heaven is the person you have become. Interestingly, you become this person, this "new creature in Christ," before you get to Heaven, during your Earthly walk. The joys of Heaven may indeed be experienced in the here and now. God's Kingdom is among us here on Earth. Christian salvation is something that we experience in a progressive manner during our current lifetime. The icing on the cake is being able to look back on our lives, during our life review after death, and hearing those wonderful words, "Well done, thou good and faithful servant."

Universalism and mental illness

One of the most difficult cases to make for universalism is that God does not hold our sins against us. Our sense of justice requires that sin be punished and righteousness be rewarded. God saves us by grace (ie.

unmerited favor), but the decision to reject God's grace must also be punished, in the interest of justice. The greatest sin of all, according this line of reasoning, is rejecting God's grace. Either way, as the argument goes, God is just in condemning people to everlasting torment in Hell to satisfy the demands of justice.

The only exception to this would be in the case of mental incompetency or mental illness. Most Christian evangelicals believe that children and mentally ill people will be going to Heaven when they die because they are not mentally competent to make informed moral decisions. Well, I personally would extend that exception to include the entire human race, regardless of age or mental condition. All of us are sinners and have been born with a sin nature or tendency to do both good and evil. We can't help ourselves. In Romans 3:23, the Apostle Paul insisted that "all have sinned and fallen short of the Glory of God." The reason some sin more than others is that their brains work differently. The decisions we make in life result from the way our brains processes an infinitely complex set of life events and human interactions.

Those of us who choose to become Christians and follow the teachings of Christ to the best of our ability do so because our brains process information differently than those who don't. If we back up the chain of causation, we must conclude that none of us should be held liable for our sins in God's court of justice. Our sins result from mental defects which were not of our own choosing. Our good deeds result from unique thought processes occurring in brains that we ourselves did not create.

Does this mean that we should not be held accountable for our sins? Of course not! However, for reasons stated above, the purpose of both human and divine justice should be guidance and correction, not retribution.

Like father like son

Children tend to turn our like their parents. Often the child, even after insisting he or she will never be like a disliked parent actually becomes like the parent anyway. Children of abusers tend become abusers themselves. Children who grow up in loving homes tend to do better in life than those who do not. The same is true when we regard our Creator God as a Heavenly Father. Christians are taught to emulate and try to be like the God they worship. This is a good thing, if God is pictured as loving, kind, fair, just and forgiving. But if God is at the same time pictured as judgmental, harsh, hateful and cruel towards those who do not conform to a certain carefully defined set of attitudes and behaviors, then we give ourselves license to behave in exactly the same way.

When we teach our children that God is loving by nature, yet hateful and cruel towards His enemies, then we give them an excuse to be hateful and cruel themselves. The reasoning goes like this. It's ok to be judgmental and hateful towards those who deserve it. To make matters even worse, not only is it ok to be judgmental and hateful, towards those who behave badly, but also towards those who might be loving, kind and generous, but who's religious beliefs differ from ours, or who are different from us with respect to ethnicity, gender orientation, political views, dress standards, and so on.

While it is true that Jesus taught us to love our enemies and return good for evil, we don't take this teaching as seriously as we should. Why? Because we believe God does not take it seriously. If it's OK for God to be judgmental, hateful and cruel towards all non-Christians, especially towards egregious sinners, then why would it be so bad for us to behave in the same way?

We look for ways to circumvent God's command to love our enemies and return good for evil. For example, we might say God forgives His enemies, but only if they repent and ask for forgiveness. We even excuse hateful attitudes towards kind and loving people, because they don't repent of their incorrect theology, sexual orientation, or moral values. When we view God as both loving and hateful at the same time and highly selective regarding those whom He blesses and those whom He doesn't, then we can justify almost any negative attitude towards those who differ from us.

The schizophrenic God described above is not actually the real God of the Bible. I personally believe that most of the harsh and cruel acts of God described in the Bible, especially in the Old Testament, are not accurate history and mostly reflect man's imperfect view of God. However, even if you accept those accounts as true and accurate descriptions of God's activities, the Bible also teaches that after judgment comes mercy, and the purpose of God's negative judgments is to teach us life lessons and help us to learn and grow. The Bible clearly teaches in both the Old and New Testaments that God's plan for the ages is to restore all humanity to a state of perfection, bliss and union with Himself in Heaven.

The Four Spiritual Laws

Many of you have heard of the Four Spiritual Laws of Bill Bright and Campus Crusade for Christ:

God loves you and offers a wonderful plan for your life (John 3:16; 10:10).

(1) Man is sinful and separated from God. Therefore, he cannot know and experience God's love and plan for his life (Rom. 3:23; 6:23).

(2) Jesus Christ is God's only provision for man's sin. Through him you can know and experience God's love and plan for your life (Rom. 5:8; 1 Cor. 15:3 - 6; John 14:6).

(3) We must individually receive Jesus Christ as Savior and Lord; then we can know and experience God's love and plan for our lives (John 1:12; 3:1 - 8; Eph. 2:8 - 9; Rev. 3:20).

Here, I humbly submit my own alternate version:

(1) God loves you and everything that happens is part of God's plan for your life. According to Prov. 16:9, "The heart of man plans his way, but the Lord establishes his steps." Even our bad choices are part of God's plan.

(2) Man thinks he is separated from God. Therefore, he doesn't always know and experience God's love and plan for his life. According to Romans 6:23, "the wages of sin is death, but the gift of God is age-abiding life." This verse has nothing to do with life after the death of the physical body. It refers to our awareness of and relationship with the God within all of us, our true spiritual selves. To be alive spiritually is to be connected with God in our conscious awareness.

(3) Jesus Christ, God incarnate, showed us how we can know and experience God's love and plan for our lives. He demonstrated to us that although God's plan for us includes suffering and physical death, God never leaves us nor forsakes us. In order for us to be born again spiritually, we must first experience death. According to John 12:24, "unless a kernel of wheat falls to the ground and dies, it remains only a single seed. But if it dies, it produces many seeds."

(4) If we obey Christ and follow his teachings and example, we can experience spiritual life in the here and now, not just after we die physically. According to 1 John 5:12, "Whoever believes in the Son has eternal life, but whoever rejects the Son will not see life, for God's wrath remains on them." Just as separation from God is an illusion, so it is with God's wrath. The experience of rejection by God, or spiritual death, may be replaced with the abundant life for those who believe in Christ and follow his teachings.

Time and Eternity

Time, defined as "the sequencing of events," exists both in our space-time universe and also in Heaven. Without time, it would be impossible for anything to "occur" or "happen" or "change" or for people to even "think." For all of these, some sort of logical sequence of events must occur. Time is not a thing that actually exists independently on its own. It is an artificial construct that we use to describe the "space" between one event and another. In Heaven, everything occurs both sequentially and concurrently, depending on the observer's vantage point and focus of attention. A series of events occurring on Earth over several millennia, may be observed from Heaven in any sequence, and the various "events" in the sequence may be individually observed at any time and in any order. It's sort of like a digital movie. The end of the story has already been written, acted out, and put onto the DVD. It may be viewed sequentially from the beginning of the story to the end. Individual scenes can be selected and instantly viewed, regardless of where they fit in the overall story line.

When viewed from a "heavenly" vantage point, we are already seated with Christ in the Heavenly places. When viewed from an "earthly" vantage point, not all are yet alive in Christ. In the Bible, the term "eternal life," more correctly translated "age-during" or "age-abiding life," has nothing to do with time. Instead it refers to life that may be experienced in the here and now on Earth, as well as in Heaven after we die. It refers primarily to the here and now. It refers to our awareness of and connection with our higher self (ie. our human spirit) and the Spirit of God within us. It refers to our ability to view our earthly existence from a heavenly perspective, basking in God's love and the love that we share with friends and neighbors.

When awakened to our true nature as beloved children of God, already loved and accepted by God in Heaven, we are able to view the people in our lives differently. Instead of viewing them as "bad" or "good," we realize that all are unconditionally loved by God. No one is inherently evil. At the core of our being, all of us are loving, kind and well-intentioned. The trouble is most of us are not aware of this and have temporarily lost our way. Like sheep, we have all gone astray, and the unseen hand of God moves behind the scenes guiding us back to our true home in Heaven. Those of us who "are in the know," realize that Heaven is not someplace far away, but coexists with the spaces we occupy on Earth. God's Kingdom is present with us now and may be experienced right now. It is not a future experience. It is a present experience. Everything we are doing right now is actually taking place in Heaven. We are actually alive in Heaven, viewing our lives as in a dream through the senses of our physical bodies, which are not actually physical at all.

To sum it up, realize that the future is now. In a manner of speaking, you are already there. You don't have to wait until you die to wake up from the dream. You have been given by your Creator God the power within you to create your own version of Heaven on Earth.

New wine and old wine skins

Luke 5:36-39: *He told them this parable: "No one tears a piece out of a new garment to patch an old one. Otherwise, they will have torn the new garment, and the patch from the new will not match the old. And no one pours new wine into old wineskins. Otherwise, the new wine will burst the skins; the wine will run out and the wineskins will be ruined. No, new wine must be poured into new wineskins. And no one after drinking old wine wants the new, for they say, 'The old is better.'"*

Most of us are familiar with Jesus' saying that you can't sew a new patch onto an old garment, or put new wine into old wine skins. Today's Christian evangelicals like to think that their theology is fundamentally different from the ancient Hebrew religion which was characterized by legalism and a very anthropomorphic view of God. The Christian belief that God tortures unbelievers endlessly in a place called Hell, has resulted from a failure to completely break away from Hebrew tribalism and a view of God as loving and kind only to a very select category of people, and very cruel and harsh towards the enemies of His favored nation. Although today's evangelicals have completely embraced Jesus' view of God as loving, kind, just and forgiving, they still cling to the tribal exclusivism of the Hebrews and have placed severe limits on the extent of God's love and forgiveness. They have been unable to fully embrace the teachings of Christ, because, like the Pharisees of Jesus' day, they have been unwilling to fully let go of the errors of the past. This is in no small part due to the erroneous view of the Hebrew and Christian Scriptures as historically, scientifically, and theologically inerrant in every respect, rather than viewing them as a progressive revelation of sorts, whereby God has progressively led His people on a journey of self-discovery. The Bible records this process from man's, not God's, point of view.

When I first embarked on my journey to discover what the Bible really teaches about God and Christian salvation, I had to put all my cards on the table, and be willing take off those cards which do not fit with the truth. One of those cards was Scriptural inerrancy. Because Christian evangelicals believe that their eternal destiny (heaven or hell for all eternity) is at stake, it would be very scary for them to put the inerrancy card on the table and be willing to take it off, if necessary. It was a step I had to take for the sake of intellectual honesty and an honest search for truth. However, as a Christian evangelical, I decided to leave that card on the table until fully satisfied that it was safe to take it off. I did not take that card off the table until I was fully convinced that the Scriptures fully support the doctrine of universal reconciliation, regardless of whether or not one views them as inerrant. Not only do the scriptures fully support universalism, but that support is absolutely overwhelming. Eventually, I felt safe in taking the inerrancy card off the table. I now view the Scriptures, for many very good reasons, as man-made documents which record God's progressive revelations to mankind, written from man's point of view. Understanding this has made it much easier to discard the "old" for the "new."

The teachings of Christ and His Apostles were a striking departure from the orthodoxy of the Hebrew religion. Since then, I believe God has continued to bless mankind with additional revelations and insights into

His true nature and how we may interact with Him. These revelations, which I believe fully harmonize with the spirit and intent of the New Testament record, have come from a variety of sources, such as NDE's, science, hypnotic regression, psychology, sociology, history, both Christian and non-Christian mysticism, and the writings of many thinkers from all walks of life. When investigating these sources of truth, we must be willing to discard some of the old garments, as we put on the new. Our search for truth is severely hampered if we are unwilling to first admit that there might be at least some flaws in our current belief system. Open-mindedness in our search for truth does not necessarily mean that we have to abandon our currently held convictions and beliefs. But, we must be willing to at least temporarily put those cards on table. In the end, we may end up discarding some of them. At the same time, however, we will be building a firmer foundation underneath the most important beliefs, the ones that are actually true.

CPSIA information can be obtained at www.ICGtesting.com
Printed in the USA
LVOW11s1548220915

455237LV00002B/439/P

9 781500 651107